The Groupwork Series

Understanding and using groups

Brenda Vernelle

Whiting and Birch Ltd

MCMXCIV

Published by Whiting & Birch Ltd
Forest Hill, London SE23 3HZ, England.

ISBN 1 87177 60 X (cased)
ISBN 1 871177 61 8 (limp)

Printed in England and the United States by Lightning Source

Contents

Introduction

Help! It's my group today

Everything seems to happen so fast in a group, how can I understand what is going on? When I join a group where the people are new to me, I'm always a bit worried. Even in a group I have been in before, I sometimes feel anxious about what others think of me. When I have to lead, it scares me. Sometimes, I think it's better to lead a group because you can have a bit more control over what happens. But then, the people in the group sometimes seem uninvolved or hostile.

There seems to be fashions in using groups. A while ago, every agency seemed to want to start groups - groups for offenders, for young isolated mothers, for mentally ill people, for volunteers, for children leaving care. Then enthusiasm faded, but now it seems to have caught on again. Are such groups any use? Where do I go to get more information about them? In my work with individuals I get some supervision, but where do I get supervision and consultation about my groupwork? We heard a bit about groups when I trained, but it doesn't seem to be much use now.

My staff group is OK some of the time, people really help one another over work, but get into a staff meeting and what happens? We all just sit there and the things that have been bothering us all week, just seem too difficult or too unimportant to mention.

Do any of these statements reflect your feelings about groups? This book is designed to help you overcome some of these anxieties and make the most of the available information. It is based on my experiences of teaching groupwork to students for twenty years, and acting as consultant to experienced groupworkers. I have practised groupwork in psychiatric settings, children's' residential units and youth work. I have learned much about the preoccupations of groupworkers and searched through mountains of words to abstract the nuggets of information I find valuable. I have formulated my own practice theories, some of which may be useful in working out your own ideas. I have learned that a knowledge about groups can contribute to understanding about difficulties at work and to inter-professional rivalries. It can also help to make sense of prejudice and hostility between groups and account for the ways in which people lose their ordinary impulses when influenced by large groups.

There is plenty of information to help you feel more at home in group situations, but much is of limited use to practitioners. Theoretical books are often based on carefully controlled experiments in psychology laboratories and it can be difficult to see how these abstractions apply to your work. There are many books with practical hints on groupwork. These can be useful, but may encourage workers to ignore theoretical understanding and rely on recipes for action. When using such suggestions, how can you discover what makes them work in one group but not in another? Such books give only limited help in developing your knowledge about groups and how best to influence them.

Nevertheless, spending time and energy reading and training will pay off in your groupwork. Knowledge has to be gathered and processed; it is more than book-learning. Some of what you learn strengthens your work by confirming the value of what you have been practising. At other times it will give the feeling that you now understand a piece of behaviour that seemed difficult to account for when it happened. Knowledge enhances your ability to observe accurately what happens in a group.

Decide which sources of knowledge are most useful for your own unique ways of learning and style of working. Take the first steps toward more effective group leadership and more productive group membership.

SOURCES OF KNOWLEDGE

First, there is the accumulated knowledge about what happens in groups. The first careful observations about groups were made in the 1940s when people began to formulate ideas about patterns of group behaviour. Many observations were made by psychologists driven out of Nazi Germany, where they had seen the power of the group used for evil ends.

Research done in the 1950s and 1960s on group processes, both in America and Britain, stands up to the practitioner's strenuous test of 'Is it useful?' Practitioners are busy people, with limited time to read. I have included theory from those years in this book, but present it in detail only where I consider that it adds substantially to understanding. Even those who do not have much enthusiasm for theory may find some that they can put to work for them.

Second, there is the accumulated wisdom of practice. If there is an experienced groupworker in your vicinity, get them to talk about their work, or better still, work alongside them in a group. This book is not an 'I did it this way' description, although I have drawn on my own experience. Other books, for example, Heap's *The Practice of Social Work with Groups*, give you a feel of sharing the detailed successes and failures of an experienced worker.

Third, there are 'how to' books describing various activities that can be carried out in groups, or helpful suggestions about problems that arise. Bernstein, who practised as a groupworker and formulated theories about group social work, edited two books (*Explorations in Group Work* and *Further Explorations in Group Work*), which give many practical hints. There are several books describing activities for different kinds of groups: Brandes and Phillips' *Gamesters Handbook* is popular, and Lennox in *Residential Group Therapy with Children* gives a practitioner's flavour to the group games. Others are listed in Appendix B.

Fourth, it is particularly valuable to be a member of a group specially designed to help participants recognise what is going on in the group, and the role played by individuals. These groups (known as T Groups) enable you to understand group dynamics and your own behaviour as a group member (and potential group leader). This is why T Groups are included in some training courses for the helping professions.

All groups are potential sources of information, including those which are part of our work. Every group can help increase understanding, if you are able to analyse what happens in it. To do this, increase your theoretical knowledge to the point where you can understand the dynamics of the group. Once you can do this, it is possible to conduct small experiments, for example, by supporting someone who seems to have a good idea (rather than leaving this to others) and test whether this has any effect. This turns a frustrating group into an opportunity for learning.

Fifth, many people begin their groupwork by starting a group and learning as they go along. Those who enjoy learning in this way may feel exhilarated and avoid depression over any failures. But this method has its dangers. It is vital not to expose agency users to situations which we would not undergo ourselves. If you are never a member of a learning group how can you know what it feels like to be on the receiving end of your style of leadership? Even experienced leaders need to return to a training group occasionally to refresh their view of what happens for the ordinary group member.

Another problem in this way of learning is that we have, personally, to make every mistake and find our way out of it. Books and theory help you avoid the most obvious pitfalls and benefit from the experience of others.

STYLES OF LEARNING

You have your own style of learning and you learn more effectively in particular situations. Some people like to find out about theory, then put it into practice. Others prefer to learn from practice and formulate the theory afterwards. Some like to work intuitively and turn to theory only when they get stuck. Some like a model to imitate. Others prefer to formulate principles of their own. Diagrams baffle some but enable others to grasp a point. Discover your style of learning and work through the route most likely to help you. You will know whether you should begin with experience, feelings or intellectual knowledge.

Feeling and intellect are not always easy to separate. Powerful learning opportunities occur through the experience of strong feelings in group situations. For example, if you are learning about group conformity, experience of the powerlessness that group pressure can engender is vital. It is important to understand this force if it is to be resisted. Both approaches to learning are needed, so be brave and seek learning opportunities which do not seem at first glance to fit your style. It is by branching out into new ways of working that learning is facilitated.

THE PURPOSE OF THIS BOOK

This book is designed to help you get the 'feel' of group situations, make sense of what goes on, and work with events. It is an introduction to groupwork knowledge and practice based on social psychology and my own experiences. I have written in the hope that intending groupworkers who read it will learn to use theory as a reliable guide for their work. It is also intended for those with some knowledge and experience who want to develop their skills further.

In presenting theory, I have tried to highlight only theoretical or experimental contributions which illuminate group situations. Where an interesting experiment has given profound insights into group dynamics, it is described in detail. I believe that most of what is included can be substantiated by academic or experimental work. However, I have reduced background information because practitioners may get impatient if they have to wade through a mass of theory to get a grain of practice information. In general I have chosen theories that are likely to be of most help in practice, and which have stood the test of time. Chapters One to Three cover this theoretical background. Chapters Four and Five consider the uses of this knowledge in practice.

Having acquired a good understanding of the ways in which groups operate, and some experience of groupwork, the next step is to extend your skills. I have described four possible ways of doing this. There are many other approaches, but those described in Chapters Six, Seven and Eight have been popular with my students, and are those I have found most effective in my own work.

In Chapter Nine, I have explained what T Groups are; these are a valuable method of learning although they sometimes create anxieties. I have therefore described the ways in which they have developed and suggested strategies for getting the best out of them.

It is impossible to understand what happens in a group without taking into account how different groups relate to each other. Chapter Ten tackles inter-group processes and describes how group pressure to conform and obedience to a leader are powerful tools in creating inter-group hostility.

The book also applies knowledge which is useful in working with agency users to those groups of which we are members in our work. We spend much time in staff meetings and committees, sometimes finding them a negative or puzzling experience. Chapter Eleven deals with the groups we encounter at work.

I end by indicating possibilities for further training, and offer useful addresses and details of books that cover areas of interest.

ACKNOWLEDGEMENTS

There are many authors and practitioners whose work I may have quoted without acknowledgement, simply because I have used their ideas so often over many years and cannot now separate out the attributions that should be made. I apologise in advance to anyone not acknowledged and can only say that their contributions were so valuable that they have become received wisdom in the groupwork field. In general I have made attributions only where the name of the originator gave a useful memory tag for the idea.

One person from whom I have learned much is Gaie Houston. Finding myself in a Gestalt group led by Gaie was a major event of my life. I would also like to acknowledge the inspiration received from groups led by Viyog Gilbert and Donna Brandes.

I owe a great debt of gratitude to the many students who stimulated my thought with their questions and helped me to try out many of my ideas; also to colleagues who joined with me in running groups at Huddersfield Polytechnic.

My thanks to John Harris who read my manuscript and made helpful comments. Ken Verity encouraged me in my task, reconstructed my grammar and sustained me with his friendship. The errors, of course, are all my own. Although I have always believed that one learns from mistakes, I trust there are not too many of these!

One

Understanding group dynamics: structures and members

WHAT IS A GROUP?

Suppose you are travelling by train in a full compartment. The people are close to one another, doing similar things like reading or dozing. But this is not a group. Imagine that the train comes to a halt in a tunnel; ten minutes go by, you are getting uneasy. People start to talk to each other, even though they are strangers. A group is starting to form, with members communicating and sharing a common concern. The train starts again, and the feeling dissipates. If the train remains stuck for much longer, further group features emerge. Some people have ideas about what to do, others offer to lead a party to find out what is happening, and the feeling of belonging to a group grows even stronger. A group is not simply an agglomeration of people, communication has to develop and a common purpose emerge before individuals form into a group.

If I am talking to one other person, are we a group? Not really. This is a face-to-face pair. Each has the other's attention and all communications are addressed to one other person.

Three people interacting start a process; it becomes important who is talking to whom and who is getting left out. Differentiation of roles happens within moments. For example, one becomes the listener or observer and the others initiate actions. But if the group gets too large, it starts to split into sub-groups. In a group of more than about twelve people it becomes more difficult to be aware of every member of the group and be in communication with all the other members.

A simple definition of a group is 'a number of people in relation to one another'. Once they are communicating, and feel a common sense of purpose, a relationship also develops to the group as a whole, not only to the individual members.

A group does not have to contain all the members in the same room. Membership of the group continues even when people who are part of it are away from the group. Everyone is a member of many groups; it would take you some time to list all the groups to which you belong. Some will be more important and longer-lasting than others. Certain groups will be recalled with pleasure, others with distaste; we do not have to like a group to be a member of it.

A large organisation has many sub-groups. These subgroups often operate much as an individual does within a group. They resemble a group in which the members are separated physically but also have a sense of a larger grouping. This means that experience of what goes on in the small group can also be used to understand some of the events in organisations.

THE IMPORTANT FACTOR OF GROUP SIZE

The first part of this book deals mainly with groups of between three and twelve members. Most groups work better and feel more friendly if they do not exceed a dozen. How many famous groups can you think of that have been made up of about twelve members?

If groups of learners exceed about twelve members, then the chances increase that some will be unheard, or contribute little. One of the problems of current resource squeezing in education is that seminar groups have been forced to exceed this number. Equal participation is much harder to achieve in a larger group, and belonging to such a group is often not very rewarding.

Eye contact is important in communication, and to maintain full participation, a group in which members cannot face each other directly is disadvantaged. When a group gets very large, organisation is more difficult, and there is anxiety and conflict about whether a strong leader would solve the problem.

When a large group reduces in size, the amount members contribute and their ability to express themselves in a group is quite noticeably increased.

Size is thus an important influence on what happens in a group; it is one of the basic ways in which a group is structured. Other influences come from such fundamentals as the time a group has for meeting and the task to be carried out. These structural elements form the basic design of any group, but play only one part in determining how the whole group functions.

WHAT OTHER FACTORS INFLUENCE A GROUP?

Each group has its own 'feel'. If members of a work group meet together outside the office, although the members are the same, it feels like a different group. A group that has worked together on a task for years may start to fall apart when one or two of its members leave and are replaced. Obviously, a group is partly a product of the people who belong to it, but is also strongly influenced by the way it is set up. Once under way, it influences itself by the way it develops. After only one meeting, it has a history, and future growth is partly determined by what has already happened.

Golembiewski, who was a Professor of Political Science and Management in America, wrote an influential book on *The Small Group* in 1962. He made sense of the many influences on a group by separating them into three categories that are the determinants of any group situation:

- the structures of the group
- the characteristics of individual members
- the processes which a group develops in order to operate

These form a framework for understanding the way in which a group functions, or, in more formal language, the dynamics of the group.

It therefore makes sense to start by analysing group dynamics into these three types of factors: structures, individual members and processes.

WHAT STRUCTURES A GROUP?

Size

Some basic ways in which the size of the group influences what happens in a group have been outlined already. Other factors which are part of the structure include:

9

Time

An important factor is the time available to the group for meetings. Timetables and appointment diaries tend to impose an hour as a typical unit of time for a group, but one hour does not allow much time to get together, plan and carry out work, or formulate a common task. Under certain conditions, an hour can be a good duration for a meeting. For example, if people are used to working together they need less time to get through the preliminaries of starting work. If the people involved have a short attention span, as do children, it may be advisable to plan shorter groups. A longer time is needed for more complex tasks, or for a group to find out about each other's ways of working. This is an example of the way the structure of a group needs to fit the requirements of its members, and the nature of the task to be done.

The amount of time available to a group before its sequence of meetings must end needs careful thought, as does the interval between meetings. Groups which are planned for a limited number of meetings can be more intense than those with no set time for ending. Limiting the meetings means that ending the group can be planned from the start, so that members know how many meetings they are committing themselves to. In addition, the hour at which meetings are held must fit in with the requirements of members. A group of single mothers will not be well attended if it meets in the evenings. A group for older boys would not be popular on Saturday afternoons.

Location

Where the group meets is one determinant of how it develops. The basic requirement of a meeting place is that it provides the amenities for members to communicate with each other. The way a room is furnished helps to dictate the flow of communication. A room arranged with a platform in front and all the seats facing forward, as in a lecture room, gives little scope for communication between members and will be a serious limitation.

A group does not flourish in a room full of broken furniture, or that is too big, too small, too cold, or too hot. Pleasant, comfortable, surroundings give group members a feeling of being valued and respected. This is not an invariable rule: street gangs like to meet in any place that will give them a sense of ownership, no matter how uncomfortable! A room that is too imposing may give people a sense of unease.

In groups of agency users, some protection from noise and interruptions from other groups is vital. A room should ensure confidentiality and privacy if trust is to develop. It must also be appropriate to the activities of the group. I recall an attempt to run activity groups for children with emotional difficulties in an inappropriate setting. The only rooms available in the psychiatric out-patient department were also used by chiropodists and oculists, who inadvertently provided fascinating play material for the children! Luckily this soon convinced the hospital out-patient department that we needed our own premises.

Obviously locations need to be reasonably accessible for group members and take account of requirements such as difficulties in climbing stairs. A less obvious need is that of each individual's preference for a personal zone around them which others do not invade. This is an example of the way the structural property of space interacts with the individuals who compose a group.

Rules

Rules can be formal, written down, as in the 'Rule Book' used by some committees, or informal but just as strict. Even very informal groups have their rules. For example, a group of friends meeting in a pub will have rules about who pays for rounds of beer. In some groups, many of the roles are laid down before the group starts. An example would be the head of an establishment, or the doctor, who always chairs staff meetings.

The rules that are either prescribed or evolve within a group are very important for the way a group develops. A stranger coming into the group needs to find out quickly what these are. The new person may be given a list of the rules, only to discover that the unwritten ones are even more significant. In joining a new staff group, for example, workers will be given a 'contract' which specifies the basic duties. However, the clause which states that they will be asked to undertake 'other tasks as specified by the department' may actually cover the most difficult part of the work. It may be some time before a new employee discovers unwritten rules about how and when to approach senior staff. Can you think of other examples from your own experience?

When rules are evolved in a group they quickly become rigid and unalterable, even when the members themselves made them. Members who challenge these rules may be seen as 'disloyal'. Equally, one way of disrupting a group is to refuse to abide by the rules. If a member breaks a rule about confidentiality, for example, trust in the group can be destroyed. So agreement on basic ground rules is vital to the success of a group.

Voluntariness

Another factor is whether the members have chosen to be in the group or not. You can decide whether or not to join your friends in a group which meets to play badminton, but have no choice about serving on a jury. Some agency users have no real choice about joining a group, although they may have consented under duress. For example, offenders in Day Centres may agree when asked to attend, but only as an alternative to a worse fate. Often, this is revealed in their attitudes.

You are inevitably in a group such as a family or ethnic group, even if you feel as if you are only a distant member. Some people feel more attached to a religious or political group which they have chosen to join than to the groups they were born into.

Of how many groups are you a member, but have not chosen to join? How does it affect your feeling about the group? Does it help to make a group valuable to you if you choose to join it? Perhaps being allocated to a group means that you will stay in it even if you have doubts about your membership?

Closed and open admission to groups

A group can be set up with members who are expected to attend throughout the life of the group; this is a 'closed' group. It means that even if members leave, nobody else will be asked to join. The alternative is to have an 'open' group with a changing membership. Open groups vary. Some are composed of a core of people who are joined by floating members at each meeting. Others do not want to close their door and exclude any other members, but do ask members to attend for a while if they enter the group. Closed groups may decide that their membership needs revivifying and invite new people to join at an agreed time, so the distinction is not absolute.

Since every group is influenced by the members in it, changes in membership will be an important factor. If a group is to have a limited life, closed membership ensures continuity. Open membership is useful in some situations where the aim is informality, or there is a rapid change in the people eligible for the group as in a hospital or assessment centre. It is more likely that a group which has consistent membership will settle to intensive work, although Henry in his article in *Groupwork* on 'Revisiting open groups' points out that groups with changing membership are sometimes able to pass on the accepted ways in which a group operates from long-standing to new members.

Patterns of communication

Sometimes in a group, the way in which people are permitted to communicate with one another is laid down by custom, for example in the army, or a street gang, where the new recruit cannot talk to the chief, but must only speak to someone of middle rank. The physical structures may influence who talks to whom, as when team members work in several rooms, or are often out of the office.

There was an experiment carried out by Bavelas in 1960, that I have repeated frequently in many training courses for groupworkers. Each time the results are much the same as Bavelas describes them. The experiment involves solving a problem whilst keeping silent and only being able to pass written messages to fellow group members in a certain pattern. Thus there is artificial control over who communicates with whom and the resulting blocks to the flow of information are quickly seen.

In the original experiment, Bavelas and his co-workers arranged for certain patterns to operate while requiring an abstract problem to be solved. They then looked at the influence of these patterns of communication on the efficiency of the group. This was measured by the time it took to solve the problem and the number of messages which had been sent. Members of the groups were also asked whether they had some satisfaction from doing the task. Finally, Bavelas looked at whether the structures he had imposed influenced group leadership.

If O stands for each group member, these patterns were:

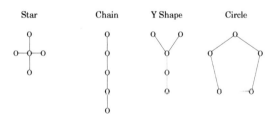

These patterns differ in two ways. The first concerns the number of links joining group members. Put another way, this means the number of people each member has to go through to reach another member. In the star, every member is only one link away from the person in the centre, but two links away from each other. In the chain, the first person is four links away from the fifth person. In the Y, the one at the bottom is really 'out on a limb'. In the circle, there is equality, since no-one is further than two links away from anyone else.

Secondly, they differ in the importance of the person in the crucial central position. In the star, the person in the centre is in direct touch with all other members. In the Y the central person is dependent on another member to get in touch with the fifth person. In the circle, there is no clear central member.

The effect of these differences is evident in the efficiency with which the group accomplishes its task, and the satisfaction gained from being members of the group. The star is usually fast and efficient. Unfortunately, the central person may be enjoying the position and working hard, but the other members get bored unless the problem is solved quickly.

The more 'democratic' circle uses everybody's knowledge and people will work on a complex task with persistence and enjoy solving the problem. There is usually more satisfaction in being a member of a circle pattern.

To summarise, the factors that Bavelas studied:

- differences in the numbers of links between people
- position of the central person
- effect on the efficiency of the group
- interest or boredom generated in the task for those in different positions in the pattern

Difficulties in solving a problem occur in particular patterns. The person in the centre of the star may not enjoy being in this position, and feel snowed under by information. Messages pile up before them, and are not dealt with. The ability of the group to solve the problem evaporates, and it is difficult for a member on the periphery to make a bid for leadership if he or she does not have the information which is piling up in the centre. It usually takes longer for the circle to solve a problem, but if there is a hitch, for example, someone is giving misleading information, then it gets picked up more quickly.

Both the chain and the Y often give difficulty. In the chain, the person in the centre not only gets overwhelmed with information, but cannot reach the furthest members personally. In the Y the one at the base is not only isolated, but sees that others have a lot more ability to communicate. If these patterns are re-arranged slightly, we get:

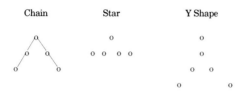

Does this remind you of any group or organisation of which you have been a member? In organisations the workers are engaged in the task of solving the problems of agency users but over them is a chain of command, many links away. In some patterns, a break in the chain can easily be compensated for. In the circle, for example, if one member gets ill, or stops talking to another, there are still ways round the break. Whereas in the other patterns, if two people stop communicating, the others are stuck, because they are dependent on that person for information. Have you met any staff teams in which this has happened?

Bavelas found that the person receiving most information is inevitably seen as the leader. This person controls the information the others get and therefore restricts their ability to operate efficiently. If this person likes leading, and has the skill appropriate to the particular task (and different tasks require different skills) then the problem will be solved quickly. But if they do not see themselves as leaders or cannot deal with this particular task, the group is stuck. This is where the more democratic circle, though slower, has a wider range of group member's skills to draw on and is not so dependent on the quality of the one who happens to be the leader. In the Y group, the designated leader may be the one at the top, but the second in charge controls all the information and so is the real leader.

Every group develops its own patterns of communication. If you want to see who talks to whom, and who gets a major share of the communications, get a huge ball of wool and have the members hand it to one another when they speak, rolling out the thread. Quite soon there will be a clear guide to what the pattern is. If you can't do this in practice, imagine the wool passing round!

It is also important to note the direction of the flow of information. Is it one-way or both ways?

One-way and two-way communication
One-way communication happens when the leader or manager gives orders but does not allow comments and reactions from subordinates. It

can also happen when communication to the leader is blocked. This is a common pattern in organisations. Orders may be issued by the person at the top which are inappropriate or impossible to carry out. A worker down the chain of command may decide not to obey the order. But without two-way communication and feedback from the workers, the person at the top thinks all is well. The leader then issues more orders, based on the idea that the first order was carried out. Each time the mis-match between what they think is happening and what is actually happening is compounded.

There is a party-game which illustrates this perfectly. One person stands with his or her back to a small group of people, and without looking at them, attempts to structure them into a group sculpture illustrating some theme. The 'sculptor' has a vision of what the group is going to look like, but without visual feedback on the effect of the orders, he or she gets a shock when time comes to turn round and see the finished product. What was planned as a graceful structure is simply a muddle, with members having to contort their limbs to carry out the impossible orders!

Don't forget this simple principle when you are in a position to issue orders. It is one of the most common mistakes in leadership.

Feedback

In a group, the more readily members feel able to be open and spontaneous about communicating with all the other members of the group, the better the task will be done. This may not seem to apply to tasks such as fighting a battle, or performing a complicated surgical operation, where one person needs to direct events very fast. But every soldier and theatre nurse can tell stories of where the person in charge was not aware of what was happening on the periphery and the result was disaster.

A hierarchical pattern of orders, without feedback about whether these have been carried out, is a common factor in many disasters where lives are lost. The danger is made worse where there is some mechanical failure of feedback equipment like videos and radios. Blockages in communication which prevent feedback can also be the result of human factors. The rivalry and lack of understanding that sometimes occur when members of a team from different professions try to work together provides an example of this.

In small groups, the factors that inhibit feedback involve both the structure of the group and members' own ways of reacting to information. Where feedback concerns our own behaviour or ways of organising, it is particularly difficult to accept. This will be considered further when the influence of the individual on the group is discussed.

What job does the group have to do?

Some groups are a way of getting people together to have some fun. But this is still the task of the group. Every group has a purpose and work to do. The nature and importance of this task or goal can be imposed from without, as in a community children's home. Alternatively it can be self-generated, as in most leisure groups or self-help groups. The task may be written down formally, or apparently so well known as not to need to be on paper. In many situations, the absence of a clearly formulated task or goal may lead to several different goals all operating simultaneously. The most important may be unspoken - the need for workers to protect themselves from press vilification or legal action is an example.

It is also important that goals have support from those both within and outside the group. Many social workers battle to uphold a goal of respect for agency users but find that their aim is not given enough priority in the organisation. This leads to alienation and 'burn-out'. Teams of diverse professionals sometimes find that their goals are not shared by fellow team members; they then feel frustrated and hostile.

Contracts with members

A contract is an agreement between members and organisers which spells out mutual expectations about the group. The nature of the contract negotiated with members also helps to set the structure of the group. Such contracts can be informal, simply a suggestion about 'getting together' for example. However, if you are to make the best use of groups in your work, the contract is best defined carefully. The way in which the contract is negotiated does a lot to set the scene for a group. If the contract is imposed on the members, this is a clear indication of the power of the leaders. If it is negotiated, membership participation is seen to be valued from the start. Putting the contract on paper also helps, perhaps in the form of a letter to members, or as a poster on the wall at each meeting.

SUMMARY

So far, this chapter has considered the structural factors influencing a group, that is, the way the group is set up. It may sound theoretical, but when it comes to organising a group yourself, or trying to change an existing group that has become 'stuck', these basic factors can have a lot of influence. If you neglect them, and arrange a group that, for example, meets too often or is too big, or which cannot communicate for some reason, your group will be struggling.

To summarise, he structural factors outlined so far concern:

- size of the group
- location of the group meeting
- time available
- formality or informality of structure
- whether membership is voluntary or imposed
- closed or open membership
- communication patterns that are imposed or develop
- whether communication is one-way or two-way
- whether the group structure permits feedback
- type and status of group goals
- contracts with members and whether these are imposed or negotiated

THE INFLUENCE OF INDIVIDUAL MEMBERS

A second set of factors that influence the group concerns the members. Everyone brings with them their own personality and ways of behaving. They also bring their previous experiences of other groups, where they learned ways of reacting and dealing with events. Every group is influenced in important ways by the behaviour of individual members.

Roles people play

In our lives generally, everyone plays many roles. Some are imposed by birth or the stages of life development. When you are a child, you have to play the role of child; too early an assertion of independence and adulthood spells trouble. There is no option but to play the role of daughter or son, though there are many different ways of doing so. There may be some choice about becoming parents and of work roles, although many find these have been imposed. Roles such as being a chairperson of a political party or a football club have to be won against opposition from other aspiring and ambitious people.

Once you occupy a role, the behaviour needed for it is prescribed by the expectations of society generally and the people affected by the role in particular. In some roles we are allowed to contribute our own ideas about how they should be played. All the roles we play add up to a considerable body of experience and help to form our personalities.

A well-functioning group depends on having people who will play various roles which further the needs of the group: someone who gives some leadership where this is needed, for example, or will be secretary, look after new members, or say when they think the group is veering off the point. Groups also need members in supporting roles to one another. You may have experienced a group where members are in leadership roles in other groups and expect to lead this group. If everyone is trying to lead and no-one will be led, little gets done. Particularly difficult is a group where everyone prefers to remain silent and expects others to do the work. The result is a group which takes a long time to make progress.

People differ in the way in which they play roles. No two people will be exactly similar leaders, or secretaries, or jokers. Moreno was an innovative psychotherapist who invented the idea of getting people to play various roles as part of their therapy. He pointed out that we differ in the intensity and the skill with which we play a role. Some appointed leaders will take the job very seriously (an example would be Captain Mainwearing in the British TV programme 'Dad's Army') while others will play down its importance (as Sergeant Wilson does). Corporal Jones in the same programme is an example of someone who is keen to be in a role but plays it without the necessary skill.

Many fictional groups rely on the comedy or tragedy inherent in the ways in which individuals fill roles more or less suitably. If you take a book, play or film which you have enjoyed which is about a group of people, you may be able to see the way in which the author has used the notion of the roles needed in a group and the various ways in which they are played. Then think of a real-life group of which you are a member, and see whether you can allocate the role each member plays, and the way in which they individually interpret the role.

Some people are not very good at picking up the skills of a new role, and will stick to the ones which they feel comfortable using. Others (perhaps most of us?) feel uncomfortable and incompetent when we are forced to take on multiple roles. An example of this might be a situation where nursery nurses are asked not only to look after the children, but to invite parents into the nursery for 'training' in child care. Looking after children and teaching adults are different skills. Roles of parents and nursery nurses can easily be undermined where this is not recognised.

Some people have a very definite preference for a role in a group. One may be the joker, another the quiet one, or the one who is always criticising others. Someone who finds groups stressful may have difficulty in becoming a member who contributes, even if they have many good ideas. Do you have a specific role you often find yourself playing in groups?

Sometimes a member may be stereotyped. A woman may be asked to make the tea, or be the secretary; a member with a regional accent may be expected to be obstinate, or to take a back seat. In some cultures, an older person may be heard respectfully and be thought of as the leader, in others they can be disregarded as 'has-beens' and barely tolerated.

It can be difficult to shake off the expectations within a group that you will play a particular role, the motherly one, for example. If you are usually the joker, your serious remarks may attract laughter. The expectations based on your own preferred role are the most difficult to discard and you may sometimes feel that you are playing a stereotype of yourself.

Previous experiences in groups will colour each member's view of how a role should be played. If you have watched a skilled performance of the leadership role, you may expect others to play it in this particular way and feel anxious if it is played differently. Membership of a group which has a strong influence on your behaviour and values can also influence the way you play a role in another group. An example would be of a male gang member who joins a group in a juvenile justice centre and finds that each group member is expected to assume responsibility for an aspect of caring for others such as making refreshments. This he sees as a girls' role and feels insulted.

The topic of roles will arise again in considering the processes that operate in groups, since some role-playing is the outcome of individual preferences and skills, while other roles are imposed by the group. It is difficult to distinguish the roles that are assumed by individual preference from those required or stereotyped by the group, since these factors interact. In situations where roles are a problem for a group, it is useful to try to separate out whether individual or group process is the main contributor.

To summarise, contributions made by individual members to role-playing within a group can be based on:

- age, gender, ethnicity, social class, education

- roles occupied in the past
- status, experience in leadership
- willingness to complement another's role
- intensity, conviction and skill in role-play
- ability to deal with multiple roles and role overload
- role preferences
- membership of important groups outside this group

Behavioural differences

Everybody differs in their ability to produce certain responses. Some people never lose their temper. Some seem to react to many situations with aggression. Some people are good at empathising with others, while some are insensitive. If a group has too many aggressive members, it will have difficulty getting started. But then, so would a group in which everyone was over-polite. A group needs a mixture of different behaviours, just as it needs a mixture of roles. So try not to groan when the 'difficult' member arrives; their behaviour is an important part of your group, giving you work to do and preventing members from becoming complacent!

Status

Everyone carries a status with them from outside the group. We are all important in some way, as parents, workers, or citizens. We are all unimportant in some contexts. For example, at work you may be in a senior position, but when you get into the company of people from other occupations, they do not recognise this. Some people drop their status with relief when they get into a different group, while others still expect to be accorded importance in a new context.

Getting other participants in the group to agree on each member's status, and in particular, the status of the leader, is one of the most delicate operations. A group in which this is agreed is much more efficient and pleasant to be in than one where there is disagreement.

Response to group pressure

An important experiment to determine individual variations in susceptibility to group pressure was done by the psychologist, Asch. He demonstrated clearly the power of the group to influence individual judgement.

Asch told male college students that they were to take part in an experiment that was about visual perception. One by one, they came into a room where five people were already seated. The student was always placed last-but-one in the row. They were shown a series of lines and then asked to indicate which of the lines was the same length as a separate line. Unknown to the student, the other five, who seemed to be taking part in the experiment, were in fact, 'stooges' and had been briefed to give an identical incorrect response. After the others had given the wrong response, the student was unsure of the evidence of his own eyes. If all the others were so confident, perhaps he was wrong? The final person in the line always agreed with the others, not him, so as the series of comparisons went on, the poor student nearly always felt forced to agree with the majority. Afterwards, the students often insisted that they had given the right answers, because everyone else had agreed with them. This is a classic example of the power of group pressure.

However, not all students in the experiment conformed in this way. Some went on maintaining stoutly that their answer was right. If the experimenter changed the rules slightly so that the last person to answer agreed with the student, then the number of times they gave the correct answer increased dramatically. It is always useful to have an ally.

Group pressure can be extremely powerful (Chapter Ten goes into this topic at greater length). Can you think of an example you have experienced? In a staff meeting perhaps, when the pressure *not* to mention something that everyone is finding difficult meant you said nothing?

Attitudes to authority

One of the psychologists who fled from Germany to America in the 1930s, Adorno, did some research into what he termed the 'authoritarian personality'. He thought there were some people who are conformist, rigid, and with little imagination. They are usually quite prejudiced against anyone who is 'different' and think in stereotypical ways. They have an exaggerated respect for authority and rules. He found that this cluster of personality traits and belief systems did in fact describe certain people. His research was confirmed when it was repeated in the 1970s.

More recently, Argyris, writing about different types of managers, thought that some people are so achievement-oriented and centred on individual accomplishments, that they find co-operation very difficult and expect conflict. Such people may themselves respond to 'strong' leadership and therefore rule through fear. If their need for this kind of rule conflicts with workers' needs, their management will be unproductive.

In studying groups, Bennis and Shepherd observed that some people dislike authority intensely. If they see a rule, their first thought is to break it. They took these characteristics - obedience to authority and dislike of authority - as being the two ends of a continuum, with all of us having a position on this line somewhere. Where would you be on such a line? Do you like a known structure with clear rules, or do you prefer less clear-cut, unstructured, situations where there are no laid-down rules?

Attitudes to intimacy

Bennis and Shepherd also thought that some people have a great dislike of behaviour that indicates closeness to other individuals. Such people feel uncomfortable when others are willing to disclose facts about themselves, or easily get into close contact with anyone else. Indeed some people cannot bear to be touched or to see other people touching, even in the most socially accepted ways. Have you ever shaken hands with someone who thoroughly disliked the touch? Or been hugged by someone you do not know very well? How did this make you feel?

Other people don't feel comfortable unless they have established a rapport with those around them, and like to develop a close, trusting relationship as soon as possible. So here is another continuum, with dislike of intimacy at one end and preference for closeness at the other. Where do you fall on this line? Most of us have a preference for one end rather than the other.

Hidden agendas

In a group which is functioning well, individual needs are respected. If members trust the group, they will be able to say what their needs are and how the group can help to fulfil these. Some needs will of necessity have to be put to one side if the group is occupied in an important task. Others may not be appropriate to a particular group and are best dealt with in another context.

Problems arise when important individual needs are ignored by other group members. This can lead to covert alliances in which members join together to further one of these hidden needs for one another. These become important but disguised items on the agenda. An example would be a situation where a group of parents of children with a disability might meet with medical staff to gain information, but convert the meeting into a complaints session. Complaints are not on the agenda and nobody mentions them officially, but somehow every item seems to lead around to these discontents. Such hidden needs must be recognised as appropriate and admitted to the official agenda.

Individuals need to feel that their needs are considered in the group, but occasionally someone may insist on gaining satisfaction for their own aims even when this is not appropriate for the group. Even more destructively, some individual aims are calculated to interfere with the task of the group. Such aims may be conscious, for example, wanting to undermine the authority of the leader. Or they can be unconscious, as when a leader is concerned to maintain popularity at all costs. The presence of one person with such aims can influence others who are drawn in to a covert pressure group which furthers the aim without making it explicit.

Hidden agendas of this type are very destructive to the group. It is important to recognise them and enable them to surface. Those based on racist and sexist attitudes undermine the progress of a group and are particularly painful to tackle. Challenging hidden agendas is never easy, but if they are interfering with the task of the group, this must be done. Developing trust in a group is difficult if there are significant hidden agendas operating. A group can be encouraged to use the problem-solving methods and communication skills on the difficulty if it can be revealed in a supportive group atmosphere. (Some of these skills are described in later chapters.)

Previous experiences in groups

Groups are frightening and anxiety-provoking places for some people. They think of all the awful groups of which they have been members over their lifetime. If the most basic group of all, the family, has been a distressing place, that is an uncomfortable base-line. But if the family has been very nurturing, this also can be an irrelevant place to start from, since many of the groups in the world outside the family are tough.

School is another place from which memories about groups remain powerful. Insensitive teachers and bullying pupils set their mark on our future expectations about what is likely to happen in a group. Although the group happening now may be far removed from those early experiences, it can still remind us of past groups. We go on building up our experiences at work and in leisure activities with the end result that some people are uncomfortable in groups while others feel at home. Probably most of us feel some anxiety on joining a new group: just what is going to happen? Is it going to be like the last one?

Sherif was a social psychologist writing in the 1950s, when he made a particular study of boys' groups. He said that, starting in childhood, but continuing into adulthood, we all have 'reference groups'. Such groups uphold rules and values which influence our personal values and standards of behaviour and which support us in maintaining those standards. This is obviously true of religious groups, but it also applies to families, friends and sometimes, politics or work. Which groups influence you in this way?

Sometimes the influence is towards behaviour that is relevant to a particular group but is seen by others as 'anti-social'. Gangs can help a youngster maintain behaviour which others deplore: getting tattooed or fighting in the street, for example. Terrorist behaviour is maintained by a close reference group which is more important than the opinion of the rest of the world. When joining a new group, one of the anxieties is about whether membership means being asked to behave in ways which are unacceptable to the reference group. A gang member sent on community service with young people with disabilities, for example, may be required to behave in a nurturing way quite at variance with his usual way of operating. In that situation it is vital that the new group quickly becomes the reference group, or the new behaviour will not last long.

A new group may also cut across the boundaries of other groups. It may be fun to join a leisure group, but socialising afterwards makes inroads into family ties. Students on social work or counselling courses may find that they are learning new values which conflict with those they are 'supposed' to hold, as far as their reference group is concerned. Have you had the experience of being attacked by family or friends who think you are 'growing away' from them?

SUMMARY

This section has introduced some of the factors that help group members to make an impact on any group they join. These include:

- the role a person prefers to play
- individual behavioural reactions
- the status each person occupies outside the group
- individual response to group pressure
- individual response to authority
- individual response to intimacy

- hidden agendas
- previous experience of groups
- the reference groups to which a member belongs and which may influence his or her attitude in another group

There is no way for the individual to avoid influencing the group; even keeping silent can be a powerful contribution. The silent member attracts attention through their silence; others may think the one who does not speak feels superior, or intimidated, or angry. Then members feel guilty, or start to get angry themselves. Powerful members gain their own ends if other members remain silent, since silence implies assent.

It usually seems as if it is the other group members who are being unco-operative or critical, but are you ever in these roles? Do you expect other group members to agree with you? This means that if a group is a difficult experience, one place to look for an explanation is into yourself. What contribution are you making? What particular needs of yours in a group are not being met? Is the group too authoritarian, or too intimate for your comfort? Could you relinquish some of your less important requirements? Or would the group profit if members resisted its demands for conformity - including you? It is important to become sensitive to your own reactions in group situations.

Perhaps the group has too many of one sort of person and needs people who can, for example, play a wider range of roles, or tolerate more democracy. Are you able to be flexible and switch roles, or play one in a different way? It sounds easy in abstract but in practice this is one of the hardest things to do.

CONCLUSION

This chapter has described the basic structures which shape a group and considered the influence of individual members on a group. These are the first two of the three factors which Golembiewski thought determined the way a group evolves. In the next two chapters, the third determining force will be described: the processes that develop as a group gets under way.

Two

Understanding group dynamics: group processes

Once the structure of the group is determined, and the individuals who compose it are assembled, it sets out, like a sailing boat rounding the harbour wall and starting its task of dealing with the elements. This is group process! It can be rough and scary, but it can also be exhilarating as members discover effective ways of coping with each other, the task, and the problems that develop.

In this analogy, the structure of a boat clearly determines its seaworthiness, but the individuals who compose the crew are also vital to what happens on any voyage. In a group, the structure is equally influential; the size, time available, communication patterns, goals, and so on, are as important as the depth of the hull and the nature of the steering gear on any boat. The way the boat is built must match the needs and experience of the crew. Sailors used to a small fishing boat will be of little use on a racing yacht. A crew composed of people who would all like the role of captain will make a mess of the most sophisticated racing gear, where orders have to be given fast and carried out without question. The interactions between individuals who compose the group and the structure are therefore an important element in success or failure.

INTERACTIONS CREATE PROCESSES

The interactions that develop between individuals and the group produce the process. Every group has a particular way of developing and working.

A group is more than just the sum of its parts. That is, what happens in a group is not just the product of the individuals who are the members, nor simply the result of the way it is set up. The impact of a group on individual members and the influence of individuals on a group, goes round in circles, so that it is difficult to sort out who is influencing what at any given moment. A skilled group observer will spot the point of influence and the mechanisms by which it is carried out. This is not easy; sometimes the group may change direction, make a decision, or select one member to speak for it with such rapidity that it requires a video-recording played back slowly to see just how it happened!

Individuals behave differently in one group compared to another, so the group is an important influence on the individual. Every group acquires an identity of its own and has a different effect on members. The impact of the group on members is more than any one individual member, acting alone, can make.

At the same time, no matter how a group is set up, it will always be influenced by the membership. To influence a group, an individual needs to make alliances, note the type of group they are in and who the other members are. Thus the process of the group develops, which in turn exerts an influence on members.

GROUP DEVELOPMENT

Every group goes through a sequence of stages as it develops. These are the recognisable markers which loom up and pass by as the group becomes one which means something to the members and which accomplishes the task for which it is convened. There are two slightly different ways of explaining the stages of group development. Some theorists believe that a group has to repeat endlessly a cycle of development, while others see the group going through a series of stages until it disbands. Probably both are true, since a group may climb from one stage to the next but also go through a series of vacillating movements while it does this. At moments of stress, the group may revert to behaviour that was characteristic of the stage before any trust between members has developed.

The easiest theory of group development to remember is that of

Tuckman, who summarised many observations and theories. He concluded that all groups go through stages of Forming, Storming, Norming and Performing. To this needs to be added that groups have to go through a stage of Ending, or Mourning, as well.

The following description of developmental stages is based on the ideas of Garland, Jones and Kolodny (in *Explorations in Group Work*, edited by Bernstein). They looked at groups from a practitioner's viewpoint and worked out a theory of group development with social work groups, mainly for children and young people. The description also seems to fit many adult groups. It is more detailed than Tuckman's. See if it is recognisable in any of the groups of which you are a member.

Stage one: pre-affiliation

This describes the anxiety experienced when a group first meets. Everyone needs to protect themselves to some extent among people who are new to them. Members have to find out if the others operate by the same rules, and whether the needs of individual group members are going to be respected. Will members have anything that they can share?

People are usually on their best behaviour at this stage, very polite and formal. They may not give anything away about themselves. It can be very quiet, or there can be a great deal of slightly nervous chatter. If someone makes a suggestion about organising the group, it is well received. When it comes to carrying out the suggestion, support often seems to melt away. If the leader does not offer to organise the group, there will be much unease.

To a certain extent the leader has to put up with this stage and not fall into the trap of over-organising people too soon. At the same time, leaders have to recognise that having convened a group, they have some responsibility for providing support through this uneasy time, and through the next two stages. It is important not to expect too much of a new group.

To cope with this situation, some members make bids for power. These can be quite subtle and difficult to detect, or blatantly obvious. They begin to search for like-minded fellow members. They seek to find out what kind of behaviour is expected, and whether this expectation fits the ways they like to behave. As this happens, the group moves into the next stage.

Stage two: power and control

Members now dispute for status and control of the group. They try out the strength and cleverness of other members, and find out what they can 'get away with'. Alliances form for mutual protection or the exploitation of others. They test what will happen if they challenge the leader's power. Children sometimes go so far as to lock the leader out at this stage! Adults are usually more subtle, and use criticism, or suggest a change in leadership. As Tuckman noted, this is a stormy time, with much conflict. It is a time when the ground rules of the group are worked out, ways of behaving begin to be agreed, and members gradually find out how to get along with each other.

Agreement on a few ground rules is helpful. These will vary with the nature of the group. When members are expected to talk about themselves in some detail, it is useful to agree that what they say will be kept confidential, but this can only be a suggestion.

The legitimate need for basic rules can be turned into a struggle for control over a group. Some members may make oppressive demands for conformity at all costs. 'Everyone in this group must ... ' and then follows a string of prescribed behaviour. 'Everyone must like each other/listen to each other/work together/not be prejudiced/sexist ... etc'. Of course it would be wonderful if we were all like this, but the danger lies in the 'must'. What happens when someone breaks these rules? What sanctions can the group apply? Is it possible to legislate for everyone to be nice? If members are going to be expelled for behaviour against such rules, will there be any group left?

If members are to feel at ease in the group, they need to be able to express how they feel, even if this expression is not popular. Possibly some curbs are needed, but they will be more effective if they are worked out over the course of the group. It is important to remember that the aim is not to end up with a group that is so similar that it just becomes a vehicle for mutual back-stroking. How can oppressive group demands for conformity be avoided whilst achieving agreement on behaviour so that everyone feels a sense of belonging?

It is this struggle for norms, or agreed ways of behaving, that helps the group to progress. If norms are oppressive and constrain members' behaviour uncomfortably, the group cannot make much progress. When norms suit most people, and the standards are understood and accepted, the group can relax.

One method of getting agreement is to start with an issue of no particular significance, such as a decision on a name or an emblem that represents the group. This begins to give members a sense of belonging together. If the group has to go out and be recognised, a mark such as wearing woolly hats or a red rose is valuable. It is an outward expression of a group's common cause.

Agreement on how the group is to be organised is vital for smooth functioning. For example, is it to be democratic, with everyone taking turns to lead, or are members to follow a clearly recognised leader? Agreement frees group members to participate in planning group activities and to contribute their own expertise.

Some members cannot tolerate the unease of this stage and opt out, either by not returning, or by withdrawing from what is going on.

If a group gets stuck in this stage, a search for a scapegoat starts. 'We would be getting along fine if it weren't for one particular person'. The topic of scapegoating will recur later in this chapter under the heading of 'roles'. It is important that the leader does not support the idea that one member is responsible for all the ills of the group.

Sometimes the leader feels like giving up at this stage. It is a time that searches out all the leader's weak spots. Members may take refuge in the idea that everything would be all right if the leader was better. Alongside such negative reactions, in a group in which the structure is well thought out and the processes are becoming supportive, individuals are beginning to think of the group as well as themselves, and to develop ways of working together. This 'Storming' stage is unpleasant, but so is a group which gets stuck at the first stage of polite triviality. Groups make progress by coping with these difficulties.

Stage three: move to intimacy

Whereas in the second stage, the emphasis was on struggles around authority, the group now has to grapple with closeness and intimacy. The transition from authority to intimacy is marked by the increased agreement about norms and ways of working. One of the reasons for the disagreements in stage two was the need to postpone any emotional closeness.

Members start to feel the benefits of having joined the group. They know one another much better, and feel at ease with what is happening. They are ready to disclose more about themselves. Needs for dependency are revealed, and some rivalry develops about who is to share the favours of the leader, or a popular member.

But this stage can get too agreeable. People can get so much pleasure, or reward, from belonging to the group that they neglect the task for which the group was set up. A group for lonely mothers may enjoy each other's company so much that they exclude newcomers and therefore do not learn to make new friends. Some staff groups meet so often that work is neglected.

It is important to enable trust to develop, but also to keep an eye on the progress of the task. It is a temptation for the leader to allow the group to rest once trust and closeness has developed, because it seems so comfortable. The leader needs to remind the group about the task, help the members avoid settling into cosy sub-groups and encourage tolerance of diversity. Rivalry and anxiety about relationships will continue, even if they do not surface so easily as in earlier stages. There may also be an over-reliance on norms and a failure to stand up against group pressure.

Stage four: differentiation

At this stage, the point of reference for members becomes the group itself. Before this stage is reached, members might still be thinking back to other groups to which they once belonged. Another group could have been used for comparison, for example, 'This group is not as much fun as the one I went to last year.' Reactions more appropriate elsewhere, for example, the family or school, may have been evident in this setting, with the leader being called 'Miss' or 'Sir'. Now, in stage four, members can differentiate between this group and other groups and feel that the task is as important as the relationships which have pre-occupied them in former stages.

People feel attached to a group which is valuable to them. A useful term for this feeling is 'cohesion' and there is more about this in Chapter Three. This feeling is based on a sense of mutual purpose and free communication. That is, members will not be rejected if they are unfriendly, but they might get some forceful feedback about how their behaviour made another member feel. Most members of the group contribute their skills and knowledge, and thus become the leader for a while, so that leadership is shared among members. The group often turns to accomplishing a task outside their own boundaries. In my own experience as a worker, at this stage a group of people who had been mentally ill turned their energies to helping a group of people with learning difficulties, with much profit to both groups.

The leader seems almost redundant, but is still a useful reference point. Many leaders hang on to information or resources at this stage, in order to justify their existence. Some leaders thrive on a group's dependency on them, but a more constructive reaction is to help the group run itself and to become a resource person. This does not mean abandoning the group to its own devices. The task of the leader as this stage progresses is to see that leadership is shared and to contribute resources for the group to draw on. The leader also has to help the group prepare for ending. Most groups have to terminate at some time, and it is better if this end is achieved as part of a plan for the group.

Stage five: separation

If the group has gone through the other stages and the final phase is a deliberate termination, this stage will provoke some anxiety but not panic. Even so, reactions similar to those of earlier stages are set off at the prospect of the group ending.

It is sometimes assumed that, although we know that ending one-to-one relationships is painful, and that endings need careful handling, a group is somehow less significant. Anyone who has been involved in an ephemeral but pleasant group such as one which assembles for a tour or a course, will know that endings always have some sadness; the exchange of addresses at the end is a way of pretending that separation can be postponed. Ending a long-term group, such as you may have experienced at college, or in a particular job, brings a real sense of loss. If members have experienced a high degree of cohesion, they will feel some regrets when the time for ending comes. When groups are set up for people who have been deserted many times, the ending can remind them of those other experiences, and they may feel anxiety out of all proportion to this particular ending.

Even if the group was planned to meet for a limited time, members can deny this. 'You never told us', some members say. If the group is to be time-limited, members need to be aware of this from the start. It is important to remind members several times before the actual ending. Members may assert that the group is still needed. Alternatively, they can compensate for the impending loss by insisting that the group has been of no use, so it does not matter if it ends. Sometimes members behave with aggression, or withdrawal, as they did in the early stages.

It is useful to help members recall the tasks they did accomplish and the ways in which the group has been useful. It is usually possible to build in some follow-up provision for contacting people in the group, or the leader, or a known figure. Re-unions are often planned but do not always happen, because members have moved on and left the experience of the group behind them once it is over.

However, there will be extra difficulties if the group has been stuck at one of the earlier stages, or if the ending is unplanned, for example because the leader is leaving. A stuck group may breathe a sigh of relief at getting out of its difficulties by disbanding, but you can be sure that members will feel particularly badly about the group experience, and this will be carried over by them into future groups. Sudden, unplanned endings leave a wreck, and there can be some very disturbed reactions.

Manage endings of groups with care, build them in from the start if possible, and provide some links when the ending comes.

To summarise, Garland, Jones and Kolodny divide group development into five stages. These are:

- **pre-affiliation:** the individual investigates whether the group is likely to be of any use
- **struggle for power and control:** members find out where they stand in relation to each other
- **move to intimacy:** members enjoy some agreement on norms
- **differentiation:** the group gets on with the work it has to do
- **separation:** preparation is made for ending and the group is reviewed and evaluated

In a group set up to fit the needs of the members, where the leadership has been constant, and the task fulfilled, the stages may be in an orderly progression from one to five, but many groups will encounter difficulties. For example, a new member may join after the start, or the venue is changed. Under such stresses, the group will regress to earlier stages. A group of people used to operating in groups and sure of their skills will sometimes be able to work through all the stages very quickly, or skip the second and third stages completely.

CYCLICAL CHANGES IN GROUPS

One theory that sees the group as going through an ever-recurring cycle is that of Bion. He was a psychiatrist who, in the second world war, discovered that groups were an effective method of rehabilitation for army personnel suffering from 'neurotic disability'. Later he used groups for therapy at the Tavistock Clinic, London. (There is a more detailed account of these groups in Chapter Nine.)

Bion thought that groups had certain unconscious and irrational basic assumptions which they had to work through repeatedly and which prevented them from getting on with the work of the group. These assumptions were:

- **dependency**: the whole group behaves as if it is totally dependent upon the all-powerful leader
- **pairing**: two group members are drawn together on the assumption that they can produce a way of getting rid of the leader and take the group over or substitute their own preferred nominee
- **fight and/or flight**: the only possible way of behaving seems to be either to fight the leader or fly from the group

According to Bion, these assumptions have to be reworked repeatedly in the group, as they arise in response to any tensions. Whenever the work of the group seems to be making no progress, one of these assumptions can be found to be operating.

Have you ever noticed how often, especially in the early stages of a group, you feel helpless to influence what is happening, and it feels as if only the leader has the power to get everyone to comply with what he or she wants? Or that the leader is getting the group into a mess, and you can do nothing about it? Basic feelings of helplessness can be projected on to a leader, and he or she can be accused of every variety of incompetence, whilst group members behave as if there was nothing that they could do about this personally. Of course, if the group is in a dictatorship's prison, or a concentration camp, this is true. Thankfully, most of our groups are not conducted in an atmosphere of ruthless, cruel authority. But we often behave as if they were.

When we are feeling helpless we tend to produce infantile reactions. Trying to grab power, or fighting authority blindly, or running away, are all the result of those feelings. Next time you are in a group that is getting heated, sit back and see if you can categorise some of the behaviour being displayed as one of these basic assumptions. The interest of this theory is that, once it is understood, it returns some power to the group members. It is possible to choose to opt out of such behaviour, even if this is not easy when group pressure is strong.

STAGES AND CYCLES COMBINED

Hartford, drawing on her experiences of social work groups, thought that both theories about developmental stages and about cyclical changes were needed to explain the ways in which a group makes progress.

She developed some helpful ideas about the first, pre-group stage, which she divided into sub-stages. At first the group is only in the mind of the organiser. Next, ideas are communicated to the agency and the practicalities discussed. Finally potential group members are contacted.

After the group starts to form Hartford thought that there is likely to be a cycle of integration, disintegration and conflict which would lead to reintegration, reorganisation and synthesis and then to a more serene group maintenance phase. However, this cycle can be set off again by events such as a dispute between members or a change in the situation of the group.

Hartford also divided the ending stage into three sub-stages: planning to end, carrying plans out, and making arrangements for the post-group stage.

Hartford's stages of group development can be listed:

first stage: pre-group planning
1. the organiser plans
2. the agency is involved
3. group members are contacted

middle stage: cycles of
• integration
• disintegration and conflict
• reintegration, reorganisation and synthesis
• group maintenance

ending stage:
1. planning to end
2. carrying out the ending
3. arranging the post-group phase

USING THEORIES ABOUT GROUP DEVELOPMENT

What are the practical implications of these theories? If a worker understands that every group goes through stages of development, there are many ways in which this can assist practice. For example, expectations of a new group can be made more appropriate. It is important to accept that people go through a stage of feeling new and apprehensive. Allow time for this to pass. Remember that a new group cannot be expected to share intimate information until they have worked through the first two stages.

Do not get discouraged when the group is 'storming' and 'norming'; this is a vital stage in getting to a working agreement. Planning should take into account that an agency can get worried when a group goes through stage two, perhaps rather noisily.

It is also vital not to confuse stages three and four. A group stuck at the third stage of facile agreement and conformity will not be able to accomplish much; one that progresses to the fourth stage will get on with the task to be done. Groups stuck in one stage can be analysed and shifted. Members often have good ideas about how to make progress from one stage to the next, as few enjoy being stuck in the early stages.

Plan for the end, and expect some strong feelings to emerge about the ending. Endings need to be built in at the beginning.

The rather discouraging ideas of Bion about the incessant re-working of the basic assumptions in a group are also useful to help analyse and shift a group going through a bad patch. Ask yourself why the group is not getting on with the work. Which basic assumption is prevalent? Are members (including yourself) disabled by a sense of dependency? Are they planning idealistic alliances and fantasy solutions? Or are they alternately fighting each other and the leader and then flying from the consequences of their actions?

ROLES

Although group members may arrive with their own preferred repertoire of roles they can find that the group insists they play the role in a particular way. An individual may have developed a way of playing a chairperson, for example, but find that this group insists on a different style.

In some situations members are forced into a role by the way the group is set up. A group may have a tradition that a particular type of member is always leader; when someone resembling this ideal arrives, that person is immediately put into a leadership role. Another way in which a leader can be forced into this position is due to the communication patterns that develop. For example, the person in the centre of the star pattern in the Bavelas experiment is forced to become the leader because all the information is coming to them.

There may be pressure to play a role that is quite unfamiliar, as when a group lacks a treasurer, so a member is coerced into playing that role even if they cannot add up. But when a group needs a member for a particular role, they look to the person most likely to be able to play it, and then put great pressure on them to occupy the role.

Scapegoats

A particularly destructive process is at work when a member is selected to be a scapegoat.

The first recorded scapegoat is found in the Old Testament of the Bible:

> And Aaron shall lay both his hands upon the head of the live goat, and confess over him all the iniquities of the children if Israel, and all their transgressions in all their sins, putting them upon the head of the goat, and shall send him away by the hand of a fit man into the wilderness. And the goat shall bear upon him all their iniquities unto a land not inhabited: and he shall let go the goat in the wilderness.
> *Leviticus, Chapter 16, verses 21 and 22*

This is an exact description of what can happen in a group. The 'goat' has to bear all the iniquities of the group. In other words, when the tensions and transgressions of group members become more than they can bear, or when they cannot address an important problem because they feel that to do so is 'wrong', they select someone who is weak and defenceless, load that person with their guilt, and eject him or her with a great feeling of righteousness.

Such action may have been soothing magic for the desert tribe, but it seldom works positively in a group. This is because the ceremonial ejection of the only one whom the group sees as being loaded with sin, does not solve the problem. The remaining members of the group still cannot deal with their own feelings and the sense of righteousness does not last. Quite soon another member of the group has to play the role of scapegoat. In a small group, if one member is ejected in this way, the group may disintegrate and not meet again. Members may feel so badly about the action that they cannot face each other. In addition, the ejection of the scapegoat has made the unresolved problem even more dangerous to tackle.

If you observe one member of a group being accused of an iniquity, you may be fairly sure the accusation concerns the central unresolved problem of the group at the moment. Remember that the more righteous the feeling, the more certain it is that the group is behaving like the tribe in Leviticus. It is important that you do not collude with this general feeling, but help to seek other solutions than the ejection of a group member.

One question that often arises when the topic of scapegoating is discussed, is whether the scapegoat invites the treatment he or she gets by some particular, unacceptable, characteristic or by apparent defencelessness. If someone is regularly scapegoated, this could mean that they are poor at defending themselves, or have a tendency to put themselves in situations which they might know from experience could be damaging. In a group of children, it is often the 'scruffy' one who is picked on, especially if they have an unpleasant habit of some kind. However, such a person will be nurtured carefully in another group. If scapegoating does occur, it is a group problem that needs solving, not just an experience of one disaster-prone individual.

To be a scapegoat, the member has to be powerless and without allies. If there is at least one member of the group who supports the scapegoat, total rejection will be avoided. Unfortunately, other members are reluctant to give support, fearing they will receive the same treatment. Often, the scapegoat is visibly 'different' in some way from other members and is therefore seen as vulnerable. Perhaps a woman in a group of men, or a black person in a group of white people is picked upon. Such oppressive behaviour will not occur if a group is willing to tackle their own attitudes and look at their own behaviour.

An exception to the notion that scapegoats are isolated and powerless seems to occur when it is the leader who is being scapegoated. But many leaders, though appointed to that position, find it is one which carries very little power, and the position of leadership isolates them. Even very powerful leaders can be scapegoated if they lead the group into disaster. Everyone remembers what the leader did, but forgets that they did not dissent at the time decisions were made. Scapegoating of the leader means that there is likely to be confusion over power issues, and the leader is playing the role of the one who is responsible for the group's problem.

Deviants

Scapegoating is very destructive in a group. However, a group can gain much profit from having a 'deviant'; that is someone who questions the group assumptions, does not behave according to group norms, and generally makes the other members think about their group conformity.

It is not comfortable to be a deviant in a group. A great deal of attention from group members is directed towards the person who is disagreeing. However, a deviant who later conforms becomes a popular member of the group. There is a sense of satisfaction in bringing the deviant back into the group, or pride in belonging to a group that can encourage and nurture those whose ideas are 'different'.

In situations where group pressure to conform becomes dangerous, a deviant who refuses to go along with the feelings and actions of other group members is essential. This is a difficult role to occupy, since even when the group ultimately realises that they were misguided, they are seldom willing to hail the one who objected as the hero.

Saboteurs

A deviant is not at all the same as someone who deliberately sabotages a group. The group saboteur usually has a 'hidden agenda' which is more important to them than the official purpose of the group. In a group in which an important issue needs attention, the saboteur may provide a negative method of escape. Alternatively, members may provoke sabotage in order to avoid the work that needs to be done.

Other roles

You will probably be able to think of other roles you play yourself in the group, or have observed in others. Redl saw young people in his social work groups as the Tyrant, the Fixer, the Seducer and the Bad Influence. You will have met the Bad Influence yourself, particularly in children's groups; he or she is the member around whom things go wrong simply because they are there. When they are not there, things seems to go more smoothly.

I have noticed Monopolisers, Trivialisers, Recognition-seekers, Silent Critics, and so on. There are also, happily, Good Listeners, Inspirers, and Calming Influences. Can you add to this list?

LEADERSHIP

Leadership is important to a group. The qualities, skills and expertise shown by the person occupying the role have a strong influence on a group. A great deal of research has been done to try to find out if the qualities of a good leader can be specified and identified in individuals. Obviously the armed forces and industry want good leadership. The communication patterns prevalent in such organisations are usually the star or the Y, which means that the ability of the leader is vital. There is a problem in defining the attributes of a good leader: there is no agreement on just what these are, or how they can be predicted. When established and successful leaders are studied, they seem to come in all varieties and succeed for different reasons.

The leader is only one member of a group, one element of the process. Leadership skills can be learned, but acquiring the skills of leadership means more than learning ways of directing and manipulating a group. Becoming a 'good leader' by using techniques and tricks means that your group may be manipulated into conformity, but will not develop trust nor will members feel that they want to contribute their abilities and energy to the group. Good leadership in the helping professions and in management is based on respect for group members and a willingness to share responsibility.

Fiedler looked at many groups in industry and the armed forces. He developed a theory that helps to explain the ways in which successful and popular leaders differ so widely. He called it the 'contingency theory of leadership'.

Fiedler thought there were three important dimensions in every group:

- the nature of the task
- the power given to the leader
- the relationship between members and the leader.

Nature of the task

A well-defined and unambiguous task is most efficiently carried out by a leader acting with authority and possessing relevant expertise. But an ambiguous task with many unknown elements needs a leader who will be able to draw on every particle of expertise in the group, and encourage shared leadership. In the helping professions, the task can rarely be defined with absolute precision. Workers have to use their initiative to deal with constantly changing situations. This means that the authoritarian leader who likes to work with a clear task is unlikely to succeed in such settings. One response of the authoritarian leader in this situation is to try to define a task precisely, wasting much time in the impossible attempt.

Power of the leader

In some situations, the leader may have a great deal of power, in others the position is only nominal. An organisation often requires a middle-ranking leader to take a large share of responsibility, but confers little authority. Some organisational structures make it easy for a leader to be by-passed. In a group of agency users, the leader's power will usually be weak. Even where it is reinforced by the courts, it may be disputed by group members.

Relationships between members and leader

Where the relationship between the leader and the members is based on equality of status and expertise, a leader who believed in being authoritarian would be most unpopular, whereas if there was a great discrepancy in status between the members and the leader, a highly democratic leader could puzzle and confuse the members. Some agency users will have encountered many situations in which they are ordered about and have very limited experience of consultation. This means they find it difficult to know how to react to a democratic leader.

The three dimensions of leadership outlined by Fiedler mean that the success of any leader is contingent upon a match between the leader's style and the group. A leader who is highly successful in one situation may be a failure in others.

When a leader is not doing well with a group, Fiedler thought that it is important to assign such a leader to a situation where he or she will be more effective. For example, the authoritarian leader may operate well with a group where the members are clearly his or her subordinates, whereas the democratic leader struggling with that same group may do better with a group of people of equal or near equal rank. Other examples of changes that can be made, involve giving a leader sole authority, or requiring the leader to consult. Giving the leader greater control over vital communications will mean that everyone will have to go to him or her for all information, which will add to the leader's power. To lessen the power, the information may be made more widely available. It may be possible to modify the task, or change the mix of the group. Training the leader to change their style, for example by teaching him or her to be more aware of how they set about being a leader, is another possibility. However Fiedler found that leaders seemed to find it extremely difficult to change their approach.

In any group, it is important to analyse these elements of task definition, leadership power and relationships between leaders and members. Think of a group with which you have been involved and see how these factors operated.

Leadership styles

Fiedler noted that leaders tend to be quite inflexible about their style of leadership. He concluded that it is easier to move a leader to a new group which matches his or her leadership style than to attempt to re-train a leader to fit a group with whom there is a mis-match.

Argyris confirmed this; he found that leaders could be divided into two types. The first type tends to be achievement oriented, to think in terms of the individual and individual success, often adopts conflict as a mode of problem-solving, and is not too good at co-operation. The second type is interested in co-operation, is personally unthreatened by other group members, prefers to seek a decision which involves all the members and welcomes honest feedback. The two types seemed to represent basic personality characteristics.

Which kind of leader do you prefer to work with? And when you lead, which kind of leader are you?

Another approach is to examine the effect of different leadership styles on comparable groups. An early experiment on leadership was done by Lewin, Lippitt and White. Lewin was one of the social psychologists who fled from Europe to America in the 1930s. (There is more information about his work in both Chapters Eight and Nine.) He wished to find out more about the impact of leadership on groups, so he gathered together a large group of boys aged about twelve and split them into three groups. They met in the evenings and participated in craft-type activities. He then trained a group of leaders in three different leadership styles.

The first style he called 'Authoritarian'. This meant that the leader made decisions, dictated the steps involved in activities one at a time and did not reveal any overall plan. He decided who worked with whom and on what, and used personal criticism as means of getting better work done.

The second style was 'Democratic'. This style involved putting all strategies and policies to the group for discussion. When the group arrived at an overall plan the leader reminded them of this when appropriate. Group members were left to decide with whom they worked, and if it was necessary to criticise, the leader did so by referring to facts rather than individual performance.

The third style was 'Laissez-faire'. This meant leaving all decisions to the group without interruption, supplying the materials but only giving information when asked, not participating in the group at all, and never criticising.

Each leader had to use each style in turn; (these leaders did not seem to have difficulty changing their leadership styles, but it was in a circumscribed situation). As they went from group to group, changing each of the styles, the behaviour of the groups of boys altered dramatically. There is a film, made in Hungary, of a repeat of this experiment done with six year old children. This confirms vividly the differences in behaviour that accompany each leadership style.

Both in Lewin's experiment and the Hungarian film the authoritarian leader was not directly challenged, and members were overtly dependent and submissive. With one another, group members were hostile and unco-operative, expressing aggression frequently and bullying weaker children. The work was carried out without enthusiasm, but productivity was high. In the Hungarian film, the children produced a neat pile of painted clay Easter eggs, which was the appointed task; but the eggs were all much the same pattern, and not very well done. Once released from the authoritarian leader, the members ran wild. The children said they would like to be a leader like this one, even though they had not enjoyed being in the group, because they could then boss the others around.

The children in the democratically-led groups had a strong preference for this leader. Their motivation to work was high, and the work produced was creative and original, but not so prolific as in the 'authoritarian' group. They were friendly to one another, and went on working when the leader left the room. The group was important to them, and they enjoyed being members.

The laissez-faire style was a disaster. The work produced was poor in quality and often destroyed. In the film, the clay and paint was mostly spread around the walls and ceiling. The children said they hated the group (except for one small boy in the film, cowering under the table and fearful of the uncontrolled behaviour going on round him, who maintained that he was having fun). There was extraordinary aggression in the film between the children, and the group became quite dangerous. The children also said they wouldn't mind being a leader like this one, since she had nothing to do.

The Lewin experiment was done in the late 1940s, in America, when it was possible that the outcome was influenced by its acceptability. Naturally people wanted to find that democracy worked. The Hungarian film shows that similar reactions occurred in a different culture. Both experiments were done with children. However, it does seem to explain some adult behaviour you may have observed in a group. If the group has no clearly defined task, no accepted norms, and a laissez-faire leader, behaviour seems often to be destructive. Authoritarian leaders produce passive members. If your group is demonstrating some of these behaviours, have a look at your own style of leadership.

This experiment also demonstrates one of the effects Fiedler was describing. That is, the way in which different leadership styles fit in with the task set for the group. The boys' groups were not so efficient with a democratic leader, but they were most enjoyable and members had a sense of achievement. Groups of agency users do not need to be efficient in the way in which operating theatre teams do. They need to learn about shared leadership and their own resources. Therefore the authoritarian style is inappropriate. Equally inappropriate is the laissez-faire style, which might work with a group of highly creative and responsible workers, but does not give the necessary structure and modelling of co-operative behaviour to a group of people unused to working together.

Leader expertise

It is important for group functioning that the leader has relevant experience which is shared by and with members of the group. One source of trouble in many teams is that the leader may come from another occupation, and have only minimal understanding of the members' concerns. This could be one reason why, for example, a doctor in charge of a team of social workers may have difficulties.

In leading a group of agency users, the possession of expertise relevant to the task of the group is vital. Anyone leading a group of children going caving had better have good knowledge of caving as well as of group dynamics. The reverse is also true. Technical expertise in caving is not enough, the leader will be more effective if he or she has some knowledge of how a group functions. If the task of the group is assisting members with personal problems, the leader needs training and experience in counselling.

Occasionally a leader will hold on to knowledge that could be shared with a group, feeling safe with the role of the 'expert'. In general, any group of agency users will profit if the leader shares their relevant specialist knowledge. Sometimes it can be useful to refuse the expert position and encourage group members to develop their own skills.

Task leaders and social-emotional leaders

Bales, whose work was inspired by Lewin's ideas, studied groups engaged in problem-solving. Observers meticulously recorded every interaction between members. From these observations, Bales was able to show the links between what people did and the decisions taken by the group. He found that in most groups, especially the ones that succeeded in solving the problem, there tends to be a leader who is concerned with getting on with the job and another leader who is good at paying attention to the social and emotional needs of the group members.

Solving a problem in a group, or making a plan, inevitably involves some members in getting their own suggestions taken up, while others find their ideas are overridden. Individuals' needs get submerged in the interests of getting the problem solved. The task leader tends to remind the group that there is a job to do, implying that the job is more important than the individual. The social-emotional leader may slow down this process, ensuring that members do not get left out, or left behind. This person watches to see that communication is open, that everyone has a say, and that contributions are acknowledged. They are sensitive to non-verbal communication and to indications of distress.

For maximum effectiveness, the group obviously needs both types of leader. Even better, this kind of awareness is best spread through the membership. Shared leadership indicates a well-functioning group, whereas rival leaders can be destructive. Flexibility in leadership roles is therefore a good indication of group strength.

The task-oriented role is not a single one. People who initiate ideas, give information, co-ordinate and summarise, energise the proceedings, criticise and evaluate, are all forwarding the task. Group maintenance roles include those who encourage, support and help set nurturing group norms. The role of defusing the tension often falls to the joker, who can be useful in small doses, but can deflect the group if the jokes hide a contentious issue that the group needs to deal with.

In a group, do you find yourself driving on with the task, or are you concerned with the effects of the group on individuals? Do you see yourself as a task-oriented person or one for whom the social-emotional factors are most important?

TASK AND PROCESS

In any group there is the drive towards accomplishing the task, and there is the process that this generates. If the task is the only focus, the group will either be hampered in its work because it ceases to pay attention to the needs of its members, or it will reach quick decisions which are not put into practice. If the group gets pre-occupied and bogged down in its own processes, no work will be done.

Attention to process is often suppressed because it involves examining feelings, or touching on painful or contentious issues. Anyone in a group remarking 'Let's get on with the job' or 'We have to reach a decision' is acting as the task leader, driving the group towards dealing with the task. Anyone saying 'Just a minute, what is going on?' or 'How do people feel about this decision?' is acting as the social-emotional leader and attending to the needs of the members and the process of the group. One member might have sufficient perspective and knowledge of group dynamics to be able to comment on the processes of the group, though what he or she says may not always be listened to in the heat of the moment. Groups that are stuck can profit from calling in an outsider to observe their processes and find the nature of the difficulty.

An observer may see that, for example, a member's contribution is being ignored because they have less status. One member may be blocking communication, or holding back vital information, or be unhappy with their role. The leader may be neglecting the fact that the group is only in an early stage, and be expecting too much co-operation. The leader's style may be irritating members. Conflicts develop, communications are distorted. The group may start to split into sub-groups. Everything may become too cosy and no work gets done, and so on. (The next chapter will outline some of the ways in which groups can get stuck, or fail to create a positive climate for getting on with the task.)

Remember that in a successful group, the need for getting on with the task is balanced with the need to attend to processes. Time needs to be given to both aspects of the life of the group. If this is done, any decisions taken by the group will be more acceptable to all group members, and will actually be put into practice, not shelved. So time invested in the processes of the group will pay off when decisions are implemented and do not have to be worked on again and again.

SUMMARY

This chapter has considered some of the important factors to be recognised and worked with in group processes. These include:

- stages of development that the group goes through
- sequential and cyclical stages
- roles needed in the group and imposed on group members
- scapegoats, deviants and other roles
- leadership styles
- the need for leadership styles to fit the type of group
- leader expertise
- task leaders and social-emotional leaders
- the important distinction between task and process

Several of the theories that increase understanding of what is happening in a group have been described. Theories may seem indigestible, but Bavelas' communication patterns, or Lewin's work on styles of leadership, are useful reference points in the mass of interactions that go on in any group.

To return to the analogy of the boat, once the boat has left the calm waters of the harbour, and is actually in rough water in the open sea, things happen in a split second; small variations in winds and waves have to be assessed rapidly and taken into account. To the beginner, the boat has changed tack before they have realised what is happening. In a group, many interactions happen at great speed, but a skilled and experienced group leader can spot what caused the change and influence the direction of what happens next. The next chapter continues the description of these processes.

Three

Getting on with the work of the group: more about process

This chapter continues the description of basic processes in groups and will outline further important factors in understanding and running groups. The final section examines the factors that make for successful group problem-solving.

COHESION

What makes a group stick together? Why do people come to a group and stay in it? Sometimes they have no choice, but there are ways of opting out, even from compulsory groups (by non-participation, for example). There is a great difference between being a member of a group that is important to us, and a group to which we are indifferent or which we actively dislike. If the group gives us nothing, there are no reasons to keep us there, and we leave it. What keeps us in the groups of which we are members?

Cartwright was one of the psychologists who worked in the tradition of Lewin and Bavelas. He analysed the forces which produce group cohesion and considered what needs to be done to foster and increase this. His ideas are useful to the groupworker in creating a positive experience for participants.

Cartwright pointed out that the more attractive a group is to its members, the more influence the group has. People need to experience positive gains from belonging to a group. This happens when a member is in agreement with the goals of the group and at ease with the size, the style and the way in which others in the community see the group. A businessman may join the Round Table even if it means sacrificing time at home, because of the group's prestige. He may make good business contacts there and enjoy the company of other men with similar interests. Although he may not be interested in fund-raising, he participates in it because it is a way of being a good group member. Similarly, someone who is assigned to a group for offenders will need to feel at home in it and not be expected to undertake activities which are too divergent from those of his or her reference group. If the activities are very strange, a quick pay-off for the new behaviour helps a member to remain and feel safe in a group.

It is a condition of being a social human being that we have a need for affiliation, for belonging, for recognition and for security. Each group we join fills some of these needs. We look to other group members for agreement with our own points of view, values and aims. If the other members of the group are attractive, or successful people, then the prestige of joining the group is high. Cohesion is therefore a product of the interactions that go on in a group, and a synthesis of individual and group factors.

There is also the consideration of the penalties of not joining a particular group. To be a member of a gang brings protection against other gangs. To be a staff member who never goes to staff meetings is self-isolating, and such a person gets left out of decision-making.

Why do members leave a group? The reasons can be listed under the headings of structure, individuals or process:

Structural reasons
- the group has too few or too many members
- it meets at an inconvenient time or place
- the premises are dreary or too splendid
- it is uncomfortably formal or informal
- there are too few or too many rules
- membership is officially compulsory
- the prevailing pattern of communication gives the new member no access to information and low status
- membership is unbalanced—for example there may be too many people concerned with their own problems and unable to relate to others

Reasons that concern individuals

- a group which makes excessive demands on its members can cut across the demands of other group values or activities
- the new member can find no congenial role, or a member of long standing is ousted from a favourite role
- the member may feel inadequate or inferior to the others
- there may be one person who is too dominating
- disagreements with other group members may make it difficult to stay
- the member may feel ill-informed or out of sympathy with the aims of the group or the methods of work it uses
- another group may appear more attractive

Reasons arising from process

- a member may feel isolated because everyone else in the group knows one another well, or sub-groups exclude them
- the group may be stuck in the first or second stage of development and have difficulty agreeing norms
- other groups may scorn this one or it may lose in a competition
- there is no agreement on leadership, or the leader has too much or too little power
- methods of dealing with conflict may be leading to repression rather than resolution of difficulties
- the emotional tone of the group may be cold or anxious

This list is by no means exhaustive. Can you think of further reasons? Under which heading would your reasons belong?

Encouraging cohesion

If, as a groupworker, you find people are leaving a group, what can be done about it? Effort can be made to make the group more welcoming, more successful or co-operative. The physical conditions of the group can be improved by meeting in a warmer, more comfortable place, or decorating the old one. The domineering or unsympathetic members need to be tackled, and the group's capacity to solve its own problems increased. How? It is not easy and this is where you need outside help, supervision or consultation, since every group has its own distinct problems and strengths. Meanwhile identifying the situation is a good start. Thinking through strategies and alliances puts you in a better frame of mind to address the problems.

A way that easily overcomes problems of cohesion, is to compete aggressively with another group. It draws a group together wonderfully.

Politicians have always known this and start to highlight difficulties with other nations when problems at home become unmanageable. Friendly competition can foster cohesion, but in it's more virulent forms, can lead to destruction of a group. This can happen not only through defeat, but also through changes that take place in a group as other aims are subordinated to the struggle.

Boys' clubs have traditionally used this tactic and fostered competitions with other clubs. Sherif did a series of experiments with boys in which he took them to camp and created competition between groups for food and other amenities. In a very short time, friends who had arrived together but were placed in different groups were sworn enemies, and the boys identified strongly with their own groups. (There is more about inter-group rivalry in the next section and Chapter Ten.)

The problem with wars and competitions is that someone has to lose. It is not easy, but more rewarding, to foster inter-group co-operation; helping out another group, sharing a joint project, for example. In this way, the cohesion of the group can be increased and the needs of individual members met without harming any other group.

COMPETITION AND CONFLICT

Scarcity

Competition occurs when there is scarcity. In a group, attention from powerful figures can be intermittent, or there may be a lack of positive feelings and respect for each other. Members of the group can be forced into rivalry by having to compete for scarce resources, or one group may find itself in competition with others for the same reason.

Competition is particularly acute in a situation where only one can win. If only one member of staff can get promotion, others may be jealous. But people seem to create a condition of scarcity where there is no need for it. One situation where this can be guaranteed to happen is known as 'The Prisoner's Dilemma'. This version was devised by my colleague, O'Byrne:

> Two men rob a bank and hide the loot. They are brought in for questioning, though there is no real evidence against them. They have promised each other to deny it all. If they honour this they will get off and get half the loot each. But they know that if one 'grasses' on the other, and the other keeps to the bargain, then the one who 'grasses' will take the

share of the other and get all the loot while the one who kept to the bargain serves his sentence! This means double gain for one and nothing for the other. Neither feels that he can trust the other completely. But if they both try to pin the blame on each other, they will loose the loot completely. That is, mutual co-operation will lead to modest gains for both players, mutual competition will lead to losses for both. Attempts to co-operate on the part of one player, when coupled with a competitive move by the other, will lead to a major gain for the competitive one and a loss by the co-operative one.

I have used an exercise based on the 'Prisoner's Dilemma' with students on a training course, in a version that substituted pennies for loot. If the students had co-operated, I would have lost £5 in pennies. They succeeded in creating rivalry and scarcity to the extent that I lost only £1. A colleague who tried this later lost £2, so it seems that some groups are better at co-operating than others!

The Prisoner's Dilemma clearly shows that co-operation is a dangerous business if you cannot trust the other person. Have you met someone who never seems to trust anyone else and who feels that if they do not watch out for themselves, nobody else will ever help them? Others may trust everyone and continually find this is not a universally effective principle. It is difficult to ensure that other parties to an agreement will stick to it if anything is to be gained by breaking away. Maintaining a co-operative situation needs a great deal of energy and sustained commitment, as those who have participated in inter-professional ventures know well.

Competitiveness

Some shortages legitimately result from scarcities, but others arise from mutual mistrust. Some competitive behaviour results from individual backgrounds, more than the objective situation in the group. Sherif showed with his boys' camps that it is very easy to create a competitive feel in a group, particularly if the competition is with another group. Tajfel later confirmed this finding with adult groups. Businessmen are clearly more interested in competition than are members of the helping professions, but if the stakes are high enough, most people, at least in Western cultures, will think competitively rather than co-operatively. Does your own culture and background encourage competitiveness, placing a high premium on success? Do you get rewards such as being praised for loyalty and fellow-feeling when you place the interests of your own group over other groups?

Being powerful does not stop individuals from being competitive. They may dread being unseated from power, or resent others with equal or greater abilities. So they use their power to increase the gap between themselves and others. There is plenty of evidence in dictatorships and totalitarian societies that the dictator, or the ruling party, has used power in this way.

Groups suffer from the abuse of power when a member or leader is authoritarian or domineering, or when one sub-group uses its power to attack another. In a group which is being torn apart by such mis-uses of power one solution is to get an outsider, preferably someone not concerned with the group in any way, to look at the uses of power within the group. What seems obscure to members may be clear to an impartial outsider. Such an observer would notice the way in which group pressure is operating. Are members feeling helpless? Is their feeling realistic? Are members being coerced into operating against their better judgement? What is impeding co-operative behaviour?

Groups also suffer when they are oppressed by a powerful outside influence. If this occurs it can bind the group together in adversity, but it also means that if there is any way of leaving the group, many members will take this escape route. (Chapter Ten outlines some causes and effects of inter-group rivalry and prejudice.)

Conflict

Are you frightened of conflict? Do you find something very important to do elsewhere if two people start an argument? Does aggression leave you shaking? If you do not feel this way, do you really enjoy a fight? It is not easy to deal with conflict constructively. What is important is to sort out your own feelings around authority, structure, and power sharing. We learn from an early age what happens when we challenge other people and want some power for ourselves.

Some conflict is useful. At a group in a residential setting, one resident came to the house meeting and tried to discuss whether another resident would let her watch 'Top of the Pops' that night. Worried staff scented trouble and insisted this was not dealt with in the meeting, but 'quietly' afterwards. But residential life is about learning to negotiate, and if staff act as buffers all the time, residents do not learn the skill for themselves.

Besides, the other members of the group may have had a valuable contribution to make to the discussion.

Dealing with problems which affect cohesion, or impede co-operation, may require some confrontation. For example, a member who is monopolising the group, or bullying others, often adjusts their behaviour if they are faced with the effects of their actions. To be helpful, such confrontation needs to convey to the other person that feedback is not the same as criticism. Feedback on how my behaviour affects others is useful. Their judgements about me are not, because such judgements reflect more about their own difficulties than they do about my problems. A group member who is not receiving any feedback may begin to feel they are getting the 'kid glove' treatment and not being dealt with honestly, or start to throw their weight about, making themselves even more unpopular.

One theory which illuminates a common source of conflict is that of Karpman. Working within the framework of Transactional Analysis, (which is described at length in Chapter Seven), she invented the notion of the 'Drama Triangle'. This deals with three possible roles which are interrelated: that of 'Rescuer', 'Victim' and 'Persecutor'. In the triangle the 'rescuer', who on the surface is trying to help others, actually starts to dominate, overwhelm and persecute them. The 'victim' blames others for his or her own problems and so becomes their persecutor. The 'persecutor' throws scorn on the 'rescuer', is critical and judgemental, and gets jumped on by the victim and the rescuer and becomes a victim. So the merry-go-round continues:

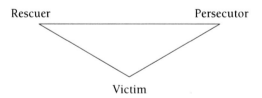

Members of a group frequently feel they are trying to help others, but only get criticised for their pains. In groups of clients, if one is singled out for 'help' by other group members, they can feel persecuted, refuse to change, and so in turn persecute their 'helpers.' Thus each is using their power to undermine others even if it based on a weak position.

Berne's notion that people play 'Games' in interactions of this kind also throws some light on conflict situations. 'Lets You and Him Fight' is instantly recognisable, as is 'I'm Only Trying to Help You'. Berne was the chief inventor of Transactional Analysis and many of his ideas throw light on the way in which conflicts can develop in groups. Can you think of some other competitive 'Games' you have observed?

A guide to dealing with conflict in the group is to ask yourself whether this behaviour is just difficult for you, or is it threatening the existence of the group? If two group members are arguing, can this group deal with it as part of the work it has to do? In fact, a group is often a good place to deal with disputes, since these usually involve the failure of both people to listen to one another. If each of the disputants can be persuaded to repeat the argument of the other person, it is clear that distortions have crept in, and they are in some way exaggerating or ignoring what has been said. It is particularly difficult to deal with disputes that centre on racist and sexist issues, since those from the dominant faction are often unaware that what they are saying or doing is offensive. Honest feedback can be useful, but sensitive feelings need to be recognised.

It is also important to be in touch with the emotional state of members in dispute. Too much anger may need calming before work can be done on the issue. A group member may be so much in need of nurturing that they interpret all feedback as lack of acceptance. Check the clarity of the communication flow at times of conflict. Anxiety often leads to complicated and unclear communication.

Above all, seek help if you are puzzled or anxious about conflict in the group, or worried that the conflict may cause the group to disintegrate. It is in situations of this kind that a co-leader is most valuable. They can check your own perceptions of what is happening and give support in sorting out the problem. There may be an unexpressed fantasy operating which predicts that conflict inevitably leads to destruction. Conflict can be valuable if it is the product of working together on a goal. But it is negative if it is an end in itself.

ANXIETY AND HELPLESSNESS

In all groups, the fact of being with other people can provoke anxiety. When those others are experiencing many difficulties, the anxiety can become overwhelming.

Menzies, who studied and worked with organisations, was asked to report on nurses in training in one hospital, as many of them were leaving before their training was completed. She found that there was no constructive way in which they were helped to deal with their feelings of distress and their own reactions to nursing sick and dying people. For example, enforced intimacy raises problems around sexuality, a taboo subject. Instead of a recognition of the inevitability and universality of these reactions, the nurses were offered defences: starchy uniforms, rigid procedures, frequent changes of location and advice on not getting involved. These defences were not sufficient for the more sensitive student nurses, and they dropped out.

Blaug used these ideas to understand a student placement in a day nursery, where the undervalued nursery nurses were grappling with defiant, unsocialised children who were very destructive, especially to each other. The defences adopted by the nurses consisted of never talking about the work or the children. In fact they hardly communicated with each other at all, so that the staff room at lunch time was often completely silent. In this way, they managed not to reveal their feelings, but also lacked any support from the group of staff.

What defence mechanisms are employed in the place where you work? Does your organisation have a receptionist sheltering behind glass, an office that is difficult to find, the telephone that remains unanswered? Is the worst sin supposed to be getting over-involved? Are you encouraged to keep a distance between yourself and agency users? In groups are you coldly professional, brisk, or distant?

Is there a better solution to dealing with these anxieties? Make a start by sharing your feelings, and find out how others feel. People involved with groups deserve the support of colleagues. If you are interested in groups and believe they are worth setting up and participating in, then it is logical to believe that groupworkers themselves can profit from being a member of a supportive group. Anxieties arise in all types of work with other people, as well as in group situations. There is much knowledge to be gained in sharing these.

Understanding the anxieties and needs of group members to take defensive positions is an important skill. Signs that a group is creating stress for a member can be seen if that person is keeping quiet, talking too much, letting others take the initiative, or blustering and bullying. You could easily draw up a list of the defence mechanisms you have observed. Which of these can you deal with, and which cause you trouble? Which defence mechanisms do you adopt when you are anxious?

PROBLEM-SOLVING AND DECISION-MAKING

'Problem solving' is a shorthand way of describing some of the work done in groups. Staff groups are obviously solving problems about allocation of work, rotas, consistency of service, inter-personal communication, and so on. Activity and leisure groups set themselves tasks which create the need for some group problem solving. Counselling or therapy groups are concerned with helping to solve problems of individual members.

In analysing the ways in which groups work, it is useful to refer again to the three factors of structure, individual members and process. In problem-solving these elements are closely related to the success of the group.

Size

The importance of the structural factor of group size has already been indicated in Chapter One. It is a crucial factor in problem solving. There is a saying that the ideal committee size is one person. Think about that - it implies that one person is able to make decisions, and then that decision will be carried out effectively by others who have not been involved in the decision making at all. Does this remind you of the authoritarian leader? Or of the problems of one-way communication?

In large groups, it is usually the voice of someone who enjoys speaking in front of others and has a vested interest in getting their own point across whose voice carries the decision. This means that other members do not feel that they have participated effectively.

In a group with more than a dozen or so members, reaching a decision becomes more difficult. It is less likely that the issues behind decisions will have been thoroughly explored. Once made, decisions taken by a large group will tend not to be carried out after the group is ended, unless a smaller group is appointed to do this. (Chapter Eleven has more information about the dynamics of the large group.)

Time

Adequate time ensures that decisions are not rushed. Bales noticed that if a group was given a problem to solve, they behaved at first as if time was very short, and wasted some time by rushing into solutions. Only when these were seen to be fallacious, did they start asking questions, eliciting more information, and thinking through what was involved in the problem. Conversely, too much time can also impede the process. It seems that many people profit from a deadline that sharpens their sense of urgency.

Agreement on aims and procedures

It is also important that the group understands its aims and objectives and accepts these. The better a group has worked out its norms of procedure and ways of working together, the more efficient will be the process. Have you noticed how in some groups the decisions seem to be reached in a pleasant and easy way while in others, even minor points are bitterly contested?

However, there may be too much emphasis on seeking agreement. This can lead to decisions which are based on failure to take unwelcome facts into account, or to consider unpopular alternatives. The 'knock-on effect' of decisions taken can be neglected. Without a thorough examination of all the evidence, decisions can show a distinct tendency to occupy the middle ground, as if group members prize agreement more than a good decision. So a group norm of careful exploration of all aspects of a problem or decision, even when this is uncomfortable, is vital to effective decision making.

Power and status

If the group contains people of very different positions of power some voices will have more influence than others. Recognising this, the Trade Union movement puts a lot of energy into training workers' representatives to speak in meetings with managers. When clients are involved in Social Service Department case conferences, they are at a great disadvantage, particularly since professionals are usually in a majority. Clients may well feel that the only way they are going to be listened to is by being aggressive.

Group members need to feel some confidence in their own ability to influence a situation. This will only be true if the organisation has delegated sufficient power and decisions are made within the limits of that power. A successful group is secure in the knowledge that their decisions will be respected and implemented.

Communication

It helps if communication is open and friendly, if members are listened to and valued, and criticism is directed towards evaluation of ideas, not persons. There needs to be shared leadership, with both the task and the social-emotional processes given consideration.

If there is a block in communication between two members, the Bavelas experiments show that this can seriously impede problem-solving. An isolated group without good communication with other groups, will begin to make some very odd decisions. You can see this in the behaviour of extremist political and religious groups.

One of the norms that aids good communication is that members should be willing to negotiate with one another. Basic skills in negotiation involve:

- careful listening
- ability to state the position of opponents
- generating a variety of alternatives
- selecting those that are closest to the stated aims of the group.

(There is an excellent book which helps with strategies of negotiation of this kind, *Getting to Yes* by Fisher and Ury.)

Strategies for effective problem solving

Effective groups often find it helps to have a set of questions to work through about the problem. This should not involve mechanical form-filling, but thought-provoking questions about:

- the definition of the task
- how much time is available
- who is going to be timekeeper and summarise the discussion
- what information is needed and how this is going to be gathered
- how far the power of the group extends over the problem
- what the knock-on effects of a decision will be
- who is going to implement the decision and what follow-up there should be.

(The group of mice who decided to put a bell on the cat, neglected to note some of these important questions.) There is a useful book on *Effective Meetings* by Tropman which is a help in organising decision making.

Groups whose main purpose is personal problem solving, such as therapy groups, also have to address these questions, though not so formally. In Transactional Analysis and Gestalt, the person asking for help with a problem is asked to state what they expect the outcome of the work they are going to do will be. In Gestalt groups they are asked to specify how much time they will need, and to negotiate with others who may also want some time from the group, so that all have a share. (Chapters Seven and Eight have more information about these approaches.)

Task and process again

Driving on with the task of making the decision will not bring success. It is important to remember that decision-making will be ineffective if attention to the process of the group is neglected. Members may seem to agree, but feel alienated from the result. This means they fail to implement decisions once the group is over, or sabotage useful suggestions during the group. A good group leader will recognise that process is important as well as task and will draw out the abilities and skills of the members. If process goes unrecognised, these will remain untapped. It is also essential to have members who can keep the component parts of the decision in mind and focus firmly on the task.

CREATIVE AND DESTRUCTIVE GROUPS

Positive groups

Randall and Southgate observed many community groups and decided that creative groups which got work done were those where the needs of the members were given priority. It is therefore essential to take time to deal with these. In this respect, adult group members are not very different from children. If members feel secure, their needs diminish and their ability to co-operate increases. In groups which have established that members' needs are considered important and are met wherever possible, and some trust has developed, conflicting needs are dealt with by negotiation. For example, you may want fresh air, others may feel cold, but they may not mind if you have the window open for a few minutes when the room gets hot. Or it may be possible to widen the ideas of a narrowly focused member by engaging their heart as well as their head. Recognising the value of the contribution a member makes is a good place to start.

One important need is satisfied by belonging to a group which successfully solves problems and accomplishes its task. A shared sense of a job well done is a powerful source of creativity and positive feeling.

A group encourages co-operative behaviour when decision-making is based on a wide distribution of power, experience of other members' trustworthiness, and agreement on goals. Members need to know that decisions will not be made behind their backs and that what the leader and other powerful group members say they will do will actually be implemented.

A group in which cohesion is high will produce co-operation. Progress to the third and fourth stages of group development will be marked by an increase in co-operative behaviour.

Negative groups

Randall and Southgate found that some groups were destructive, with little reward for membership from fellow members. Such groups are characterised by:

- power struggles
- de-skilling between members
- disagreements over aims
- dislike of new ideas
- scapegoating
- overdependency on a leader, or inability to accept that the leader has any power.

To work remedially on such groups, first analyse what is going wrong, then see if anything can be done about the elements: a change of membership, a redefinition of the task, or another factor which is exercising destructive influence.

SUMMARY

This chapter has considered further important factors that influence the process of the group:

- cohesion, or what binds a group together
- competition and conflict
- the way the group develops mechanisms for dealing with anxiety and feelings of helplessness

It has also applied ideas about group processes to assist effective decision-making. The impact of these factors is crucial:

- size and time
- agreement on aims and procedures
- power
- communication
- attention to task and process

The final section shows how these combine together to become a creative or destructive experience for their members.

If you give attention to the way these factors are operating, and the style of their operation, your group experiences will be more positive, creative and stimulating.

CONCLUSION

Taken together, Chapters Two and Three cover the processes you can expect to find in the groups of which you are a member, and those you will be leading. Analysing what is happening in a group is a skilled task, and reading about it is like reading a book on sailing and then expecting to be able to manage a boat. Chapter Nine makes some suggestions about taking part in groups that are designed to help members to increase their understanding of group processes and of themselves as group members.

As with all knowledge, awareness of what happens in groups can be used positively or negatively. That is, it can be used to further the aims of the group and individual members, or to sabotage and manipulate the group in ways that make members feel badly. One positive effect of having this knowledge, is that ways can be found to counteract negative influences in groups and build good group relationships.

Four

Using groups in social work and health care

WHY BOTHER WITH GROUPS?

After the preceding sections on conflict and competition, the misuse of power in groups and the negative experiences that groups can provide, is there any point in going on? Does it confirm all you worst fears?

But there is no escape. We are enforced members of groups such as staff meetings, and, if we want to enlarge our own horizons and have an impact on the world, there is no way we can do that in isolation. Politics is about the opinions of groups, not of the individual. Our favourite leisure pursuits need other people, if only to play football or go to a concert. So, if you cannot escape, then it is important to learn about groups and how to use them constructively. In doing so, you will gain in understanding and knowledge about the groups that you want to run in your work.

REASONS FOR USING GROUPS

Many people arrive as users at a social work or health care service because they have trouble with groups. They are either in the 'wrong' group, such as a teenage gang, or a drug-users group, or they are isolated, as is the young mother in high-rise flats, or the elderly person whose family has left the district. Youth services have a long history of providing services to counterbalance the power of the socially unco-operative teenage group. Community centres, day care facilities, residential 'homes' all provide antidotes to isolation.

Until recently Social Services and Health Care teams confined their work to the individual, or at most, the family. For a worker experienced in the dynamics of self and client, or patient, groups may seem a place where the worker has less control over what happens. Suppose a group were to damage fragile people, or an unsuitable member take over the leadership, or members insist on chatting aimlessly rather than engage in problem-solving! If a worker fails to deal with such events, the failure is very public in a group.

Increasingly, it is important to overcome these fears. Patch-based work in local offices involves co-operating with a variety of workers from different backgrounds in an attempt to help people in a neighbourhood form their own effective groups. Community care involves the setting up of specialist group care facilities needing a high degree of skill. Juvenile justice and alternatives to custody programmes use day and evening groups in preference to the prison living groups that have such a negative influence on offenders. Health visitors can see that there is a great need for young mothers to meet together. Health centres are setting up groups for patients and their families. People from different ethnic backgrounds find that, in many cultures, the original groupings of family and homesteads have been disrupted and getting together has become an important need. Workers in many settings are using groups to draw people together who have experiences in common. In this way, clients and patients can participate in the healing power that a good group can generate.

POSITIVE GAINS FROM GROUPWORK

For the member

A group can offer a stimulating experience. The adrenaline runs high in a group situation. There are more people to learn from, more models of alternative behaviour. If a young man sees his probation officer as conventional, middle class, perhaps of a different racial or ethnic background, he may have trouble identifying with what the officer is saying. In the group there may be people to whom he feels much closer, who can provide more powerful role models.

It feels more 'natural' to be in a group than to be sitting opposite a person who is of higher status, or 'different' to you, as you will remember when you think about the first time when you, alone, faced a manager who was going to supervise your work. People in trouble may 'dry up' when asked to talk about themselves to a worker, but find their voice again in a group.

A group gives all participants the opportunity to play an important role, even if it is that of group clown. Someone has to make the tea, or notice if a member is upset; it can just as well be a member as the leader. Thus status and power is equalized to some extent. The person who has seemed to be inadequate in the foreign setting of the office, may well be able to demonstrate some unsuspected skill with other people. Those used to being 'helped' can experience being a 'helper'.

Most important, a problem can be shared and the discovery made that you are not the only one who is suffering. You can listen to others who have to deal with difficulties that make your own seem less overwhelming. Above all, there is the generation of hope that can be fostered in a group. Together, much can be accomplished that would not be possible alone.

A group provides a safe setting for trying out new behaviour. A depressed woman may regain her sense of competence and start to become more assertive with encouragement from the group, before trying this out on an unsympathetic family. Youngsters can be more caring, and harassed mothers more aware of their own needs. New behaviour can be practised before tackling the unco-operative world outside.

The purpose of convening a group is to have a stronger impact on the behaviour of people in the real world, not just in the office. The alcoholic, for example, may be full of remorse in the clinic, but facing up to a group of fellow alcoholics who are sceptical is a searing experience. This is one of the reasons for the current development of group techniques relevant to the problems of sex offenders, who are usually well entrenched behind concealment and their own justifications.

For the worker

If information needs to be conveyed to several people, it can be more easily given in a group and then discussed amongst group members. A worker may find her or himself constantly giving out the same information. Why not call a group together? The evidence is that people remember information better if they have a chance to discuss it. Most students, for example, prefer seminar discussion groups to lectures.

Group support is useful for leaders. For example, a critical or aggressive group member may attribute hurtful behaviour to the leader. Other members, rather than the leader, might have a better chance of showing that person that they are actually angry with someone else who is not present. They can help the angry one re-direct their feelings to the person who is creating problems for them.

The leader therefore does not have to do all the work, and can safely leave to other group members some of the important roles. Social workers and health care professionals are often intensely 'responsible' people who have difficulty allowing others to help. Within a group, this can be reflected back to a worker, and some of the responsibility shared.

Another vital use of groups for professionals, is as support for the worker who has to do a difficult and sometimes dangerous job, very often alone. If anxieties and ideas can be shared with others in the same field, this can make the difference between becoming 'burnt out' or mastering the job.

CRITERIA FOR USING GROUPWORK

When I worked in a day care mental health setting, the first question that was asked about anyone who was referred, was whether there was any reason why they should not be in a group, since almost all the patients participated in groups of various kinds. But many agencies only use groups as a second line, and prefer to see people as individuals with individual needs, neglecting the group dimension of their troubles.

It is sometimes assumed that, although groupwork is useful, if someone has a problem too idiosyncratic to be resolved by a group, or if they might do harm in a group, they need individual work. However, group homes and day care settings often successfully serve people whose problems are more usually treated individually, such as alcoholics, or substance abusers. Gathered together, they can make good progress in a group. This also applies to groups of perpetrators of sexual offences run by specialist agencies such as the National Society for Prevention of Cruelty to Children (NSPCC), where the nature of the problem would alienate someone in a group of people with variegated problems, but where the agency can gather together enough people who share a problem to make up a group.

A potentially difficult group member can sometimes be helped by bringing together a group specially for their benefit. An aggressive and unco-operative child, for example, can be helped by a group of calmer children. Adults with learning difficulties, or with certain forms of mental illness, can also benefit from a supportive group of this kind.

Another assumption is that some clients need individual 'parenting' or are functioning at too infantile a level to be able to share the worker. In the day hospital where I worked, this sometimes happened, but we found that such people might tolerate a group in conjunction with some individual sessions. Realistically, it is not usually possible for workers to 'parent' effectively, and to attempt it may create unrealistic expectations. The notion of the 'key worker' used in residential settings can also be used in groupwork situations.

A group may be unwilling to help an individual who has alienated other members. This happened in the day hospital, and a member had to be temporarily excluded, but instead was offered individual appointments. Some clients or patients believe they will only profit from individual help, particularly if they feel guilty or different from others. A group may help them at a later stage.

In fact, in the day hospital, almost everyone was able to profit from group membership, and some users could lead groups of people with similar interests. The groups ranged from one that ran the canteen and served tea and coffee, to intensive group discussions. There was a drama group, a group for making its own musical instruments and playing them (led most successfully by the patient who at one point was excluded from the day hospital), an occupational and an art therapy group, and many others. One volunteer ran a popular group for the children of parents attending other groups. If there was no group that appealed to a member, he or she would be invited to start one around their own interests. Groups waxed and waned with the energy and enthusiasm of the members, but this is natural in such a setting.

Groups are often used with offenders, and many of the alternatives to prison rely heavily on groupwork. They have to work out clear and strong guidelines for the regulation of offending behaviour, and use written contracts with clients. A difficult situation arises when group members are in danger of breaking the law, particularly where this relates to child abuse. There are many good examples of the use of groups for parents whose children are at risk of injury. The NSPCC, which works closely with such families, has an excellent record with people in these difficult circumstances.

Pound describes Newpin, a service which has started in London, and is being extended to other areas. This is a befriending scheme for isolated mothers, many of whom are seriously depressed. Newpin uses groups both for training volunteer helpers and aiding mothers who can get to a centre. Such work must be done in liaison with authorities who can be consulted and brought in when the possibility of abuse becomes a probability. Guide lines for such situations should be planned well ahead of the time for their use. Some very creative groupwork is done with clients who present risks, but it is usually in a strong structure and with good back up services. Do not tackle such problems alone.

Some problems cannot be dealt with in groups, and it would be foolish to pretend that groups are a universal panacea. An example might be someone who is totally unable to acknowledge their own difficulties. Such a person would be unwilling to join a group of people whom they see labelled 'offenders' or 'ill', or having a problem they cannot see as their own. They therefore refuse to identify with the group, and if forced to attend, will be there in person but not for real. They may use the group to further distance themselves from the others in the group whom they consider to be quite different from themselves.

It is essential to remember that we all need some time either alone, or with one or two other people valuable to us. Groupwork settings sometimes overlook this, and run the risk of driving a group member into total withdrawal brought about by the exhaustion of over-exposure to the group!

GROUPWORK AND ETHNIC VISIBILITY

Black workers and potential agency users become very tired of the notion that black issues represent a 'problem'. In considering the uses of groups for black agency users, the white worker is sometimes the one who does not perceive that a 'problem' may well be one to be owned by the worker who is white. Where groups are racially and culturally mixed it is poor practice to avoid the issues raised.

I have encountered situations, for example, where a white worker has assumed that they are the only person who can lead a group of agency users from different ethnic backgrounds and that this presents them with no difficulties. If white workers are the only people available to initiate a group, this itself makes a statement about the agency they represent. Groupwork undertaken with black clients needs to involve people identifiably from the community, as co-leaders and consultants. Black leaders with groupwork skills have an important role to play in training white leaders. It is important to ensure that workers and voluntary helpers get appropriate opportunities to obtain training in groupwork skills and ethnic-sensitive practice.

Muston and Weinstein in their article in *Groupwork* on 'Race and Groupwork' point out the difficulties that are raised when the group leader is white and some or all members are black. For groups of racially-mixed composition, they advocate the appointment, wherever possible, of black/white joint leaders. They also discuss the advantages of working with groups of people with a shared background, pointing out that members who have experienced severe alienation and oppression, such as some older black people, feel more at ease with others with similar experiences. Such groups require a leader who understands the background from which members come.

Mistry and Brown in an article in *Groupwork* on 'Black/White Co-working in Groups' point out the absence of helpful writing on this topic. They agree that it is essential to involve black and white co-leaders in any group where the issues of racism are to be tackled. They point out additional factors that need to be taken into account in such co-leadership. For example, there might be an unspoken assumption that racist issues become the responsibility of the black leader to tackle. They consider it vital that black group leaders have access to a supervisor who is black and can understand the issues.

A white leader may be aware of the need for sensitivity to the needs of black group members, but still do and say many things that make members uncomfortable. They may not, for example, always hear the import of prejudiced remarks made by white group members. Thoughtless and prejudiced remarks cause offence and injustice to black group members although these may have been made in ignorance rather than with malicious intent. Prejudiced behaviour cannot go unremarked but is difficult to tackle. (Some background theory that could help with this is considered in greater detail in Chapter Ten.)

RESIDENTIAL WORK AND GROUPWORK

In residential work there is inevitably an on-going group of residents and staff. Group dynamics are important to the quality of life and when understood, can be made to contribute positively to the well-being of residents. An old people's home, for example, often has a fairly rigid pattern of communication between residents, and a recognised series of sub-groups, each with a different status. In a home for young people there are disputes over territory and possessions in which certain dominating individuals always seem to come out on top. Some of these uncomfortable dynamics in group homes can be dealt with by changing the structure of the group, for example by making a change in the setting such as re-arranging companions in shared rooms. Some processes that are operating against the interests of the group or an individual resident, as in scapegoating, need intervention. Brown and Clough have treated this subject in detail in their book *Groups and Groupings*.

There is also a staff group, who have to get along with one another in what is inevitably a task that never ends. Study of the structures, membership and group processes that develop among staff and residents, widens the understanding of what is happening. This leads to less emphasis being placed on personal responsibility for difficulties, and greater appreciation of the part played by structures and processes.

Special groups in residential settings

In addition to the inevitable group living that is the basis of residential life, many establishments are now using groups in a more deliberate and planned way. There are, for example, reminiscence groups for elderly people and leaving-care groups for young people. Using her experiences in a children's home, Lennox advocates groups for children in care to help them come to terms with their personal difficulties. She asks residential staff why they are not running groups, since they are so valuable.

There are some particular problems in running such groups. One feature of groups in residential settings is the difficulty involved in getting the group together. If people live in one place, it might be thought they would be available to attend. But because they do live there, they see it as home and treat it accordingly. That is, they guard the right to do as they please, when they please, in their own house. Plans for groupwork in residential settings have to take this into account. One possible approach is to make a contract with all prospective residents before they arrive, to establish that groups are part of the way of life in the home.

A staff member can have difficulty in setting up a group, unless this is agreed to as an integral event well beforehand. Bringing in outside leaders to run a group may be more popular with residents, as they are not involved in the caring role. It is important to choose an appropriate activity. Aims must be clear to both staff and residents. Setting aside time from schedules and regular activities is not easy. I have seen a group founder on the fact that one member of staff was absent when the time for the group was agreed, and so had sent most of the residents on another activity at the specified time. Or staff can be suspicious that what is happening in the group is undermining their authority outside the group.

In spite of problems such as inertia, ineffective communication and staffing, many residential establishments do run creative and successful group meetings and special groups with residents. If you work in residential care and think that this would be appropriate, persist, and obtain help to run such groups.

This can be accomplished without the formal use of 'therapeutic community' techniques, but if a conscious use of groups is practised, it is likely to make the community more 'therapeutic' for those who live in it.

Therapeutic communities

The term 'therapeutic community' refers to a residential or day-care setting in which the living group experience itself becomes therapeutic for the users. Therapeutic communities were originally set up in psychiatric hospitals, and involve a thorough and comprehensive use of groups. The whole group of staff and patients meet regularly and attendance at group therapy is usually a requirement. Ideas from the therapeutic community movement have spread to day facilities and specialist units.

This is a technique that needs to be used with discretion. One of the ways it founders, for example, is where staff are only notionally committed to the idea of group decision making. Powerful leaders untrained in group membership persist in making decisions without reference to residents or fellow staff members. It can also happen that residents or day care attenders are frightened and confused by the groups that are on offer, and do not wish to participate. Implementation of a therapeutic community approach needs exceedingly careful preparation and commitment from all members of an agency.

Kennard, who has made a particular study of this approach, and writes from the practitioner's viewpoint, gives a good summary of the basic ideas involved and suggestions for further reading. Before setting up as a therapeutic community, it is vital to understand what is involved and to train for the specialist task, for example by taking a course with the Richmond Fellowship, (whose address is in Appendix A).

DOES EVERY GROUP HAVE TO BE A THERAPY GROUP?

Groupwork is a term that embraces a wide variety of uses and group situations. For example, a small group of three or four people engaged briefly in an activity such as cooking, and a long-term, intensive therapy group can both be described as groupwork. Some workers are reluctant to start because they have a vague idea that all groups must be 'deep' experiences in which participants look at themselves and their histories and restructure their personalities. This is not the only way of running groups; as an over-enthusiastic ideal for groupwork, such a notion can be quite destructive.

For a start, the word 'therapy' is a problem. It means, according to the Oxford dictionary, 'The medical treatment of disease', and as so defined has no place in the major part of our work, since most of us are not doctors, and are not treating clients' illnesses. The possible exception is the case of mental illness. However, leaving aside the controversial question of whether mental illness is physically or environmentally induced, what we are very often concerned with is the secondary effects of mental suffering, such as isolation or the inability to conduct oneself in a socially acceptable way.

But there is another sense in which the word 'therapy' is used idiomatically, to mean 'helping someone feel better'. If I say 'That party was much needed therapy for me.' I am implying that it did me good. Hopefully, any group in which you participate as a worker will be designed to help members feel better about themselves and gain a sense of control over their world. This can be accomplished in a group devoting time to mending motorcycles, or sharing the problems of being a parent of a child with a disability, or learning to cook for the first time after being in an institution for many years. The central factor is that the needs of the members are fulfilled by the activity of the group. Similarly, a group of workers engaged in building their skills, or participating in an 'away-day', is expecting to benefit from a group. My point is to emphasise that many types of groups are not 'therapeutic' in the dictionary sense, though they may be so in the idiomatic sense.

A reluctance to go too deeply into personal problems can be useful if it implies a cautious approach to helping participants to avoid going too fast, too far, too early, into their own personal traumatic situations. To do so could make them feel uncomfortable about their contribution. As trust develops in the group, the young man using a motorbike repair workshop may refer to some of his troubles, and begin to learn that it helps to talk. Maybe this will unlock a need for him, one that he can best explore in another situation; the motorbike group has undoubtedly had an effect on him. A young mother may role-play some of the situations she cannot cope with which involve her children, and learn something about her own ways of handling situations. She does not have to recall her own traumatic childhood experiences in order to develop her sense of competence. However, she may need to do just that at a later stage, if it is appropriate to her own difficulties.

Meanwhile, start a group with limited aims if you are new to groupwork. There will be plenty of interesting developments which may be therapeutic!

PSYCHOTHERAPY AND COUNSELLING

In many settings there is a need for groups that explore personal difficulties and help in solving problems of group members. The questions arise: who should run these? Can they be deemed to be 'psychotherapeutic'? In some medical settings, the doctors try to maintain a 'pure' approach by insisting that it is only medically qualified personnel who can run such 'psychotherapeutic' groups. But the need very often arises because there is no local psychiatric service that provides any form of groupwork. Does this mean that nobody should be offered such a facility? It could be that the local psychological service offers some groups, but this is not common, and many patients have to wait for several months to see a psychologist for individual therapy. Outside large cities, the availability of any form of psychotherapy is usually limited. Community psychiatric services have been developed, and nurse therapists can be found who offer psychotherapy in some areas. Even less frequent are psychotherapy groups for non-residential clients or patients: where these are available they are often set up by organisations such as Mind and other voluntary organisations promoting mental health.

Psychotherapy needs to be distinguished from psychoanalysis, which is a long-term method of treatment based, usually, on the theories of Freud, or Jung. Psychoanalysis is practised by some doctors, but many psychoanalysts are not medically qualified. The Institute of

Group Analysis in London is a centre for the practice of psychoanalysis in groups.

What is psychotherapy and how does it differ from counselling? Attempts to deal with this question get bogged down in linguistics. One answer is that psychotherapy is done to patients by doctors, or other medical personnel. Patients, by definition, are ill people. But what is happening when a group run by social workers meets in a day centre for people with mental health problems and works on the personal concerns of members? Or where parents who are thought to be endangering their children come to a 'parent effectiveness' group at the local NSPCC? Or where young people who have broken the law meet at a juvenile justice unit and discuss their family problems? I submit that these groups border on psychotherapy and the only reason they are not called by this name, is that they are not run in medical settings.

Individual and group counselling led by experienced and trained non-medical leaders is concerned with the same difficulties within and between members as medical psychotherapy. Both patients and non-patients can come to such groups. Non-medical leaders will sometimes conduct groups in National Health Service premises. Moreover, some medical personnel set up groups, for example for women patients who have had a mastectomy, which are activity- or discussion-based and have no psychotherapeutic aims. So it is of little use to draw up a neat table indicating which 'treatment' applies to which 'clients' or 'patients'.

There is pressure to restrict the use of the term 'psychotherapist' to those qualified either medically or in clinical psychology. A situation in which anyone can set up as a psychotherapist, without adequate training, is obviously unsatisfactory. But those advocating restriction have a difficult task of definition, both of the activity of psychotherapy and the extent and value of the training. They also have to tackle the problem of medically qualified people who set up to practise psychotherapy without training. The basic training received by psychiatrists contains very little information on psychotherapy, but some go on to take a course after medical qualification. The situation is possibly even more confused in establishing whether a leader is appropriately qualified in group psychotherapy.

Dealing with patients who are seriously mentally ill is made more difficult without the backing of an establishment which has staff on duty at all times. However families of mentally ill people are often expected to look after relatives with minimal institutional back-up. Increasingly, such people will come to day care facilities for help. Sometimes, for example if they are depressed, a group which explores their difficulties can help. At other times, they need something less emotionally stressful, such as an activity group.

It can be useful to someone enduring mental distress, to attend a counselling group which does not label them as 'ill'. There can be advantages in calling a group together for 'counselling' rather than psychotherapy. The promotion of positive mental health (rather like the provision of 'well-women' clinics) implies dealing with problems and difficulties before they reach the point of breakdown. Groups that help people deal with the stresses of life can be said to be in this category. It is better if the word 'therapy' is not attached to such groups, and 'counselling' is a less threatening term.

But the definition of 'counselling' itself has problems. In the past, it has been synonymous with the practice of non-directive, client-centred, approaches, based on the teachings of Carl Rogers. The Marriage Guidance Council, now known as Relate, has made this type of counselling widely available in Britain. Increasingly, however, counsellors have extended their skills by using the newer theories such as Transactional Analysis and Gestalt, or a variety of the many others now available. Some counsellors focus on short term work and others on longer term skills. They may use intensive approaches which rely on behaviourist, cognitive or humanistic theories. Thus a number of approaches have come to be known, collectively, as 'counselling'.

Meanwhile, it is convenient, if arbitrary, to categorise counselling as taking place over a short period. Counsellors have at least a basic training but may also have further or specialised training in a particular field such as working with the bereaved or supporting victims of crime. The term psychotherapy can then be reserved for long-term approaches which are undertaken by those with more intensive training and which deals with more intractable personal problems. Increasingly, courses in counselling are offering further training in psychotherapy to those completing the counselling qualification. Hopefully, there will soon be more courses specifically offering training in a variety of approaches to group counselling and psychotherapy.

Both counsellors and therapists may practice a variety of approaches. These can be based, for example, on psycho-analytic theory, Roger's person-centred approach, Gestalt psychology, Transactional Analysis, Psychodrama, Cognitive and Behavioural theory. This list is not by any means definitive. What each theory and therapy has in common is a search for a method of making sense of the experiences and behaviours that beset most of us, but oppress some people more destructively.

COUNSELLING IN GROUPS

To run a counselling group with therapeutic aims it is not necessary to be medically qualified. This statement would have been highly controversial a few years ago, and may still be so regarded in some entrenched medical circles. But the biggest growth in treatment of mental illness in the last few years has been in the development of therapeutic groups in non-medical organisations like Mind and Newpin. Many nurses, social workers, teachers and youth officers have undergone training and tackled therapy in groups, often with excellent results. Such groups have been used, for example, with young people in juvenile justice schemes; as alternatives to custody for adults; with school 'drop-outs', and with people who are having difficulty coping with serious illnesses.

If you are asked to participate in a group which involves counselling and sets as one of its aims an expectation that members will look at some of the reasons for their own behaviour, you will need to look further at ideas and theories that help group members understand what is happening to them. (Chapters Six, Seven and Eight give some ideas for these types of groups.)

If you are to be involved in a group where the aim is counselling and personal problem solving, make sure you get the training, co-leadership and supervisory back-up that is essential for those engaged in this kind of group. (Chapter Twelve gives further suggestions for doing this.) Those running groups for offenders, alcoholics, drug users, perpetrators of sexual crimes and others who test the worker to the full, need strong support groups of their own and the encouragement to continue their own skill development.

The purpose of counselling in groups is not to provide a more cost-effective form of treatment, but to employ the particular effect of the group for the benefit of all the members. Issues can be worked on which involve inter-personal relationships and personal effectiveness.

The ability of people to recognise their needs, express these and gain some fulfilment, deal with unsatisfactory relationships with parents, spouse, children, friends and colleagues, are all central to the work of the group. Sometimes this means exploring damage inflicted in childhood, or painful events from recent history. Some of the difficulties participants bring are the result of life-span developments such as growing independence in adolescence, early parenthood, bereavement or ageing. Others result from oppression and persecution, or difficulties arising from events such as becoming unemployed, enduring a child's illness, or a parent's increasing frailty.

All of these form the subject of individual counselling, but in the group, these can be talked over with others who may have similar experiences. New and more trusting relationships can be formed within the safe boundaries of the group and different ways of relating explored.

Remember that all groups, taking place for whatever purpose, have a dynamic and a process of their own, which, if not understood, can sometimes be destructive. This includes counselling groups. Understanding the ways in which groups work is a powerful tool in using them for positive change.

SUMMARY

In this chapter several practical aspects of running groups have been considered:

- reasons for using groups
- positive gains from groups for the members and for the worker
- criteria for using groupwork
- using and leading groups with and for people of varied ethnic backgrounds
- particular aspects of groupwork in residential settings
- definitions of counselling and psychotherapy
- participating in counselling in groups
- the different levels of 'therapy' which groups can offer.

Groups may be difficult to set up initially, especially where there is agency inertia, but they are often rewarding and stimulating to run. They can be very supportive to agency users and to staff. Make use of the positive backing a group can give to you, as well as setting up groups for others.

Do not be put off from running groups because you have no experience. Start with a small activity-based group, use your powers of observation and understanding of group dynamics, and get some skill development training. You will soon feel much more at home with groups of all varieties. Do not be deterred by the feeling that all groups must be psychotherapeutic to be 'proper' groups, but get the training that will enable you to run counselling groups where these are needed.

Five

Planning and running groups with agency users

Chapter Four considered the range of situations in which groupwork can be useful. This chapter looks at the practical aspects of setting up and running groups. Groupwork which involves self-help groups and volunteers is also considered.

STARTING A GROUP

The section on group development in Chapter Two referred to Hartford's pre-group stage which includes an important planning phase. The planning stage of the group is vital to its success.

PLANNING A GROUP

Issues for the worker

First decide on who is likely to profit from the group you have in mind. Are you targeting workers or agency users, sufferers or carers? What benefit will the group provide for these potential members? In what ways can it be useful? What aims do you have in mind? What is the best method of achieving your aims?

For example, is the group to be centred on an activity such as art or motorcycle maintenance, or is it a discussion group? Are potential members to be told if one of the aims is some personal problem-solving? One situation that workers sometimes set up for themselves is to pretend that the group is purely for leisure, with a personal hidden agenda that it will develop into a counselling group. This can lead to resistance when the group is asked to move towards the worker's hidden aims. Stewart gives an account of a group set up for older girls which met twice a week. One evening was to be for activities, and one for personal problem-solving. The girls became so interested in discussions that they asked to spend more time on that and less on outings and activities. This shows that it is not always the group members who are reluctant to look at personal issues; sometimes it is the worker who feels inhibited about asking people to do this.

The need for clarity about aims is demonstrated in current developments in group therapy with child abusers and sex offenders. In such groups, workers find that it is essential to set an unequivocal aim: to examine the offences honestly and then work on the personal sexual behaviour that has led to these. This is difficult for the workers, as well as the group members. Being clear about aims means being honest with oneself and with potential members.

It is important, early on, to decide whether the leader is going to work alone, or involve one or more co-leaders. Children's activity groups usually need more than one leader, if only for physical safety! But many groups can profit from having a co-leader, since this provides back-up for the leader and gives a more diverse target for any problems that members may have about authority. If you are planning to work with others, involve them at this stage. (The issues raised by co-leadership will be discussed later in this chapter.)

After the aims have been clarified, and possible members targeted, structural issues of time available and size need to be planned. Is the group to be open, for people to join and leave from time to time, or closed, with a defined membership for the duration of the group. What contract is planned for prospective members?

Issues for the agency

It is important that a group is not set up to be yet another unsatisfactory experience for participants. Many agency users have a history of failure and being let down. To set up a group but let it run irregularly, or bring it to a premature end, only adds another negative experience. Adequate agency support is vital.

Agencies have a tendency to approve of groups because they think they are cheap. A well-run group is time consuming; planning, talking it over after each session, keeping a record, getting help from consultation, all need resources. Shortage of time for any of these tasks robs the worker of opportunities to develop his or her skills and places vulnerable people at risk. A group can be an effective way of using resources and of achieving changes, but cannot do this unless it is properly resourced.

Agencies can usually find some money for expenses and a place to meet. Many agencies now are more aware of the need for a pleasant group room easily accessible from the main office. Some are able to transport members to the group. But agencies which are not concentrating on groupwork often find it difficult to free busy workers to be consistently available at set times for a group. Duty rotas and emergency cover play havoc with regular commitments. Some disruption is inevitable where there are staff shortages, but staffing requirements should acknowledge that groups recur at set intervals, and need regular and adequate time from the worker.

Agencies may not understand the need for confidentiality in the group. Negotiate with colleagues and other agencies who have clients or patients joining the group, so that they are aware that feedback about a member is given to workers outside the group only with the consent of that member. Alternatively, if this is not the way the group is to operate, make it clear to prospective members that information given in the group can be passed on to other agencies, and under what circumstances this will be done.

There can also be an unwillingness to recognise that groupwork needs supervision and consultation. The need for supervision of those who work with individuals is generally understood, but it is less often provided for groupworkers. There are experienced people outside the agency who would be willing to act as consultants. You could find them by applying to your local college or university or consulting a directory such as the one published by British Association of Social Workers (BASW). (See Appendix A.)

PLANNING FOR CO-LEADERSHIP

There are benefits and pitfalls in co-leadership. It is not enough to assume that, because you have found one or more people interested in running a group with you, that there is agreement on methods and styles of work. It is essential, at this planning stage, to have several sessions before the start of the group in which important areas of work are made explicit. Consider the following points carefully:

Aims

Are you agreed on the aims of the group? For example, is one of you more interested in counselling than the other? Have any of the prospective co-leaders a hidden agenda? Compile individual lists of what you want to achieve. Do this first without comparing notes, then share your ideas. The aim is to discuss these and end up with a list that is acceptable to all co-leaders.

Methods

Are you agreed on the way in which the aims of the group will be carried out? If one of you has training in a technique or a specific skill, will the others take steps to inform themselves about this? How are you going to deal with setting up and keeping the rules of the group? Can you each make a commitment to be available for the entire life of the group? If not, what back-up or substitutes can be arranged? Are you all prepared to give time for planning each session, sticking to the plan, and meeting afterwards to discuss what has taken place?

Roles

Which roles are you each going to play? Is one to take the major responsibility and be designated leader? If so, how do the others feel about that? It is not enough to assert that everyone will take an equal share; such a plan often fails. It is much better to start by designating who is responsible for what, even if this is re-negotiated later. The description 'co-leader' is ambiguous. It could mean two equal leaders, or one leader with a helper. Determine which meaning is appropriate for you.

If one is to lead, what does she or he want from the other co-leaders? Is one leader there simply to provide feedback to the co-leader, watching the process of the group, or is one leader to play the task-centred role and the other the social-emotional role?

It is often useful for co-leaders to be different kinds of people: one male, one female for example. And in a group of participants from mixed ethnic backgrounds, it is essential to have leaders who can be identified by members as similar to themselves. These very differences mean that special care has to be taken to avoid misunderstandings between co-leaders.

Working together

There may be other vital differences. For example, do you differ in status in the world outside the group? How far do your values agree? Are you both comfortable with similar degrees of structure? Do you like rules or not? If you disagree, how will you deal with this?

How do you envisage working together in the group? How are you going to convey to each other what you want during a meeting? Do some role-play before you start the group, and decide how you will tackle predictable situations. Can you agree on a written contract about all this?

Without this clarification, problems will have to be dealt with in full view of group members, which produces distress for them and unnecessary blocks to group progress. With planning and follow-up, co-leadership can be of great help to leaders and provide an excellent way of developing one's skills.

A booklet by Hodge, *Planning for Co-leadership,* raises further issues to consider in detail. Mistry and Brown's article, referred to in Chapter Four, gives valuable advice for workers planning to work together who are from different ethnic backgrounds. They point out, for example, that group members will often defer to the white leader as the senior partner, and co-leaders in this situation must be agreed about how they will tackle this problem. Often the black worker is left with the task of identifying and tackling racist issues; co-workers need to anticipate this and share the responsibility. They note the cross-currents where racist and sexist issues interact, so that a black woman working with a white man may be at a particular disadvantage. They emphasise the crucial need for plenty of time for reflection and discussion after each group, and for adequate consultation. The black worker will also profit from having a black consultant and the white worker needs to be aware of this.

GETTING THE GROUP OFF THE GROUND

Once you have decided the character and structure of the group, seen that there is enough help available, and determined to go ahead, will it all just happen? Not necessarily. One of the most puzzling things for groupworkers is that they get to this stage, the group is planned, there seems to be a need for it, fellow workers or other agencies have been encouraging, but then very few people are referred. This means that you have not convinced agencies or potential members of the value of the group. If you believe that you can make a contribution to agency effectiveness with a group, this can be discouraging.

Preparing the agency

There has to be a stage of 'selling' your idea to those who can influence potential members. You may have to go to other agencies and talk to workers there. Senior personnel can help, but those who are in touch with agency users can actually recruit members; these are the important people to convince that a group is effective. You may have to explain to each of them what you plan to do.

It is natural to feel frustrated if impediments arise at this planning stage. I recall an attempt to start a group in a residential setting, when the only time said to be available for the group was at the same time as a popular television programme. On another occasion, a group day care facility for people with mental illness was set up but was shunned by local doctors and psychiatrists. It is natural that others may feel threatened by your offer. Are you implying any criticism of their ways of working? Is your skill just a new fashion? Understanding and planning for these eventualities may take time, but it is vital. Much thought has to be put into presenting your projected group in terms that show the benefits to be gained. This is particularly valuable when collaboration is required from other professionals, or people in power such as magistrates or head teachers

Preparing potential group members

It is useful to interview prospective group members before you begin. You need to prepare a short written statement about your group aims that can be shown to any potential members and referrers. Be sensitive to the fact that some potential members may not have literacy skills. Members need information about when and where the group is to meet, whether transport is available, how many meetings are planned: in other words, the expectations of the extent of their commitment to the group. The contract already partly formulated in the mind of the worker can be revised at this time, in the light of potential members' comments. They also need to be aware, early in the proceedings, if any kind of feedback is to go to their referring worker or agency and what form this will take.

Evaluating your chances of success

You have ensured you have time to run a group and found co-leaders and a consultant. You have established the need for a group and defined your aims and membership. You have engaged help from your agency and fellow workers and found prospective group members. If you have discovered serious problems in one or more of these areas, do you press onward? Draw up a list of what is in your favour, and what is against. If possible, tackle any of the factors threatening the success of the group that can be changed. Then assess your chances. Do not hesitate to ditch the idea if there is a serious flaw. Try again later!

SUMMARY

So far, this chapter has been concerned with the pre-group phase of planning. The points covered have been:

- issues for workers: setting aims for the group, deciding who members are to be, the methods to be used, what structure the group is to have
- issues for agencies such as support, resources, confidentiality and consultancy
- points to clarify with a co-leader: agreement on aims, methods, roles and working together
- getting the group off the ground, recruiting and preparing clients, dealing with obstacles such as lack of clients, lack of co-operation from colleagues and other agencies, and making a commitment to the group

WHEN THE GROUP IS IN PROGRESS

Early meetings

You have decided to go ahead - it is your first meeting and the 'ship' has left harbour. What do you do?

The first task of the group is to get to know each other and start communicating. One way of doing this involves the use of a short activity suggested by the leader. This kind of introduction can lighten the anxieties of the start. For example, in a group of young people, one way for members to begin is to introduce themselves using a description which starts with the same initial as their names. 'I'm Charlie and I am Cheerful.' 'I'm Miriam and I am Mystified', and so on. There are many exercises of this kind to break the ice.

If you feel the light-hearted approach would be seen as flippant or irrelevant, use one of the more serious ways of effecting introductions.

One way to do this is to suggest members work in pairs. Each pair talks to one another about themselves. Then the person to whom each has been talking introduces them to the whole group. This avoids having to talk to the whole group about yourself early in the proceedings. It is usually easier to introduce someone else than oneself. (These exercises, with many other useful suggestions, can be found in the books listed in Appendix B.)

Using this method of starting may not be appropriate to your particular group. If there are members who are seriously withdrawn, an activity such as sitting quietly behind some piece of equipment and getting on with a task may be the best choice. Art easels, or large machines such as a motorbike, are ideal shelter! Such groups need time before members are ready for much communication.

One way of starting which should be avoided is that used in T Groups (see Chapter Nine), where initiatives are left almost entirely to group members. In groups with agency users, it is important for the leader to have several alternative and flexible plans for the start of the group. When members are better acquainted, their ideas and suggestions are likely to be relevant and important, but in early stages it is reassuring if the leader does exercise leadership.

Planning and using exercises

It is a good idea to have several short activities prepared, but be ready to jettison these if the group gets going and is making progress without them. I find it useful to have several index cards, each of which has details of an activity or exercise on it prepared beforehand. Preparing them brings the format to mind, ready for use, and prompts me to gather materials that may be needed. Most need little more than pens and paper, but some require quite elaborate preparations. If the directions are complex or my memory fails, the cards are at hand to consult.

In general, do not over-use exercises from a book. Bear in mind the points made in the section later in this chapter on 'choosing a group activity'. Make sure that you are not using these exercises as props for your own uncertainties. Let the group have time before you start on those which require real self-disclosure. Allow members to be quiet sometimes without feeling that you have to supply something to do. Allow plenty of time for each exercise, and for de-briefing when it is completed. People usually want to talk over the experience that the activity has given them.

Other ways of helping a group to relax in the early stages are to provide some refreshment and to start with a topic or short activity which is neutral or non-threatening.

Tasks for the new group

Remember the stages of group development and do not rush the group. Be alert to withdrawn members, testing-out behaviour, bids for monopolising the group.

Early in the meetings, clarify the task of the group now all the members are together. Go through the contract with the group, defining what you are undertaking, what resources are available, and what is expected of members. When members are ready, ask them to define their expectations of the group and what they hope to gain from it.

Start with any rules which are important in the group, like those about confidentiality, and letting others speak. Observe the group norms that are set up, and what happens if these are broken. See that leadership gets spread around and that tasks and social-emotional work both get done. Do not let members settle into rigid roles. For example, who is to make the tea every week? Observe who speaks to whom, who does a lot of talking and who gets left out. Be alert to the factors that arise from the group process.

Involve members in planning future activities. It may be too soon for this on the first meeting, as plans made at this early stage tend to be unmade later in the group, but it is useful to hear what ideas members have for the group.

Remind the group when it is near the time to stop, and end with a short review of what has taken place in the session. If possible, find out gently how people have felt about the time they have spent in the group, and whether they feel that this group might have some potential for them. This process of review gets easier as the group continues to meet, so do not push too hard for this too early.

After members have left

When members have departed, review what has happened. If you can, involve your co-workers, or supervisor. If none of these are available, sit down yourself and recall what took place. Were you aware of what was going on in the group? How did you influence what happened?

Make a brief record of the group proceedings as soon as possible afterwards. If you have co-leaders, take this chore in turns. It will pay off handsomely as you progress through the life of the group. You can get a much better understanding of the sequences of events that develop over several meetings by keeping a record. If you have the time, try to record one meeting in more detail. This is particularly useful if the meeting has developed problems. Simply recalling the order in which events happened can clarify what triggered a sequence of behaviour.

Review whether the structure you first decided on does, in practice, fit the group, or whether you need some rethinking. Is it the right size, does it meet in the best place? Go through the structural factors again.

As the group continues over time

Keep the notion of group development in the front of your mind. Recognise that some group behaviour will represent transitions from one stage of development to the next. Expect the 'Storming' phase and do not become discouraged by it. Do not allow the group to settle irreversibly into the third stage of facile agreement. When the fourth stage comes, where the work of the group can make good progress, bear in mind that you need to step back as leader and allow members to lead wherever possible. If the group regresses to a former stage, or spends much time on any of the three basic assumptions, of dependency, fight/flight or pairing, analyse the reasons for this and take action if this is indicated. Remember that you are not the only person who is responsible for the group; co-leaders and other members can also help if anything needs to be done to influence the processes.

It is tempting to concentrate either on structure and process or on the individuals who compose the group. It is almost impossible to focus on an individual and the group at the same time. This is an area in which a co-leader can be helpful, since they can adopt a complementary role to the other leader.

If the leader is concentrating on the ways in which the structure is influencing the group and the processes that are developing, it is easy to lose sight of individual members' needs. An example would be a group which is aiming to win a trophy, where a member who is suffering stress through trying too hard may be ignored. Even in a group doing excellent work with some individuals, group processes can develop which mean others are distressed. An example would be of a member stuck in a role which gives them no opportunity for development. It is possible for scapegoating to occur but not to be noticed because other group members are making good progress. Restrictive norms can be set up. One member may be left out of the communication network. Some members may be treated as if they are more important than others.

If some work is being done with an individual, it is important to bear in mind the needs of other group members. If one member has been taking the group's time and attention, ask the others how they are feeling when there is an opportunity and make sure there is plenty of time allowed for this.

Recognise the norms that are developing for dealing with tense moments. How does this group manage conflict, or a member who monopolises, or one who is left out of communications? Are the norms helping the group to make progress in coping with these points of discomfort?

Sometimes the needs of the group are more important than those of the individual. For example, a group member may bring up a major concern at the end of a group. If the group goes on too long, members will get tired, miss buses etc. So the member with the problem must be asked to save what they want to discuss until the next meeting. If the problem is life-threatening, it may need action immediately, but the kinds of problems that are brought up at the end are seldom of that variety and usually represent something the individual is having trouble in telling others. Remember it at the start of next meeting, and give that person the opportunity to start again. Keep both group and individual needs in your mind and write these down whenever possible.

There are sure to be unforeseen problems with co-workers, colleagues and the agency. Analyse these. If your co-worker seems to have an approach divergent from your own, talk to her or him about this. Do not expect instant resolution of difficulties, but also make sure that you preserve your belief in the value of what you are doing.

Any group will search out your weak spots as a group leader. This is where you need co-workers and consultants. You will not know exactly how to deal with all eventualities automatically. Watch your style of leadership. Are you being authoritarian? Or leaving too much to the group at this stage of their development? Make a note of the times when you felt you did not cope and discuss these, taking further training opportunities where possible. Note where you got it right and treasure these occasions!

One possibility is to set up group supervision sessions with fellow-workers. Co-workers need to meet together. It may also be possible for several people involved in groupwork to meet, even if they are from different agencies. This is an effective way of developing your skills and sharing difficulties and triumphs.

GROUP ACTIVITIES

In deciding on an activity for your group, the starting point is the interests and capabilities of members. Activities can be graduated from those which give nervous new members a chance to shelter behind a temporary barrier, through those which stimulate group interaction, to those which place emphasis on intensive participation. Some activities mean that people can be reserved, others entail self-disclosure. (In Chapter Nine there is a description of the Johari Window, which is a device for analysing different approaches to self-disclosure in a group.)

CHOOSING AN ACTIVITY

The primary concern in planning the activity to be used in a group is the interests of the members. An example would be a group of parents of children with disabilities, who have many concerns in common, and will want time to discuss and share these. They may also want to hear from someone whom they feel is more expert than themselves. If the leader prepares a schedule of talks by experts without asking members if this is what they have in mind for the meetings, the parents could get the idea that this is one more professional who acts without consultation. However, they may want a particular speaker whom the leader knows is not available, so expectations need to fit available resources.

Vinter, drawing out principles from his experience of social groupwork, made a useful analysis of possible group activities. He says that activities have three components:

- the physical space in which they take place
- the performance, or skills, required by the activity
- the behaviours evoked by but not essential to the activity.

The physical space, equipment and staffing needed for rounders, for example, is different from that for cricket. The skills required for rounders are much simpler than for cricket. In addition to skill with bat and ball, there are skills that will be developed in teamwork and co-operation. A game goes on without spectators, but is much more enjoyable if there are people to cheer.

Vinter says that practitioners need to be aware of the ways in which different aspects of these components are likely to influence group members' behaviour. He thought there were six 'dimensions' that need to be considered:

1. **Prescriptiveness**
   the rules for conduct

Rules can be highly prescriptive, as in cricket, where every move is governed by a rule. Or they can be low in prescriptiveness, as in informal swimming sessions. Many young people resent too many rules and do better with a game of low prescriptiveness. A useful outcome of the safety rules of an activity such as climbing is that members can see that some rules are essential. Other activities, such as personal problem-solving, may seem to need few rules, but in fact do profit from structured exercises and ground rules.

2. **Control**
   how behaviour is decided

Controls may be decided impersonally, as a cricket umpire does with the aid of a thick rule book. Or they may be more informal and at the discretion of a leader or another member of the group. In a discussion group there may be only a few basic rules such as a requirement that members listen to each other. This can be mutually enforced, members being equally responsible for keeping the rule.

3. **Provision for physical movement**
   the extent to which participants are required to move about, or are restricted

This must fit the abilities of the participants. The space available should provide safety for the activity. If participants are being asked to take risks, for example as when people with disabilities go on activity holidays, they need plenty of help around. This applies just as much when the risk taking involves self-disclosure, or close personal interactions with relative strangers.

4. **Competence required**
   the minimal level of skill needed to get pleasure out of the activity

Some activities require few skills. Informal swimming requires only a tolerance of water. Water skiing needs many sessions before participants can begin to enjoy themselves. For those with a low tolerance for frustration, activities requiring minimum skill can begin to build up their sense of competence.

High levels of skill can be difficult and frustrating to acquire. One group of children that I was involved with decided on a session at a shooting range. One boy came home in a rage. He had thought that all you had to do was point a gun at the target and pull the trigger. Not one of his shots went in. It may have been a salutary lesson, but he gave all the other children a hard time for days afterwards.

Talking about oneself could be another skill that is hard to get right at the first try.

5. **Interaction between participants**
   the way in which the activity stimulates participants to
   actions involving each other

Some games are solo efforts, others require team participation. An activity such as the preparation of a meal, which encourages interaction, can be the stimulus that gets a group to look at how it functions and how individuals react. A solo activity such as presenting a project, highlights differences in ability and leaves other members out of interactions.

In counselling or skills training, it is important to involve all members as much as possible. If there has been a session where a member has been working on their own situation, this can make others feel left out. This can be prevented by involving members in role-plays which centre on others and asking how they feel about what has been happening.

For many group members, especially young people, activities are more likely to engage their interest if there is no chance of their being 'out'. Opportunities to rejoin the activity are essential if their initial efforts are not successful.

6. **Structure of rewards**
   types of rewards available, their abundance or scarcity, and
   the manner in which they are distributed

Rewards can be given to a team, in which case all profit, or to a single prize-winner, when others who helped get left out. Children's groups profit when rewards are frequent and each member gets a reward at some time. Are adults so different?

Vinter has some recommendations for groupworkers. He thinks the worker needs to be enthusiastic about an activity before the group can get really involved. Activities should end just before the point of boredom and fit in with other routines, especially in residential situations (for example, no horseplay before bedtime). Rules should be changed if necessary, to fit those in need of maximum participation, frequent rewards or fewer prescriptions for behaviour (for example, in rounders, change the batter or bowler for every ball). He believes it is important not to put too much emphasis on a highly finished product, at least early in the group's life, and to be ready to switch activities if one starts to lose the interest of members. Vinter advises group leaders not to be too competent at an activity themselves, as this can discourage members: let members teach you wherever possible.

Vinter's ideas were worked out with children, but they also fit adult groups, particularly where members are not used to the activities being introduced into the group. If the activity is discussion, the notion of skills and rewards is relevant and useful. In introducing varied activities, the importance of balancing individual and group needs shows clearly in Vinter's analysis.

Ending

Plan early for the ending of the group– preferably right from the start. As members tend to forget that the group is time-limited, remind them again well before the end. Endings should never come as a shock.

Remember that members often regress when a group is about to end. One way of dealing with this is to evaluate with members what has been achieved. Get members to help with the evaluation well before the ending of the group. Evaluations can be done verbally or in written form. The original aims of the group should be restated and examined to see if they have been achieved. Leave enough time for this process to do any work that has not yet been accomplished, or to tackle a member's aim that has not been met.

Plan some follow-up for the group. For example, some groups like to make a date for a reunion. Make clear any arrangements that will offer individual, or further group help if this is needed. This does not have to be within the agency. In the day hospital where I worked, for example, some of the members went on to participate in adult education groups. Also arrange a follow-up study that can help you evaluate the outcome of the group for its members, so that you have some positive reasons for starting a new group. This could involved contacting members by telephone or letter some time after the group has ended. Another way is to look at official records. Let members know if this is your plan.

If there is to be any kind of report back to other workers in contact with clients or patients, remind members that they agreed to this. Where possible, get members to formulate the report with you, or better still, work on these with the whole group, so that everyone gets feedback from other members.

To summarise, this section has not aimed to cover all aspects of running groups, but only to give a flavour of the work involved. This necessarily varies depending on the kind of group you are aiming for. An activity group differs in many respects from a counselling or discussion group. However, all groups are dependent on their structure and the members who compose them. All groups develop a process by which they operate.

The group dynamics described in preceding chapters are all relevant to setting up and conducting groups; those which particularly apply to this section are:

- stages in group development
- building cohesion
- leadership
- task and process

The practical points in running a group which have been discussed in this section are:

- planning a group
- using knowledge about group processes
- keeping both individual and group needs in mind
- using consultants or supervision
- early meetings
- planning and using exercises
- tasks for the new group
- continuing over time
- choosing an activity: Vinter thinks that activities have three components:
    - physical surroundings
    - skills involved
    - associated behaviours
- each activity also has six dimensions:
    - prescriptiveness, or the rules laid down for behaviour
    - controls and the enforcement of rules
    - provision for physical movement
    - competence required
    - interactions that are stimulated
    - how rewards are structured
- ending the group
- evaluating the effect of the group

WORKING WITH GROUPS OF USERS AND VOLUNTEERS

I have included the two following sections as they often give groupworkers cause for concern. These are:

- What extra factors need to be considered when working with self-help groups?
- What particular points may arise when co-workers are volunteers?

SELF-HELP GROUPS

Many voluntary organisations flourish entirely on their own efforts and skills. Examples of successful groups of this kind include Alcoholics Anonymous and Gingerbread. There are also many smaller organisations, such as the Sickle-Cell Anaemia Association, and Arthritis Care. One important aim in many of these groups is to get information about the problems faced by sufferers across to those professionally involved, such as nurses, doctors, social workers or other officials. Other groups are involved in direct care of sufferers or helping to deal with associated problems. Many are small and struggling, although the popularity and importance of such groups is growing.

Many nation-wide groups employ paid organisers. These organisers may ask professional care workers to participate in a management committee or contribute specialist knowledge. This can place the worker in an unfamiliar role, since their experience of management or training may in fact be limited within their own work, and the experience they do have will be in a different, professional, situation. However, they may be expected to demonstrate the skills of the new role without adequate preparation. Organisers and coordinators may also have to search for appropriate training for their volunteers among professionals who have little experience with their particular service users.

Organisers of voluntary agencies sometimes struggle with difficult management committees. The problem is one of composition, since the local citizens they attract, combined with professional workers who are keen to demonstrate their expertise, make for a disparate management group. The status of each member outside the group may be high, and there could be an unrealistic expectation that this will be recognised and respected by other committee members. Power struggles are difficult to bring to the surface and deal with, since committee members are there for altruistic reasons, ostensibly, and not for personal satisfaction.

Locally, there may be groups set up by people with a medical or social problem to help fellow-sufferers, or constitute a pressure group for consumers. Some of these local groups approach groupworkers at a local level and ask for their participation on user groups or committees. Such groups may lack the central backing that the nation-wide groups have and are liable to flourish when local issues are in high profile but wane when enthusiasm fades.

Increasingly, agencies are developing ways of involving consumers of their services in the management of the agency. Empowerment of users is becoming an important principle. Such management groups can be set up with enthusiasm but then prove difficult group experiences. Anyone not accustomed to having power inevitably struggles as they acquire experience in using it. These groups within agencies have many of the characteristics of inter-agency work between self-help groups and professional workers.

Professional workers can have difficulties with self-help groups. They may try to dominate such groups with their expertise. They may not be available when needed, for example in the evenings, and may get discouraged by the anti-expert stance of such groups. Self-help groups may distrust professionals; members can relate discouraging stories about lack of understanding and care. They need to be able to consult with professionals as equals, as consumers, specifying where they need help, rather than having it prescribed for them. Volunteers put in a lot of work without financial reward, and know that others get paid.

But there are many ways in which a groupworker can be of use. Locally, self-help groups are sometimes short of knowledge about how best to deal with meetings, or make the best of resources. They may get bogged down in the problems of individuals and would appreciate some help with this. They may be concerned with a large number of people who have had negative experiences, and get overwhelmed with the resulting depression or aggression. There may be rivalry on the committees, or competing bids for leadership. The worker can act as a consultant, but it may be more rewarding to participate as one of the regular members of such user groups, at least at the start of your contact. This way you will learn more about the problems of the members and their great strengths in dealing with these.

Anyone invited to become a member of a voluntary service management committee, or to help voluntarily, needs to asses whether they have the backing of their agency in undertaking this work and whether they have adequate time available. It is discouraging to voluntary organisations when people join committees without having enough time and energy to contribute adequately. Find out what the commitment will mean and think carefully whether this can be fitted in with your existing schedules. The amount of energy demanded by the work will almost certainly be more than you are anticipating, as you get drawn into the concerns of the group.

The skills of the groupworker can be useful, either to a group just forming or to one which is feeling stuck. These involve the ability to analyse the structure and process of the group, bear in mind the task and the process, and not lose sight of individual needs or the needs of the group. For example, someone with experience of groups might help work out or revise norms and procedures, assess what talents are available and fit these to an achievable task. They can emphasise the need to summarise discussions, keep to the point, draw out the silent ones, and see that all are involved.

There may be tension between being a member of an agency and involvement in helping a group to get better service out of that same agency, or other agencies with which you work closely. Workers who have tried to empower disadvantaged groups have sometimes been charged with inciting revolution against the very people who pay their wages. It is never easy to change anything in one's own agency, but sometimes it needs to be done. Alliances are useful in this situation.

Membership of user groups and voluntary committees can therefore involve a groupworker in all varieties of role conflict. Expectations of the role to be played need clarification and skill development. Potential role clashes between the worker operating in different agencies can be anticipated. The worker in the new role needs to be aware of the subtle influence of the new kind of power and respect that the new role will impose. Instances of well-intentioned people becoming authoritarian when appointed, even in a minor chairing role, are not uncommon.

To summarise, in self-help groups and management groups of agency users, the groupworker may be involved in a variety of roles, for example:

- as trainer in groupwork skills
- as a participant groupworker with agency users
- as a committee member or chairperson

These roles need clarification and skill development.

Problems encountered can include:

- role conflicts for the worker
- conflicts arising from group composition over which the worker has no control
- disguised power struggles
- the impact of unfamiliar power on the worker and other committee members

In general, the professional is a partner, not a leader, in self-help groups and the aim is to be a resource for group members. It is important to build up the skills of the members, and to participate in sharing of leadership.

WORKING WITH VOLUNTEERS

Social work and health care agencies are using volunteers in their agencies in increasing numbers. Their contribution is found to be invaluable in many situations. Many groups are aided, or run by, volunteer workers. They give up their time and energy to helping and do not ask to be paid for this, but do it because of their interest in other people and a desire to contribute to the community. Their contribution is often very valuable. But volunteers are not simply a useful extra. Their willingness to give needs to be matched by an equal contribution from professionals. Volunteers deserve attention to their needs and careful planning so that their work is effective.

Particularly in an agency which uses groupwork, volunteers can assist professionals by undertaking tasks as varied as transporting members to the group, or running a group of their own. In the Psychiatric Day Hospital in which I worked, for example, volunteers set up and staffed a group which looked after the children of mothers attending a therapy group. Volunteers also ran a most successful drama group which put on several excellent stage shows with day hospital attenders. Volunteers took over the task of welcoming new members and official visitors. This puzzled many visitors, who looked in vain for any distinctions between staff and members. In fact, volunteers outnumbered doctors, psychiatric social workers and nurses by about five to one. Many of the volunteers were patients, ex-patients, or relatives of patients. Those who led groups participated with staff in governing the whole facility, through a management group. Some joined a weekly meeting known as the 'mutual training group' which used group supervision for both staff and volunteers.

The description 'Day Hospital' was in many ways inappropriate, but it was so designated by the local hospital management board, who could only conceptualise what was happening by using such a term. The small clinic saw about three hundred patients a year, through the combined efforts of volunteers and professionals. Volunteers played an important role in making it possible for the Day Hospital to stay open from 10am until 10pm. Patients' experiences of psychiatric help would have been much poorer without this partnership. Many would have become in-patients but at the Day Hospital they recovered without hospitalisation.

Another organisation which uses volunteers extensively is the 'Newpin' scheme in London (described in Chapter Four). This organisation provides help and support for isolated and depressed mothers. With training and backup from Newpin, the volunteers have tackled the problems of isolation and depression among mothers of young families in inner city areas. Pound and Mills have written about these and evaluated the impact of Newpin on group members.

These examples show that voluntary help can give an organisation great strength. To get full value from their work, it is important to pay attention to the role, status, place in the communication structure, and degree of expertise of any volunteer helpers. Their skills need to be assessed and their contribution planned. They need appropriate induction and continuing training to develop their skills. The organisation needs to define and value their role. They also need support in their work, just as the professional does. If volunteers sometimes 'fade out' or become unreliable, it is often because they feel undervalued or unsupported, or are perhaps, left to work unaided in situations for which they do not yet feel ready.

The use of voluntary workers may cause some anxieties for professionals. Issues of confidentiality, determining who is responsible for the work, what happens if it is not done, or done badly, need sorting out before the work starts. Volunteers can make professionals feel uncertain. One worker said 'If the volunteer does not do the work properly, I may have to spend more time putting it right than it would have taken to do it in the first place. If the volunteer does the work very well, I feel redundant!'

A well-prepared volunteer who is given support should be doing a job which is appreciated by both clients and professional workers. For the people they work with, volunteers can seem less remote and official than professional workers and closer to their own experiences of life. Often they are doing that part of the work that the paid worker does not have the time to do. Occasionally, a volunteer will be given a job that the paid worker is afraid to do, such as visiting a family known to be aggressive to persuade one to come to a group. Volunteers need to be able to say 'No'! They also deserve the same protection from danger as professionals.

Many organisations offer their volunteers excellent training. Relate, the Samaritans, and Citizens Advice Bureaux are leaders in this respect. Training is important in helping voluntary workers to feel they are valued by the agency. Agencies need to provide continuing support and supervision, essential if interest and enthusiasm are to be maintained.

Sometimes a person volunteers to help when they are in more need of help themselves. Newpin finds that this happens occasionally, and volunteers are then counselled. In time they may become useful helpers. In a day care centre or hospital, patients and ex-patients can help with groups, improving their own mental health as well as that of the people in the groups. Very occasionally, the motives of a volunteer are suspect. There is a requirement that anyone who is paid to work with children is subject to investigation for a criminal record. This is planned to be extended to voluntary helpers. There is no evidence that clients or patients are subject to any worse risks from voluntary helpers than they are from paid workers, some of whom are also, unfortunately, capable of exploiting vulnerable people.

Your local Council of Voluntary Service, or other volunteer organisations, will be a good source of information and have contact with many voluntary workers. Many of these organisations have also developed useful expertise on getting the best from voluntary workers. Use them, and look for ways of working with volunteers wherever possible.

All good workers can be exploited or asked to carry too much responsibility. Voluntary workers are usually able to give only a limited amount of time and should not be asked to make financial sacrifices. Nor should they be exploited by being manipulated into doing a professional's job. It is neither fair nor honest to expect them to plug all the gaps.

To summarise:

- Volunteers are valuable; they should receive resources, support and skill development from the organisations they serve.
- Their work needs to be planned and integrated into the agency.
- Their value increases in proportion to the clarity of the expectations from them and the refusal of an agency to exploit their goodwill.

CONCLUSION

One student in a course on groupwork, after wrestling with the intricacies of group dynamics, put in an anguished enquiry. 'What do you actually do in groups?', she asked. I hope that this chapter gives some answers to her question. It has dealt with the planning involved in setting up a group and what you actually do when the group is going. It is not, of course, a comprehensive guide. Other chapters in this book are also relevant to what is actually done.

Since groupworkers often liaise closely with self-help groups and volunteers, some consideration has been given to these areas.

Having reached the point where you have set up and run some groups, and consolidated your learning, you will probably be ready to develop and increase your skills. The next three chapters indicate some ways in which this can be achieved.

Six

Developing methods of work: social skills and assertion training in groups

Learning about the methods involved in social skills and assertion training can enrich and extend your work with groups. They are closely allied approaches, based on ideas developed in behavioural psychology and by social psychologists. Both methods are useful in a wide variety of situations and can be used with adults or children. They apply not only to those who come to agencies in need of help, but to those of us who accept that there is always the possibility of improving our social or professional skills. Assertion training for professionals can help prevent burn-out and deal with stress. It is also effective in helping isolated and oppressed clients to gain their rights.

Social skills and assertion training can be the focus for a series of meetings. Where this is the plan, prospective members need to be told about the methods to be used and given some explanation of what can be achieved by these techniques. Both methods work on the ways in which we manage our interactions with others. The basic technique is the use of role-play. This provides the opportunity to rehearse exactly what needs to be said and done to improve our ability to get clear messages across and let others know what we need. Questionnaires and check-lists are also widely used to establish which skills require development.

These methods can also be useful as a response to the demands of a particular situation. For example, in the course of a discussion or counselling group, a member may be describing a difficult situation at home or at school. A worker skilled in either of these methods might suggest that role-play of the situation could be helpful, on the grounds that it is often better to act out a situation than talk about it. This needs to be done with discretion; the member should be invited to try out one of these approaches and their hesitations respected.

It is possible to use skills training with an individual, but it is a lot more effective in groups. A group gives a wider choice of people to play various roles. A learner often chooses someone to play a role who resembles in some way the real-life person with whom they have difficulties. In a group there is likely to be someone who can be identified with the problem person, and this can assist the transfer of learning to the real situation.

Much can be learned from watching others working on their skills. There is also a great deal of support, both emotional and practical, available in a group. Sometimes it is possible for group members to work together on practising the new skill outside the group. This can happen in schools, or health-care settings, where several members are participating in skills training.

SOCIAL SKILLS TRAINING

Everyone differs in ability to manage social interactions effectively, that is, to achieve what they want from a social situation. Skills in communicating with each other involve the ability to adapt one's own behaviour to that of others whilst at the same time gaining something for ourselves. A well-handled social situation gives a sense of pleasure, even if it is only of the 'How are you today?' variety. 'Making a good impression' involves many different skills. The ability to communicate your feelings, ideas and needs in a way that will enable others to understand and meet them is vital. Without this ability, our lives are poor indeed.

Deficits in social skills

Social skills are usually learned early in life, and much parental effort is devoted to teaching these. Even more gets learned from imitation. But some people grow up with limited skills. This can happen if the family does not provide adequate models or gives confusing messages. Schools can limit the aspirations of pupils and the range of activities offered for them. People with learning difficulties have the additional problem that they need constant reiteration of the steps involved in learning a skill; sometimes those dealing with such children find the necessary repetition more than they can manage. Most of us could improve our skills in communicating with people who are not from a similar background.

Even if social skills are learned in childhood, these can be lost, for example through mental illness or ill treatment in later life. And in a society rife with inter-group hostility, a member of a group which is discriminated against may give up trying to establish social rapport with other groups.

Many people seen by health care or social workers have failed to learn the basic skills needed in our technological world, for example, with the telephone. Others react with understandable hostility and aggression to frustrating situations such as visiting government offices. Many are isolated because of their poor skills. Others, such as some of those involved in sexual offences, have never learned appropriate ways of relating to anyone of the opposite sex.

Improving existing skills

Above average social skills can be seen in counsellors, social workers, salespersons and others who have built up expertise in dealing with people. Even these workers can always learn more, and take their skills to a higher level, by using skills training methods. Many managers started by becoming proficient in different skills before they moved into posts needing new skills. If they can actually recognise that this is a skills deficit, it is possible to remedy this with skills training.

It can be difficult to acknowledge personal deficits or skills which can be improved. Problems in communication are often explained by projecting the problem on to other people or objects. For example, have you ever found yourself blaming the tool rather than your poor skills? Or reflecting how much easier life would be if only other people were not so dishonest, aggressive, or unco-operative?

One use of skills training that has proved its worth is in helping business people who go to far-away places to understand and imitate the social skills of the culture which they are visiting. If you are hoping to do business with the Japanese, for example, it is useless to meet them with a hearty handshake and get straight down to work. Japanese people dislike the physical contact and prefer a formal bow, and use a preliminary period of exchange of compliments and presents to ascertain what sort of person they are dealing with. This period can baffle and bore the businessman. Without this understanding, alienation sets in, on both sides of the interaction.

Just as valuable is the recognition that what seems quite natural to you may be deeply offensive to someone from a different ethnic or religious background. The way you dress may be interpreted to your disadvantage; looking another person in the eye may be thought of as disrespectful. Such non-verbal cues are important in establishing communication and can easily compound any difficulties in language which in themselves create barriers. Skills training can help to avoid this kind of misunderstanding.

To provide a remedy for deficient social skills, or to improve good ones even further, techniques of social skills training have been devised. There are different approaches to skills training, each based on a different, though related, theory. What follows is a brief description of three possible ways of approaching techniques of training: behavioural, cybernetic and experiential.

BEHAVIOURAL APPROACHES TO SKILLS TRAINING

The basic idea in this approach is that all behaviour is learned and can therefore be re-learned.

The components of behaviour

Behaviourists start by defining the behaviour that is causing a problem and then breaking it down into small component parts. It is then possible to work on each part. The emphasis is on observable behaviour. Hudson and her co-workers, for example, ran a group for men involved in sexual offences who were in prison. She found that they had little ability to talk to women, so she taught them skills such as hand-shaking, looking the woman in the eye and making small talk. Later, she helped them to extend their own reactions to what was said, enabling them to talk to women without making sexual overtures. This illustrates two of the basic principles of behaviourism: that behaviour needs to be considered in basic units, and that steps in learning should be small and manageable. Each step needs to be mastered before going on to a more difficult component.

Reinforcements for behaviour

One important idea in this approach is that behaviour becomes habitual because it is reinforced or rewarded. Sometimes this is an obvious reward, as when a parent buys sweets for a child in order to avoid a confrontation in a supermarket. The child then learns that the threat of a tantrum gets rewarded. Sometimes the reward is more subtle, for example, where a child learns that no-one notices when they are being good, but when they cause trouble, everyone attends to them.

Every individual is susceptible to different reinforcements. You may like a hug as a reward. Another person will dislike hugs but appreciate a cigarette. This means that it is important to find an effective reinforcement if someone is to practice and retain the new behaviour. Some reinforcements come automatically, as when a person engaged in conversation by the learner becomes more friendly and gives him or her some positive affirmations. The group can also help by applause, congratulations, and so on. After a successful session it is important to find some way of getting a reward from others outside the group.

Rehearsal and repetition of new behaviour

Continuous practice in a supportive environment is essential. Fellow group members can develop a variety of 'prompts' and rewards. One used by Hudson involved holding up placards as prompts while members were role-playing. Placards can provide suggestions, such as 'Smile!', 'Look her in the eye' and so on. Another technique is to have someone standing behind the person practising, offering suggestions from time to time as the practice proceeds. The best reward comes from within the learner, as they start to feel a growing sense of competence.

The behavioural approach works well with younger people, who are less inhibited by role-play. They appreciate the good sense of practising different approaches to difficult adults, or coping with bullying peers in their lives. Adults have more inhibitions. It is important that the leader is comfortable with role-play techniques, or their apprehensions will be passed on to members. To be at ease with the technique, leaders should have practised role-playing themselves.

A basic plan of work

Using a method rooted in the behavioural approach, the plan would be to work through a sequence such as this:

1. Decide with each member what behaviours are to be worked on. If appropriate, use a diary or questionnaire to determine exactly the areas in which the group member needs to try new responses to a situation. Get people to be specific. For example, if a child wants to work at 'getting on better with my teacher', encourage the child to set an aim such as approaching a teacher and asking for some special help. Another example would be the adult who wants to 'learn to relate to someone of the opposite sex'. This could be narrowed into the specific skill of talking to a person after being introduced. Ensure that the goal is realistic and limited to something achievable.

2. Evaluate the learner's existing skills and strengths, and bring these out.

3. Separate the behaviour into component skills. (e.g. securing the teacher's attention, using a particular tone of voice).

4. Select an appropriate method of acquiring the new skills. The most useful way is for the group member to role-play the situation, actually doing it rather than talking about doing it. This can be done in pairs or in sub-groups, as well as with the whole group.

5. 'Sell' this to the potential learner, e.g. by using another group member as a model who can say how much they benefited from using these techniques. If the model can demonstrate that they made some mistakes before they gained confidence in the new skill, so much the better.

6. Set an appropriate standard for this particular person, not an impossibly high one. For example, the pupil may not need to astound the teacher, but just make an impression. Star quality in the new skill is not necessary.

7. Decide what is perceived as a reward by this particular person. Being noticed may be a reward for one, but be disliked by another. Ask what pleases this person? Introduce the notion that rewards given to oneself are very powerful. For example, if someone is pleased with the way they have handled a situation, they can give themselves one of their favourite treats. (It is important that they do not reward themselves indulgently if they have not practised the new behaviour!)

8. Carry out the first practice, role-playing the situation that is causing difficulty. Members of the group can play the other participants as appropriate. Fellow group members can also switch to playing the person with the problem if they have a good idea of how to tackle the

situation, modelling better ways of coping. However this should only be done occasionally. It is easy to overwhelm someone by dealing with their problem with greater competence. Keep all role-plays light and short and do not let people get involved with lengthy scenes which show up their deficiencies.

9. Supply feedback on how the person has tackled the problem.

10. Together, evaluate how well this exercise went.

11. Repeat stages 3 to 10 several times, preferably in the same session. Emphasise the points where the skill is improving.

When I am working with people in this way, I sometimes encourage them to start with a really negative way of tackling the problem, just to break the ice. For example, the pupil could start by telling the person playing the teacher all their grievances and resentments! This is not intended as a way of approaching the problem in reality, but only as a warm-up for a serious attempt to find a way of getting their viewpoint across. After demonstrating the worst possible way of going about the task, subsequent attempts must be an improvement!

With others, it may be possible to get only an approximation to the desired behaviour at first. Some need help to even think about being in the same room as the person they want to talk to!

12. Set homework so that members can practise what they have learned. Ensure that this is an easy task; the learner should not be exposed to failure without the support of the group. Homework also needs to be appropriate. It is not a good idea to suggest to an offender with a history of attacks on people that he approach a passer-by and say 'Hello!', as one student did. The offender's reputation in the area was such that the person he approached ran away!

13. When one behaviour has been mastered, repeat stages 1 to 12 again until all the learner's aims have been dealt with.

14. Remember to practise and evaluate the individual's ability to generalise the experience and transfer skills to life situations.

A plan of this kind needs to be used with sensitivity and flexibility in skills training groups. When working with this behavioural approach, bear in mind that it is not a good idea to stop at the point where the principal effort is directed towards getting someone to stop behaving in a particular way. It is also important to substitute other skills which bring alternative rewards to those gained from the negative behaviour. This is probably why training designed to stop people smoking, or eating too much, is so notoriously unsuccessful. The immediate relaxation and sense of wellbeing that reinforce smoking or eating are difficult to replace.

A book which can help with understanding the basic ideas behind this approach is Hudson and Macdonald's (1986) *Behavioural Social Work*. There are several manuals for social skills trainers, each dealing with a different set of social skills; (some of these are recommended in Appendix B).

Training in controlling anger

A development of skills training which is designed to help people to control their anger has been devised by Novaco. His methods have been used with some success in work with violent offenders. He starts by discussing the situations in which clients are prone to anger and what they perceive as provocation. Participants keep a diary which records the frequency and extent of their outbursts. They are then encouraged to discriminate circumstances in which anger is justified from those for which it is harmful. He demonstrates to clients that their interpretations of what happens to them are an important factor in deciding the outcome.

This type of therapy goes beyond the bounds of pure behaviourism. It also draws on ideas from cognitive therapy and cybernetics.

CYBERNETICS

Welford developed a theory based on the idea that everyone is a channel for information processing. In communication theory, every 'signal' from both internal and external stimuli contains information, transmits along communication channels, and is governed by feedback control. In any situation, there is an input of sensory impressions such as speech and visual cues.

These first register on the senses and are then translated into recognisable information. This information is assessed against individual experience and emerges as a reaction to the situation. The reaction is then itself subject to feedback from action. This is illustrated in the diagram overleaf, adapted from Welford.

This diagram may seem unduly complicated; even so, it leaves out many of the complex links in the chain. It has the advantage of helping us to see where the deficit in skill may lie. For example, in the

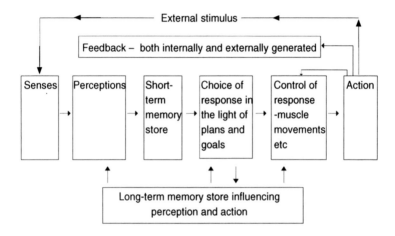

'Senses' box, if the person has poor eyesight or hearing, that may be a basic difficulty which accounts for the problem at the level of input of the senses.

Every individual has different expectations of an interaction, and most compare the present one to others in the past (the Long-term Store). If their experiences have been negative, they will expect this one to be bad too, so may interpret a friendly overture as a snare. They may never have learned the response that helps the other person in the interaction. They can lack the physical skill to put it into action (Effectors of action). Some people never get straight feedback about their behaviour, perhaps because others are frightened of them. So an analysis indicating where the problem is located can be helpful.

One young man in residential care had the habit of sticking his foot out whenever anyone passed him, causing them to trip. This naturally aggravated the other young people, and they often attacked him. He was frightened of these attacks, but was unable to see that his own behaviour had anything to do with their hostility. Using the diagram above, it is possible to analyse the problem. He saw and heard well, so the deficit was not at the first stage. He had not been found to have a serious learning deficit and was in full control of his movements. If his behaviour had made others angry repeatedly in the past, why could he not learn from this? Was this simply a case of negative behaviour being reinforced by attention? This explanation might be some help, but attempts to provide this young man with alternative sources of attention failed.

Perhaps the deficit arose from inability to de-code feedback from external sources, or to generate feedback internally? Explaining the problem in this way did link with other difficulties he was having. He often seemed puzzled and unable to connect one action with another. If this was the case, then the remedy lay in devoting some time to strengthening his ability to remember what he did that caused others to react. Concentrating on this aspect of the problem would demonstrate sympathy with his difficulty rather than irritation. Such analysis can help carers deal with an apparently inexplicable skill deficit.

The emphasis in this approach is on planned control of behaviour and on cultivating ability to moderate further behaviour in the light of feedback. Much depends on the individual's ability to read signals coming from the other person sensitively and accurately. There is also useful information to be gained from analysing mistakes; there is more learning in those sometimes than in a perfect performance!

This approach differs from that of the behaviourists, in that it stresses the need for the individual to generate his or her own skills once the principle on which the skill is based is understood. It is important that the learner takes the new knowledge into familiar situations where these can be maintained and modified.

RELATIONSHIP SKILLS

Duck, a psychologist who has studied social and relationship skills, has developed applications to the complex skills involved in making and sustaining intimate relationships. He has used the notion that people learning a new skill need the ability to understand the principles that lie behind relationship skills. He divides these skills into three stages:

- getting into the situation where one is likely to meet someone special
- making the first approaches and responding to the other's approach
- sustaining and nurturing the relationship once it is formed

He points out that a common way in which people try to help someone who is isolated is to offer suggestions about where likely mates or friends can be met. But the problem only starts there. Difficulties in the second stage mean that even if there are plenty of opportunities, some people will not benefit, as they lack the skills to appear interesting and friendly to others. Once the relationship bond is established, not everyone has the skills to nourish it, so relationships start in a promising way but soon disintegrate.

How would you analyse such skills into component parts? One author who has done this is Nelson-Jones, whose book 'Human Relationship Skills' is subtitled 'Training and Self-Help'. He has analysed the component skills of making effective close relationships and devised a plan of skills training which could be very useful, not only in relationship counselling, but also to those working with the isolated or unsocial person.

Another approach is that of Beech, in 'Staying Together', who uses a combination of behavioural and more experiential work, with many check lists to be filled out both individually and jointly. This could be done by couples or by individuals and couples in groups.

Parenting skills are another area where ability to make and sustain relationships is vital. A useful book which describes several approaches to this is Gordon's *Parent Effectiveness Training*. It has been used in units such as the NSPCC and has resulted in significant changes in parenting behaviour. An organisation which will train workers further in conducting groups in parenting skills is the Centre for Fun and Families, (details of which are given in Appendix A).

EXPERIENTIAL

This is an approach based on humanistic psychology in which the whole person is the focus, in contrast to the approaches which emphasise learning and communication. The unique nature of each individual's experience is central. Learning which is valuable and endures over time is considered to be gained through experience and action rather than through intellectual achievement. Groups using this approach often say that their aim is to help participants achieve 'personal growth'. Such growth comes from establishing more authentic relationships which preserve and add to the sense of self-worth of both participants. These groups use 'discovery' methods such as role-play of situations from the individual's past history, simulations of real-life situations and games designed to enhance sensitivity. There are several books giving examples of these games; Brandes *Gamester's Handbook* and Lennox's *Residential Group Therapy for Children* are both useful.

This method can be practised in Encounter Groups where the

emphasis is on open and direct feedback about members' behaviour. These groups can be rewarding but are sometimes stressful (more information on them is given in Chapter Nine). It can also be used in less intensive groups where the main activity involves games and exercises. The most comprehensive of the handbooks covering the latter type of group are those by Priestley and McGuire, whose books on personal and skill development in specialist areas are listed in Appendix B. They give suggestions for working with individuals and groups. Their ideas are applied to a variety of different problems and types of people. They have also applied their ideas to those in the helping professions. For older age groups, Smith's *The Best is Yet to Come* provides many ideas.

There are no hard-and-fast lines round these different approaches. Most practitioners use some techniques from all of them; Priestley and McGuire, for example, use a combination of behavioural and experiential approaches. Books differ in their selection of approaches. For example, Lennox gives three - Behavioural, Transactional Analysis, and Encounter. Variety can be confusing, but all these authors are concerned with the encouragement and practice of new behaviour, though they differ in the emphasis they place on inner mechanisms that determine behaviour.

Whichever method is used, it is essential that the leader is sensitive to the feelings of the group members. It is easy to pressure people into self-disclosures that embarrass and distress them and may drive them from the group. For this reason, try to start with behaviour which is not too much of a problem, such as tackling a teacher, before you move on to more intimate problems such as tackling a parent. Some quite innocuous-sounding exercises can provoke a great deal of emotion. (Remember the section of 'using games and exercises' in Chapter Five.) This is another reason for trying these techniques out on yourself before you apply them to others.

If a member has been through intense feelings during a session, it is important to provide the opportunity for them to return to the present after they have completed an exercise or role-play. This can be done by reminding them gently that they are in this group, that they are now among friends and are not under stress. Participants should not leave the group with emotions in turmoil. There needs to be a period at the end of these groups where some ordinary, even trivial, matters are discussed. Evaluating the events of the session is one way of accomplishing this.

Drawbacks

People who are insecure about learning new skills (these can include counsellors as well as clients!), can bring defence mechanisms into operation during training. The defence most often heard is the assertion that 'Role-play is un-natural'. Some just feel embarrassed, others believe firmly that it is useless. Like all such assertions, these are most firmly held by those who have never put them to the test. Those who have overcome their fear or embarrassment usually find that there is much of value in the technique. No-one should be compelled to role-play if they feel they cannot do this, but withdrawal leaves a person outside much of the learning available in a group.

Another defence mechanism is the self-defeating 'I know I'm hopeless so it's no good trying'. Someone feeling defensive about their skills can swing to the opposite behaviour, so that, for example, one who usually talks a lot and dominates the conversation may react by keeping totally silent. Opening your behaviour and problems of communication to the possible judgments of others is a risky business and most people experience anxiety when doing this.

Sometimes skills deficit is only part of a greater problem, and little progress will be made until that is tackled. It may also be true that tackling the skills problem helps solve another, apparently unrelated, problem.

Behaviour that could be labelled 'unskilled' may in fact be a valid defence against oppression; for example, from an intrusive parent, spouse, employer or teacher. This is where Assertion Training can sometimes contribute, but it is important to remember that oppression needs to be tackled and the victim helped to find their own solutions.

And there is the usual proviso that any leader should do some skills training as a learner before they start on others!

To summarise, so far this chapter has been concerned with skills training. It has separated the different types of training into:

- behavioural approaches, which concentrate on learning easily managed portions of behaviour and repetition and rehearsal of these behaviours
- cybernetic approaches, which emphasise the learning of communication and relationship skills and relate the practice of skills to the context of behaviour
- experiential approaches, which help a group member examine

behaviour towards others and practice new behaviours in a trusting environment

These are not unrelated categories, but for the practitioner to look at different ideas behind skills training can encourage some experimentation with various approaches and applications to different situations. It also helps to identify the approaches that other skills trainers are using, which is important if you are going to work together and support each other as trainers.

ASSERTION TRAINING

Assertion is an important social skill. To be assertive is to make a constructive impact on a situation without leaving others with a sense of being crushed. It is not the same as being aggressive.

Assertion training is a development and extension of the ideas to be found in social skills training. It draws on elements from behaviourism and from the experiential approach. What follows is an introduction to the ideas of assertion training; it is not intended as a manual, only as a taste of what can be accomplished by using this method. It is a useful method of encouraging group members to look at their interactions with others and develop more effective ways of dealing with situations in which they perceive themselves as powerless.

The aim of assertion training is for the individual to recognise that their needs and feelings are as important as those of others and that they have rights to self-respect and dignity.

Assertion training is usually done in groups. A group has many advantages, for example, to see someone else wrestle with a problem is a great help in dealing with your own bouts of non-assertiveness. The basic technique is to get members to play out situations in which they have not been assertive, and practise new responses. This means that further opportunities for learning can take place as members role-play the person who is provoking angry or guilty feelings. It is useful to portray a critical teacher, parent or boss; this gives a fair idea of what it feels like to be on that end of the interaction. The support of a group of people whom you trust is essential if any real changes in behaviour are to be achieved.

Aggression and non-assertion

Assertion and aggression can easily be confused. But aggression is often the result of not knowing how to achieve your aims assertively. Assertion maintains self respect in yourself and others, and is appropriate in standing up for yourself. Aggression is an act against others which results in their feeling put down. It frequently produces counter-aggression.

We all have areas in which we could be more assertive. Dickson calls these our 'crumple buttons', implying that we become non-assertive when someone touches one of these psychological weak spots.

Even the thought of being assertive in some situations is enough to produce anxiety. It can also induce guilt. One book by Smith on assertion is called *When I Say No I Feel Guilty*. One aim in assertion training is therefore to achieve a reduction in the level of guilt and anxiety that many people feel when they are asking for something for themselves or standing up to unreasonable demands.

Non-assertive people neglect their own rights and give way to others. They put their own needs down as unimportant and give priority to pleasing or appeasing others before they please themselves. They often have low self esteem and a chronic inability to set limits on the behaviour of others. Most of us are non-assertive in some situations. It is as if we have a 'crumple-button', which gets pressed by a particular set of circumstances or people.

Personal rights

Personal rights are, of course, not the same as legal rights. But they constitute the basis of mutual respect between people, often sadly lacking in both personal and professional relationships. The idea of personal rights also implies that if you are asking for these rights yourself, you are prepared to acknowledge those of others. There are several different interpretations of these rights. I use a version based on Dickson's list.

Your rights as a person

1. I have the right to be treated with respect as a capable and equal human being, provided I accept that the other person also has this right.
2. I have the right to my feelings and the right to say how I feel.
3. I have the right to say 'yes' or 'no' for myself.
4. I have the right to state my own needs and ask for what I want provided I accept the other person's right to say 'no'.
5. I have the right to be seen as a person, not only as someone who fills a role.
6. I have the right to make mistakes.

7. I have the right to express my opinions and values, provided I am being assertive and not aggressive.
8. I have the right to change my mind.
9. Where rights are not clear, I have the right to question, discuss and clarify.
10. I have the right to decline responsibility for other people's problems.
11. I have the right to deal with others without being dependent on them for their approval.

Do you believe you have these rights? If you don't, you are not likely to convince others! Discussion of the ethics of these rights can be useful in a group and you may want to rewrite them to suit your particular group. For example, do you have a right to take actions that are potentially harmful to yourself?

There is no definitive list of rights that can guard against every attempt to use the ideas aggressively rather than assertively. The safeguards lie in the aim of using assertion as a positive way of approaching relationships, guarding against aggression and ensuring that everyone has an equal right to dignity and self-respect.

An example of the difficulties involved in asserting a right is shown when it is necessary to use the simple right to say 'No.' Many people will hedge their refusal with so many words that they have created the impression that they said 'Yes.' An exercise to illustrate this involves group members in refusing a request such as 'May I borrow some money?' or 'As you are only watching TV, could you ... ? (but it is your favourite programme.) Try this out for yourself. The examples given may not be so difficult for you, but how do you respond when someone makes an inappropriate sexual overture?

To take an example of the strategies group members can work out: a worker is feeling angry about his or her professional relationship with a consultant psychiatrist. They describe a situation in which a patient's future is at stake and a report is needed. The worker telephones the doctor's office and is told by the secretary that the doctor is too busy to write a report. The group considers different ways of reacting. A non-assertive response would be to sigh and wait, perhaps writing a letter to confirm the request, knowing it will be ignored. The worker is neglecting their professional need for co-operation and paying a lot of attention to the demands on the time of the doctor, as well as accepting the secretary's view of the situation.

An aggressive response would be to tell the secretary that they are not earning their money, or are incompetent! This is only going to produce counter-aggression as the others defend their position and waste time on the conflict rather than on the patient.

Deciding to practice assertion, this time the worker considers the fact that he or she has a professional need for this information. The patient, and the other agencies involved, have a right to have the report. So even if it does hurt the doctor to ask him or her to do some extra work, the worker has a right to ask. There is a right to question the secretary's decision and a need to speak to the doctor. If the doctor refuses to provide a report, the worker may have to appeal to a higher authority, but gentle insistence on the rightness of the request may well carry the day. It is worth trying!

In a support group for workers, various strategies for achieving the desired aim can be tried out and assessed for effect. Members can practise assertive responses to situations they find difficult, identify crumple buttons, and gain confidence in professional interactions.

The same applies in a group of agency users. An example would be of a mother whose teenage sons are refusing to help with the household finances. She can be non-assertive, put up with the situation and be exploited. She can argue and nag aggressively. Probably she will do both and nothing will change. If she sets out her requirements, the contributions needed, and the fact that there will be no food if these are not complied with, she is making a start. If she practices this with a group, she can learn to speak with conviction and deal with the aggression she could encounter when the sons find their behaviour is challenged.

The first step is to convince yourself that you have these rights. Then it is easier to persuade others of your rights, and learn to use negotiation.

Some protective skills
In learning to be assertive, there are some protective skills which can be used as strategies for achieving your personal rights.

1. Broken record
This is a calm repetition of what you are asking for. It means refusing to be drawn into side issues. If the son says to his mother 'I can't pay anything, I have to buy cigarettes', it is no use giving a lecture on the evils of smoking, since that distracts attention from the main point. 'I

understand that you like to smoke but I must have money for the house and for food', would be an assertive response. If the son then says 'Anyway, you're a rotten cook.', anger at the slur needs to be suppressed (although it can be expressed safely at the next assertion training group!) Playing 'broken record' means responding to the taunt without emotion: 'I must have money for the house and for food.'!

2. Fogging

This is acknowledging that there may be some truth in the critical opposition, but maintaining the request. 'You social workers are all alike, if I ask you for anything, it is months before I get it.' 'Yes, it is often far too long before we are able to respond and that must be aggravating, but can I have the report on Mr X for the court hearing on Friday?'

3. Selective ignoring

This is refusing to respond at all to irrelevant or unfair remarks. It means the person making them soon gives up because they are not getting a response. They realise they are just not pushing your crumple button.

4. Avoiding apologies

When avoiding apologies or remarks like 'I'm afraid that..' or 'I'm terribly sorry ..', use the request without the padding and it will sound more assertive. Although politeness is important, beware of over-using 'please' which can weaken a request.

5. Disarming anger

This means offering a contract and negotiations. 'When you pay me for your keep, I will be able to have your girl-friend for a meal'. 'I can come and collect the report tomorrow if that would help'. In other words, avoid achieving total victory that is hard for the other person to swallow.

These are some techniques for protection against aggression. They do not come easily to most of us, though of course we pretend that they do. We like to argue back, score a point, express our frustration, and in doing so either 'win' and leave the other person feeling badly, or 'lose' and not get our point across. These skills need practice, and in a group, can be tried out repeatedly until they feel more comfortable to use.

Becoming more assertive

Role-play of a difficult situation is useful and provides the opportunity to try out one's own responses in a safe situation. Other techniques are:

- keeping a diary to record incidents where you felt unassertive, how you used your new assertiveness and how anxious it made you feel
- use of this record to measure progress: the aim is a reduction in anxiety and guilt as well as in increased assertiveness
- 'homework', or a specific task to try out and then report progress to the group

Limits to assertion

It is important not to set up yourself or clients to fail. There are some situations where withdrawal is better than assertion, notably when the other is using physical aggression. It is not much good standing in the path of a tank, offering negotiation, as the TV cameras demonstrated vividly in Peking during the student uprising of 1989.

If a woman has a violent husband, asserting her rights may only make the situation worse. But Assertion Training will begin to show her that such a husband has no right to hurt her, even if he is claiming it is because of the mistakes she has made. That may lead to higher self-evaluation and eventually leaving to set up a life of her own. Meanwhile, a woman whose husband is violent to her may find her children beginning to duplicate his behaviour. She could perhaps learn to deal with this aspect of the violence.

Assertion training and work

Assertion training is useful for workers as well as clients. We all need to be assertive in the work situation. It is easy to see the need for assertion when arguing the case for a client but it takes more practice to use it to further your own professional and personal aims. People are often drawn to the helping professions because they place much emphasis on the value of others. Assertion training is a good way of extending this concern to one's own rights as a worker.

Assertion training can be used in support groups for workers and in team-building events. It is also a valuable way of finding solutions to knotty problems which occur in team-building and inter-professional relationships. Assertion training can help a worker to stand up for their rights as a professional, to define a clear role for themselves and their team and resist aggression from powerful sources. It can enable a worker to define their needs in difficult situations and plan assertive, not aggressive, ways of negotiating changes. It is therefore a powerful tool in helping to prevent burn-out and disillusionment for workers from the helping professions.

To summarise, this brief description of assertion training has covered:

*   the distinction between assertion and aggression
*   dealing with non-assertive responses and crumple-buttons
*   anxiety and guilt associated with being assertive
*   personal rights
*   saying 'No' with conviction
*   protective mechanisms which are assertive
*   techniques of diary keeping and homework
*   limits to assertiveness
*   support groups for increasing assertiveness in work situations

CONCLUSION

This chapter has referred to the theories which have inspired some of the varieties of skills and assertion training. The main ideas are rooted in behaviourism and learning theory. It is also possible to pursue this path using a humanistic perspective in which the whole person and their experience is the focus.

If you want to use these techniques Appendix B has a list of relevant books. As with all the other theories and techniques, avoid passing on to clients what you have not been prepared to try out on yourself.

Seven

Developing methods of work: Transactional Analysis

The previous chapter dealt with skills and assertion training; these are methods of dealing with relationships and becoming more personally effective. This chapter will present an introduction to the ideas of Transactional Analysis. The following chapter introduces Gestalt. All these approaches offer ways of developing counselling skills and personal problem-solving for use in the group.

Terms such as TA (the usual abbreviation) and Gestalt sound at first hearing like technical jargon; beginners need to know something about these ideas when they hear them being discussed. These two chapters are offered as a taster of the theories; short summaries of this kind can only give a flavour of the richness of these approaches.

The strength of the TA theory is that it gives down-to-earth, easily understandable, ways of making sense of feelings and experiences. It appeals to people unused to 'psychologising' because the language is easy to understand and fits their feelings so well. It also provides a series of tools for finding out more about oneself and relationships. This can be useful for groupwork, both as a tool to help members think about the development of the group, and to stimulate them to seek straight transactions in the group and in interactions outside the group.

TRANSACTIONAL ANALYSIS

Berne, who was a psychiatrist and psychotherapist in America, devised the basic theory of TA. This offers an explanation of the significance of ordinary communications that pass between us, as well as helping us to understand some of the less rational aspects of ourselves and our relationships. The idea of the 'Drama Triangle' was referred to in Chapter Three and you will see how notions like 'Games' and 'The OK Positions' make sense of some of the ground already covered.

EGO-STATES

Berne suggested that all of us have a 'family within' of ego- states which represent the PARENT, ADULT, and CHILD. This is true no matter what stage of life we have reached. For example, there is an Adult in every child, as you will have observed when children are being 'logical' and thinking out a problem. There is a Child in every adult, though it can be squashed by the responsibilities of being grown-up.

The Parent is that part of us which looks after and dominates others. It has two sides, the Critical Parent and the Nurturing Parent. Critical Parent is the part that likes to boss others around, tell them what to do, and criticise their behaviour. Nurturing Parent is the part that likes to care for others.

Each has a positive and a negative aspect. The positives about Critical Parent are evident in a situation where people are imparting new knowledge or skills, analysing ideas, or rejecting domination. The negative aspects appear when criticism which undermines and deskills others is used destructively; it can also be very harmful when turned inwards on oneself. Nurturing Parent is an essential part of human interactions, it is the part that considers the needs of others and delights in giving, but in the negative aspect it involves smothering or over-protecting the object of affection.

The Adult is that part of us which reasons, is logical and systematic. Adult reactions are open and honest, not concealing hidden agendas or manipulative motives. But the negative side of Adult is boring! Staying in Adult when a caring, Nurturing Parent response is more appropriate, or when the humour of Child would lighten the situation is just as difficult for others to manage as any of the other ego-states in negative mode.

The Child is the part of us that likes to play, to be looked after, to be irresponsible. Child's two sides are those of Free Child, who is the

creative, fun-loving one, and Adapted Child. Adapted Child can be
conformist, obedient and 'good', but it can also be the rebel, the naughty
child, the one who likes to do the opposite of what others are asking.

To summarise these aspects of 'the family within':

PARENT contains:

Nurturing Parent
which can be:

positively:
able to love and care
for others and self

negatively:
oppressive, smothering
and dominating

and

Critical Parent
which can be:

positively:
willing to change people
and society

negatively:
destructive, critical
and hungry for
power

ADULT contains:

Positives
which can be:

able to reason and
systematise
to be straight and
honest

negatives
which can be:

boring and
insensitive

CHILD contains:

Free Child
which can be:

positively:
creative, fun-loving

negatively:
irresponsible

Adapted Child
which can be:

positively:
conformist and
co-operative

negatively:
rebellious, defiant

Everyone has within them all these ego-states, but in varying proportions. People in the caring professions tend to have a highly developed Nurturing Parent, with a rather neglected Free Child. Academics and administrators seem to have well-developed Adult and Critical Parent states but are low in Nurturing Parent. Perhaps this is one reason why co-operation between caring professionals and administrators is so difficult.

How would you allocate your 'family within' between the ego-states? Are there areas of yourself that could do with development? Are some areas over-developed?

In groups, members who talk when others are concentrating, or always arrive late, are using negative Child. Those who always make the tea, or look after others, are stuck in Nurturing Parent and may stifle the development of the group, even though they feel good about their own nurturing behaviour.

We sometimes talk to ourselves, using Critical Parent. 'Why on earth did you do that?', or 'You could do better' are messages often given internally. Try practising Nurturing Parent on yourself occasionally, and give yourself a credit or a treat.

A group member may feel that no matter how hard they try, they cannot gain acceptance. Such a person is often using the internal Critical Parent. Alternatively, the group may be colluding with each other to ensure that this member is often in the wrong; the group operates as one massive Critical Parent.

TRANSACTIONS

When we come to communicating with others, or to having dialogues with ourselves, we do so from one ego state to another. For example, if I ask you the time, and you reply '12 o'clock', that is a straight Adult to Adult transaction. If you reply 'Don't say you have forgotten your watch again!', you are replying with Critical Parent. If your response is 'Who cares?' you are using your Free Child. These are crossed transactions, and leave unpleasant feelings. Can you think of some examples from your own experience?

Straight transactions are the result of communication from one appropriate state to another. For example, if an infant is hungry and gets the response of being fed, that is a straight Child to Nurturing Parent transaction. But if the response is to tease or play with the child, then that is a reaction from the negative part of Child and is a crossed transaction that will puzzle and upset the infant.

In groups, members can get enmeshed in crossed transactions; the ability to see what is happening is vital. If one member is sad, but another member responds with 'Are you moaning again?', Critical Parent is in evidence, leaving the other feeling put down. Another member may use Nurturing Parent negatively: 'Don't be sad, everything will be all right' might be such a response.

The sure sign of a crossed transaction is a sense of some part of the exchange being not quite right, or a feeling that one has been put down or disregarded. It is not always members who cross transactions. The Adult in a leader may arrange a trip; but the disruptive Adapted Child changes the plans at the last minute but forgets to tell the co-leader!

GAMES

Do not be misled by the innocuous word 'Games'. The notion that we play complex Games instead of acting in a straightforward way, is a serious one. Berne thinks that Games are basic ways in which we deal with unsatisfactory relationships and avoid being authentic with each other. This is because we fear true intimacy with others. We do not trust them with the power this might give and dread the hurt they could do to us. Instead we substitute Games, which Berne defines as 'a series of complementary, ulterior, transactions progressing to a predictable outcome'. They are complementary since they have to involve others whom it suits to play with us. They are ulterior because their true purpose is hidden. They are predictable since the outcome is planned from the start.

'Kick Me' is a Game in which the player starts out to get a negative stroke. He or she usually finds someone, like a parent or member of staff, who is used to playing the Game. The player selects a piece of behaviour that is unacceptable, and the Game begins. At first the other chosen player may not respond, but then the behaviour is stepped up, and in the end, a reproof, or even a blow, will be provided. This is the predictable outcome. It is particularly successful when the complementary player does not like the one who has started the game. In that case, both are playing an ulterior 'hand'. The initiator's 'hand' is of behaviours designed around 'please notice me' and that of the other player is 'show me again how awful you are', but neither would confess this is their motive.

Another example is 'If It Weren't For You'. In this Game, the aim is to find someone who will put up a block to prevent you from doing something that you say you want to do. 'If it weren't for you, I would be able to do ...' But would you? Would it be very threatening to attempt this? Is it safer to be prevented? How many of you tried hard to get on a course, or get a promotion, but then felt you had undertaken more than you could manage? If only someone had stopped you from getting what you wanted!

Games which are often played in groups include 'Let's You and Him Fight' and 'I'm Only Trying To Help You'. The first occurs typically when someone stirs up a situation and then sits back. The second involves repeated offers of advice or even criticism which are said to be designed for the 'good' of the other.

A favourite Game with social workers and health care professionals is 'Harried'. This is a version of 'If It Weren't For You', since you think of all the things you would do if there were not so many other things to do. It also protects you from the demands of others, when skilfully played.

All Games have a dramatic quality, but some are potentially lethal, such as 'Alcoholic' and 'Jealousy'. Many people play a game of 'Uproar', in which they do not feel alive unless there is a drama going on, and this may have disastrous qualities. In a group, a member playing 'Uproar' is capable of sabotaging the proceedings for many meetings.

Unfortunately, the main effect of Games-playing is to rob us of the ability to relate to each other with straight transactions.

An example might be:

'If I weren't so busy, I would run some groups'.

'Well, let X do some of your work while you start a group'.

Oh dear, now I have to get started on groupwork and I am not so sure I know how to do that. Unless I can find another excuse, such as:

'I'd love to, but there is no room available for a group.'

Playing 'Yes, But ...' is a possible gambit to get you off the hook.

What this transaction avoids is an admission that you do not feel competent. You are therefore not offered any further training, so you have to continue to pretend that you know it all. If the transaction had been straight, your Adult would have acknowledged that you would feel better about taking a group if you could get some more training, support and supervision. Without clear communication, you are unlikely to get what you need.

Games come to a halt only when the payoff for them ceases. One player may refuse to continue to play or call the other person's bluff. In the film 'Charlie Bubbles', the wife says to the husband 'If it weren't for you, I could have made something of my life.' He replies, 'Yes, I robbed the world of a first-class shorthand typist'. Ouch!

In groups, games playing leaves a bad feeling and prevents members from getting on with the work of a group. A popular group game is 'Advice Shop', where members spend a great deal of time telling one person how to deal with a problem, only to be met with a string of 'Yes but..' responses. The problem with 'Advice Shop' is that members enjoy giving advice. It shows off how clever they are and means that they do not have to admit to their own difficulties, provided they prolong the game until the time is up. Another game played in groups is 'Therapy' where a member demands attention for their own problems and prevents the group from solving any of its set tasks. Games can be distinguished from straight transactions by the language used and the feeling created.

THE OK POSITIONS

There are four of these:

I'm OK, You're OK	this is a basically healthy position, but needs to be realistic
I'm OK, You're not OK	this is a paranoid position in which a person lays the blame on others
I'm not OK, You're OK	this is a powerless feeling which can lead to withdrawal, even suicide
I'm not OK, You're not OK	this brings a sense of futility, loss of interest in life, even psychotic states

These states can either be a deep underlying framework for our way of relating to the world, or ephemeral moods. You may have one of those days in which your predominating feeling is of 'I'm not OK' and 'You're not OK', and feel hopeless and helpless. A change in circumstances soon alters this temporary feeling to a more comfortable position. But if anyone adopts this as a basic view of life, they will have severe problems relating to others and dealing with situations at work.

It is often useful in a group to start with a short round of 'How I feel today', using the OK notions. It helps to remind the group that all members have a life outside the room, and some may have had a trying journey, or a disagreement with their partner, before arriving at the group. Using these ideas helps people to understand that if they or others are a bit scratchy, it is a feeling that relates to the world outside, not to the happenings in the group. But if a member is habitually feeling 'I'm not OK' or 'You're Not OK', then it is important to recognise this and help them tackle the reasons for their discomfort.

Unfortunately, we can convey to others that they are 'Not OK' in subtle ways. Children often get this message from parents and others in authority. We brand others as 'Not OK' every time we discriminate against them because of their ethnic origins. It is particularly difficult if you are judged 'Not OK' for a characteristic you cannot change, like skin colour or gender, being disabled or being old.

Groups can provide a much-needed opportunity for people branded as 'Not OK' to find a common 'OK-ness'. An example is the group recently started in London of fat women who are banding together to affirm their 'OK-ness', since they are universally branded as not OK. Their aim is not, note, to get thin, as the rest of the world thinks they should in order to be OK, but to achieve a more positive self image.

TRADING STAMPS

These are feelings collected and stored rather than expressed when experienced. They are then 'cashed in' at a later date. They can be Gold, for good feelings, Red for anger, Blue for depression, or Brown for negative feelings.

Some people specialise in one kind of Stamp. A dedicated collector of Brown Stamps, for example, does not notice the opportunities to collect Gold ones. For such a person, compliments are ignored but criticisms stored up avidly. When the book is full, there is an explosion, often against someone who is not connected to the incidents in any way, or over some unconnected incident. People differ in the ways in which they redeem their Stamps, some use them in frequent but minor ways, some cash them in one big blow-out. That way of cashing Stamps can be dangerous, and may lie behind some major crimes such as rape and murder.

In a group, a member may sit fuming about what is going on for weeks (collecting Red Stamps) before there is an explosion over something possibly quite trivial. This enables the member to feel justified about their reaction, which appears to others quite out of proportion. Members can help each other to notice Gold Stamps and collect them for a group celebration.

STROKES

In TA, there is a saying that negative Strokes are better than no Strokes at all. That is, we all flourish when given recognition by those around us. Positive validations help develop sociable personalities. There is nothing worse than being ignored, so an individual will work to get negative Strokes if there are no positives around. You may have observed a group member doing his or her best to get criticism or make others angry. This is a sign that positive Strokes are thin on the ground.

WARM FUZZIES AND COLD PRICKLIES

One particularly attractive piece of story-telling in TA concerns a village where everyone possessed a Fuzzy Bag full of Warm Fuzzies. When one was given away they made the recipient feel warm and fuzzy all over. People were always asking each other for one of these and the giver would reach into his or her bag and as soon as the Fuzzy emerged it would grow and blossom.

There was never any shortage of Warm Fuzzies since everyone passed them round so freely. Then a wicked witch came to the village, angry at seeing everyone so happy. She spread the rumour that Warm Fuzzies were being given away too easily and soon they would all be used up. People started to hoard them, or reserved them only for close family. Soon there was a terrible shortage; there was always a Warm Fuzzy in the bag when anyone reached in, but they were afraid that it might be the last one and so they felt for one less and less often. People started to play tricks to get them off one another, even to try to steal them.

People began to sicken without their lovely Warm Fuzzies, so the witch devised a bag for each person which contained a substitute; Cold Pricklies. These made people feel cold and prickly but they did give villagers something to live for. The trouble was, when someone reached into their bag no-one knew whether it was for a Warm Fuzzy or a Cold Prickly; they became uncertain and confused. Some villagers made plastic Warm Fuzzies but nobody was taken in by them as they did not warm and comfort at all.

The villagers were in despair when a warm-hearted young woman came to live in the village. She seemed not to have heard about the shortage and gave out Warm Fuzzies freely. Even though the grown-ups tried to stop her by making free Warm Fuzzies illegal, the children loved her Warm Fuzzies and started to give them out unasked.

The story can be finished in any way you choose. Does the law of the grown-ups prevail or does the children's example convince people? Will the supply of Warm Fuzzies dry up?

In a group, will there be plenty of giving and receiving of Warm Fuzzies, so that no-one has to worry about a shortage? Or will people hand out Cold Pricklies? Is the warmth between people freely given and received, or does it have a feeling of being false and plastic?

SCRIPTS

People get an idea early in life about what kind of person they are. Is this child going to be pleasant and compliant or a rebel? Is that child going to be surrounded by adoring people eager to carry out his or her bidding, or a loner? This early notion is the foundation for their 'Script'. It is put together from parental messages about the sort of person their child is, and what his or her future is going to be. 'He is just like his Dad' can be a negative message if Dad is a failure. It can be encouraging (or daunting) if Dad is a success. Either way, it indicates to the child that he or she is expected to imitate the behaviour of the model. Parental ideas about what behaviour each gender should display carry much weight. Equally influential are the reference groups to which parents belong. Scripts are the prescribed life stories that develop from these basic notions.

Sometimes the names given to children convey subtle messages, for example, calling a girl by a boyish name, or weighing a child down with a religious name. In a group, it is a useful exercise to ask each member how they acquired their name. Some will have been named after relatives, others will be given a name that immediately reveals their parents' reference group. For most, there will be some story attached to their name.

Steiner thinks that an important clue to our Script in life is given by the fairy tales we favour as children. The girl who loves the story of Cinderella may grow up expecting to find a prince, and the boy who delights in Jack and the Beanstalk may rashly seek out dangerous situations! Which was your favourite story?

Basically, Scripts can be either Winning or Losing. A Losing Script would be one that starts with a message such as: 'We didn't want a child when you turned up' and goes on to expect a child to compensate for the mistake. A Winning Script could start with a welcome into the world and continue with encouragement at each stage, but it might also include an expectation that the person would be good, or clever, or successful. Each Script has its own Drivers (described below), such as 'don't trust other people' or 'succeed at all costs'. Most Scripts are difficult to live up to, since they are wished on us by others. However, each person has an individual way of deciding which behaviour best fits the Script.

For all of us, our lives could be a book, a play or a film, and a very interesting one at that. What sort of novel would your life make? A quiet story of duty done, or an epic of difficulties overcome heroically? An exercise useful at around stage three in the development of a counselling group, involves members in describing the type of film that could be made out of their lives. This does not mean telling the story of their lives, but thinking of the type, or Script which life has formed so far. A trained TA counsellor might use a formal 'Script Analysis' which is an advanced exercise, to be used with care.

DRIVERS

Internalised messages received early in life, usually from parents, become Drivers for action as adults. A common Driver is 'be perfect', or 'be good'. Some are negative, such as 'don't be as clever as your older brother/sister', or 'show everyone who is boss'. All have an irrational quality. The internal Driver can rarely be satisfied. It is difficult to be good enough and impossible to be perfect. Can you identify some of your Drivers?

Powerful Drivers in individual group members may be about conformity: 'Don't rock the boat', or rebellion: 'Don't let them tell you what to do'. Drivers operate around the intimacy/distance dimension and many others of the individual characteristics that influence groups.

TIME STRUCTURING

Berne thought that there were six ways of passing the time that has to be spent in transactions with others. These are:

• Withdrawal

- Rituals
- Work
- Pastimes
- Games
- Intimacy

It is possible to **withdraw** from one another and cease to communicate. This is a good defence for brief periods of time, but if it continues too long, can lead to mental disturbances.

Berne thought that the safest form of interaction was to engage in ritual. **Rituals** can be very simple, as in the vague phrases that people use when they meet. Rituals regulate our behaviour and transactions to a greater extent than we realise. Violations of ritual exchanges are experienced as disagreeable and offensive.

In **Work** the rules are less rigid. Much of the time rituals get us by in work situations, but success at work means that behaviour has to be more flexible and we need to interact with others to engage in problem-solving. In work, it is the external realities which dictate the transactions. We can shelter behind the task.

Pastimes, Berne thought, were not as stylised as rituals but were fairly predictable. Going to football matches or going away on holiday would be two examples of pastimes. There is another form, which can be seen operating in groups, in which some play 'Did you see the match?' and others, 'Where did you go last summer?', thus avoiding any real closeness.

Games, though basically destructive, pass the time beautifully. Transactions in Games may appear intimate, but instead merely hook players into spending time and energy and end by feeling cheated.

Intimacy is the final, most trouble-free, but most risky, way of relating to others. It means stopping games-playing and avoiding crossed transactions. People can live with a partner, or have life-long friends, but never risk real intimacy. Intimacy is a candid, mutual relationship in which both partners give and receive freely and equally to each other.

Ritual, work and pastimes can be useful in groups, helping members with few social skills to interact more easily. However, rituals and pastimes can defend the group from moving into areas which are risky, such as feelings and relationships. Helping members to become aware of this, and of the alternative possibilities of authentic, Game-free transactions is one aim for a group.

TRANSACTIONAL ANALYSIS AND GROUPS

Berne always practised Transactional Analysis in groups. He said it was more effective that way. He would work with one of the members, and let the others learn from watching. Only later did counsellors and therapists who followed Berne's ideas find that TA is also effective in work with individuals.

In groups, I have seen TA used in Intermediate Treatment with rebellious youngsters who learned and applied the theory to their own situations. In another example, Ross worked with a group of young school underachievers. She found that some knowledge of TA gave the children resilience in dealing with the 'put-downs' they got from school. A thoughtless Head Teacher gave some luke-warm praise which sounded more like criticism, after the group had worked hard and presented a topic for school assembly. 'That was a Cold Prickly', one eight-year old commented. Understanding of this kind fosters a sense of competence and helps gain some power over one's own situation. Pitman gives many other examples of work with both children and adults in her book on *Transactional Analysis for Social Workers and Counsellors*.

Recent developments in TA have led to a wider use of the group. Members are now encouraged to help one another, not just rely on the therapist. Exercises and questionnaires have been devised which ask members to look at their ways of relating to others in TA terms. These can be worked on in sub-groups. There is a particularly useful book by Jongeward and James, called *Winning with People* which gives many exercises for use in groups.

Such exercises include individual explorations of favourite fairy stories and titles of the book that could be written about your life. They deal with understanding the behaviour of others, such as the tendency to collect Trading Stamps, or see that a Critical Parent ego-state dictates much of what we experience from others. Using these exercises provides a method of understanding the crossed transactions that often occur in groups. They are valuable as an aid to introducing TA ideas and can be taken at a simple level as Pastimes, or developed into work on individual and group problem situations.

SUMMARY

This section has introduced some of the basic ideas of TA:

- ego-states of Parent, Adult and Child
- Games
- the OK positions
- Trading Stamps
- Strokes
- Warm Fuzzies and Cold Pricklies
- Scripts
- Drivers
- ways of structuring time

It has also indicated some of the ways of using TA in groups. If you want to know more about these ideas, there are several books mentioned in Appendix B which are relevant. I hope there is enough information to show that as well as helping you to understand behaviour, the people you are dealing with can also make use of these ideas to make sense of their lives. This gives them more power over their actions and helps them feel more OK! It is possible to practise some Transactional Analysis after reading about it, particularly if you are already aware of the basics of counselling and groupwork. However, as with other theories, it is always preferable to extend and develop your skills by taking some further training and using the notions on yourself.

Eight

Developing methods of work: Gestalt psychology

Do not let the name put you off. 'Gestalt' is a German word meaning 'configuration', 'whole', or 'pattern'. The basic ideas were developed in Germany; during the 1930s several Gestalt psychologists fled to America. There their ideas were developed and influenced many areas of psychology.

Behavioural theory stresses the importance of external stimuli and of splitting behaviour into component parts. Gestalt theory emphasises the inter-relatedness of what is perceived and the whole experience of the observer. This approach views the person's ideas, feelings and actions as related aspects of the whole personality. Gestalt psychology asks how we make sense of our world and how we use our experiences.

I have personally found Gestalt ideas a great stimulus to groupwork and individual counselling. Further, these ideas have helped me make sense of my own experiences and given me strengths as a worker. In particular, I am impressed with the way in which Gestalt ideas fit with Buddhist and Zen traditions. It is sometimes forgotten that it has taken Western thinkers thousands of years to reach the wisdom that was formulated in the East long ago, but Gestalt theory seems to relate these ideas to modern problems. Gestalt theorists also anticipated modern Systems Theory and provide a humanistic antidote to mechanistic tendencies in current ideas on psychology and management.

One of the early Gestalt psychologists, Wertheimer, coined the phrase 'The whole is greater than the sum of the parts'. (Used in Chapter Two to introduce group process.) He pointed out that a group is not just the sum of the people in it, but has a life of its own. No two groups are identical. Groups change people and people change groups. Groups achieve different aims from those of the individual, and have greater power.

From this was developed most of the early experimental work on group processes. Lewin was among the Gestalt psychologists who left Germany in the 1930s and reached the USA. He initiated investigations into leadership styles and communication patterns. It was understandable that psychologists who had witnessed the tremendous power for evil of the group in Nazi Germany should be interested in finding out more about using this power in beneficial ways, for example in promoting health and personal well-being.

Gestalt psychology was developed into a therapeutic method of dealing with people's problems and fears by Perls during the 1950s and 1960s in America. Perls was a doctor and an unconventional psychotherapist who started work in Germany, escaped to South Africa, and finally reached America. 'Therapy' is usually thought of as dealing with illness, but one substantial element of Gestalt therapy is about promoting positive good mental health. This means that Gestalt techniques are useful in many areas of personal development and decision making. Perls' ideas are related to those of the original Gestalt theorists, who were particularly interested in explanations about processes of perception and thinking.

I will outline some of these notions and the ways in which they can be used in groups.

UNFINISHED BUSINESS

Perls believed that psychological unease and disease stems from incomplete relationships and unfinished tasks. These can be from our past history or from significant relationships in the present such as those with partners and fellow workers. These unresolved feelings and ideas go on worrying us and need to be worked on. At an unconscious level, such feelings influence our reactions to situations which remind us of past events. Sometimes these bits of unfinished business are minor irritations, but if they concern close relationships, they may cause emotional blocks which prevent us from getting on with the current issues in life.

Another way of explaining this idea is to say that the person involved in these relationships has only been allowed, or allowed themselves, to experience an event or feeling with one component part of their personality. That is, they have not been able to use ideas and feelings or have blocked the actions that would deal with the situation.

In counselling groups, one way of dealing with these problems is to have the group member imagine they are having a conversation with someone with whom they have unfinished business. An example would be of a boss who has behaved unfairly but who is risky to tackle because they have power over future career developments. Or it might be a long-dead parent, with whom there were always unspoken issues that were never resolved. These conversations are not rehearsals for dealing with a situation, as in Assertion Training, but a method of working on personal issues. The work done in this way may lead to better relationships, but the immediate aim is to change the person's ideas and feelings about a situation, or help them overcome a 'block' in thinking, feeling, or ability to act.

Within any group, some unfinished business will build up between members as the group progresses. One of the aims in a Gestalt group is for personal authenticity, where these incomplete situations can be faced and worked through, so that they do not cloud future sessions.

Two-chair method

In a counselling group, a member who is working on issues which concern people outside the group is gently encouraged to use two chairs, one for themselves and one on which they imagine the other person sitting. They provide both sides of the conversation, but when they are speaking as the other person, they change chairs.

An example would be of a person who feels that they never received approval from a parent, and as a result have some unfinished business with them. The person working on this issue sits in their 'own' chair and begins to talk as if the parent were sitting in the other chair.

They may start by saying:

'Why did you never tell me that I did something well?'

The person doing the work then changes chairs and speaks as if they were the parent:

> 'It does a child no good to be paid compliments, they get too big for their boots.'

This needs a reply; the person needs to speak for themselves again, so they change back to their 'own' chair and say:

> 'You might have managed to tell me I did well when I won the school trophy!'

This dialogue can be continued, with the person involved in it expressing their anger or sadness at the effect of this treatment. They will be encouraged to speak in the present tense, telling the parent all the things they never were able to say in reality, re-working the experience. If they go back periodically to the chair occupied by the imaginary parent, they can also develop their understanding of how the parent may have felt, and so begin to come to terms with their sadness and anger.

Could you develop a dialogue of this kind for yourself, or imagine one that was relevant for you?

LANGUAGE

One of the ways of overcoming blocks is to alter our language, which influences ideas about our own interactions. It is common to distance ourselves from emotion by using 'you' instead of 'I'. 'You feel bad when someone ignores you' is a typical statement. Owning the feeling by saying 'I feel bad' is the start of changing our reactions.

Language can obscure our own responsibility for a feeling. 'I can't face it' translates into 'I will not face it' and thus into a start on working on ourselves. 'It' is another word that often covers up a feeling. 'It's no use.' What is this 'it'?.

'Should', 'ought' and 'but' are words to be explored. I should get up early every day and complete this book. Who says so? Is it my own idea, or a voice within nagging me with 'could do better'? Maybe I could work faster in the evening? Where does the 'should' come from? It only serves to make me feel guilty and so slows down my work. Can you think of an example about one of your own 'shoulds'?

In a group, members are encouraged to use 'I', and not shelter behind 'you' or 'we'. 'We do not like what you are doing' translates into 'I do not like it', which is accurate. You cannot speak for others, without finding out if they agree. They must take responsibility for themselves. If you feel other members support you, check this out with them. Is your feeling accurate? If not, on whose behalf are you speaking?

VOICES WITHIN

Most of us have several voices within our heads which offer comments, criticise, encourage and debate. Do you often think over a decision, telling yourself what will happen if you take one line rather than another? This internal dialogue is usually uncomfortable but benign, though the critical voice can tell us things we would never let anyone else say, and is often slow to offer congratulations.

In some mental states, these voices become malevolent and feel as if they are uncontrollable. Once this happens, the voices harass and persecute the unfortunate individual who is generating them; such a person is usually convinced that the voices come from outside themselves. This development is far removed from our usual internal dialogues.

In Gestalt groups, the internal dialogue is externalised, and the individual encouraged to go through the dialogues out loud. Once this is done and heard, the irrational nature of many of the statements is self-evident. It is possible to see the unfriendly nature of some of the voices, to identify them as coming from parents or other powerful figures, and to answer back, using the two-chair technique. This strengthens the positive voice and weakens the negative one.

'HERE AND NOW' NOT 'THERE AND THEN'

It is important to stay in the 'here and now', while working on one's own problems. Concentrating on my feelings now will give me much relevant information. Dealing with unfinished business does not mean going over and over uncompleted events in the past. These events need to be reinterpreted in the light of the person you are now. Two people may have similar and traumatic experiences in the past, but each will make different sense of them now. One may use the experience to make them more suspicious, while the other uses it to make them more sympathetic.

Describing the event as if it were happening now is a powerful way to recapture previous experiences, but it is important to remember that those events happened to you as a younger, less powerful and knowledgeable person.

HOLES AND BLOCKS

If there is a lack of contact with events and people in the outside world, or with internal feelings, 'holes' develop in the ability to perceive and make sense of our environment. We may be oblivious to pleasant sensations, or beautiful surroundings, or worse, to feedback from others. So we have holes where there should be eyes, or heart, or ears.

Blocks develop between ourselves and our senses. When expression of needs is blocked, there is interference in the ability to get on with the task in hand. For example, you are studying a book. You begin to feel thirsty, or need a cigarette; not just to escape study, but as a way of maintaining your efforts. You decide not to be self-indulgent, but gradually, the need begins to take over your attention and you can no longer concentrate. In some situations, it is easy to stop one activity and satisfy the need, but in others a moral judgement is made, and the desire is blocked. Constant blocking of a need can result in a sensation that one can never be satisfied, or 'completed'. When the blocked-out needs do arise, they are physically locked in by the muscles. For example, anger is held back, the jaw clenches, arms tense, and muscles undergo a painful strain. If this is applied to relationships, these neurotic self-regulations can rob both the individual and the partner of satisfaction.

In the group, members are asked to pay attention to the sensations they are receiving from their surroundings and become aware of the mass of information and feelings that pass through our minds all the time, but which are largely ignored. They are also asked to notice their body posture. Which part of them is tense, or held tightly? They may be giving out subtle messages with a posture. Becoming sensitive to these messages is an important part of becoming more aware of what their body is doing.

One of the main rules in Gestalt work is that the individual is the expert on the meaning of her or his own images, postures and dreams. No group leader, therapist, or counsellor has any special 'Inside information' about the significance of these images for another person. This is the very opposite of Freudian ideas which attribute universal significance to images and dreams, and which reinforce the expert status of the therapist. Ridding oneself of this status is a notion that is vital to any group leader, whether trained in Gestalt or not. It is quite difficult to surrender the idea that one's own knowledge is superior. But in groupwork which centres on counselling and therapy, it is not the special nature of any knowledge that you have which makes you a good group leader, it is the ability to draw awareness from others.

PROJECTIONS

At one level, most people have an idealistic view of themselves as honest, loving and well-meaning, even if they also feel misunderstood and unappreciated! This applies to thieves, murderers and concentration camp guards as much as to policemen, nurses and social workers. Inevitably, parts of the personality do not fit in with this unreal image. At a deeper level, feelings of worthlessness and critical ideas about personal deficiencies trouble many. It is not easy to take responsibility for these hidden areas. One way of dealing with these unacknowledged parts of the personality is to disown them. When this happens, it seems as if others are behaving to you in these ways, not as if you are the one displaying the behaviour. This is projection.

An example would be of a critical and judgemental person in a group who is afraid of the way other members might criticise them. They might say: 'You are all so difficult to please. I can do nothing right.' They are projecting their own attitudes on to others.

One exercise that can be tried in later stages of group development, is to ask each person to record anonymously three criticisms of another member. The paper with these records is then put in a hat and each person picks out one list of criticisms and tries to guess, not who is criticised, but who is doing the criticism. It is surprisingly easy to spot the originator! This illustrates the way in which the actions and ideas that most annoy us about others are those that others see in us.

TOPDOG AND UNDERDOG

Perls thought that authentic learning is a process of discovering meaning for oneself. Instead, we internalise other people's judgements about what happens to us. This splits the self from experience and surroundings, and leads to polarisation of feelings, thoughts and actions. Thus we develop a Topdog and an Underdog in our personalities for dealing with these splits. Topdog is the moralist, the nagger, the part that is full of 'oughts' and 'shoulds'. Underdog is the whiner, the one who is always 'trying' to do things better and making excuses. These two form a large part of the dialogue that goes on in our heads. How about putting your Topdog on one chair and your Underdog on the other and get them to talk to each other? Would you discover anything about the differences between what you expect of yourself and what you accomplish?

FORCE FIELD ANALYSIS

Lewin developed a theory that we are all subject to two sets of forces; one from our surroundings and one from our own internal dynamics. These make up the 'field' in which we operate. These forces keep us in balance. Sometimes they keep us stuck, so that we cannot make a decision, or take an action, even when we want to do so. An extension of the idea of the dialogue within is the notion that decisions are often made as a result of such an internal debate. You know the sort of thing: 'I really want to give up alcohol, or smoking ... but my good intentions never go far'. Or 'Why can't I make up my mind whether to move house, or job, or exchange partners, ...' and so on.

Lewin thought that the forces that govern our decision-making are of two kinds, those that impel us towards change ('I know it is bad for me') and those that restrain us from making the change ('but it gives me a lot of pleasure'). He pointed out that it is often useless to pile on the reasons for changing. Campaigns that picture the evils of drugs, alcohol or promiscuity are notoriously ineffective. It is more effective to reduce the forces that prevent change. If a man drinks because he likes to go to the pub, that is a force that keeps him drinking. If he finds another place to go in the evenings, that is likely to curb his drinking. If a woman would like to find another job, but what inhibits her is the fear of moving to another area, then it is that problem which she needs to tackle before she can solve the one that seems on the surface to be more important.

If group members have a decision that needs to be made, or a change that would bring improvement but never seems to get done, then get them to draw up two lists. One is a list of all the factors that make it important to change, and the other is a list of all the forces that are keeping them in the present position. Then decide which are the most important and which can be tackled. Sometimes we spend a great deal of time regretting decisions that we took in the past, forgetting the weight of the factors that decided us, so it can be useful to go over the reasons for past decisions using this approach.

In groups which are meeting for counselling or discussion on personal issues, one exercise that can be used is to divide into subgroups of three and help each other on any problems of this kind. Napier and Gershenfeld describe this technique in detail.

TIME-LIMITED WORK

One useful device employed in Gestalt groups has wider applications to many types of groupwork. Time-limited work involves a negotiation at the start of each group in which each member states the amount of time they need from the group. If several people want time, they negotiate further about how this will be allocated and in which sequence each will take a turn.

For example, if three people ask for some group time for working on a personal issue, each says how long they need and whether they want to go first, second or third. The first person may want an hour, whereas the second may only ask for ten minutes. If the sum of their requests runs over the amount of time available, they negotiate for each to have less time.

This device is not appropriate for the first stage of group development, but often works well when the group is in stages three and four. It prevents one member from monopolising the group and provides boundaries for work on individual issues. It needs one member of the group to play the role of timekeeper, warning each person when their time is nearly up and saying when it is over.

GESTALT IN GROUPS

Perls, like Berne, liked to practise his therapy in groups. He would narrow his attention on to the person who elected to sit in the 'hot seat', making all the other members concentrate on that particular person. When their work was completed, Perls would sometimes invite other group members to say what had been stirred up for them by what they had witnessed. He was never interested in other members' opinions about what had just occurred, since he was only concerned with the significance of the work for the individual doing it. He thought that all interpretations about what was going on in other people were simply projections of one's own thinking. However, he sometimes encouraged group members to make an 'I' statement such as: 'When she talked about her father, I remembered something that had happened to me.'

Perls valued the group setting, using other group members as a stimulus to individual work and a useful check on each others' contributions. In his groups, members became skilled in detecting a 'phoney' response, and in receiving projections from others. This was a help in becoming more objective about their own behaviour; they also learned from the work done by others. Perls, however, was not interested in further group interactions and by firmly taking the leadership/therapist role himself, hoped to ensure that the group was a secure place where members could work on painful personal issues.

More recently, some Gestalt practitioners have tried to utilise group dynamics as part of the therapeutic effect. Houston has written (and illustrated) a *Red Book of Groups* in which she gives some useful advice about dealing with common group situations such as confrontation and blocks put on the proceedings by members.

Philippson and Harris, who work at the Manchester Gestalt Centre, have developed many creative ideas about Gestalt groups and published a short and humorous book called 'Gestalt: working with groups'. They base their thinking on the whole body of Gestalt ideas, which include those of Goodman (the co-author with Perls and Hefferline of 'Gestalt Therapy'). Lewin's notion of the importance of the environmental field in which individuals operate is considered to be crucial to an understanding of groups. They distinguish between groups set up for therapy and other kinds of groups such as teams and families. They also use Gestalt theory to account for some of their experiences in large groups.

They consider that the basic themes of therapy groups are around awareness and responsibility. Increasing our awareness about ourselves and how we manage interactions in the group is the first aim. As this develops, so too does the awareness of how some experiences and actions are avoided. Group members are encouraged to take responsibility for their feelings and behaviour. As the group progresses, members feel able to experiment with different ways of feeling, being and behaving.

As group leaders, Philippson and Harris do not aim to create artificially a safe emotional climate. Instead they ask members to note how safe or unsafe they feel, and actively experience and take responsibility for their own discomfort. They recognise the influence of group interactions on the individual but ask members to recognise their own part in these interactions and come to see themselves as active rather than passive in this process.

As the group develops, Philippson and Harris use a model in which the group is seen as a social system in which individual and group functioning are inseparably linked. They believe that the process of the group and the members growing awareness of that process is most important in any therapeutic change that may occur. The therapist's task is to establish a 'well-functioning and healthy social system', encouraging members' awareness of individual and group process and their responsibility for themselves within the group. Individual work is viewed as 'embedded' in the whole group system. Over time, the therapist works towards taking a less prominent role as the group learns to mobilise its own resources, until the leadership functions are shared amongst all the members. The group is thus seen as 'co-created' between members and leaders; each group works this out in its own unique way.

Philippson and Harris's work demonstrates the way in which Gestalt theory has been developed by practitioners who are concerned to adapt and extend the original ideas of Lewin, Goodman and Perls to their work with small groups, families and organisations. Gestalt ideas form a stimulating and fertile source for practitioners in all these fields.

To summarise, creative ideas abound for the groupworker, but I have found the Gestalt approach one of the most exciting. This chapter has outlined the basic notions of:

- unfinished business and two-chair work
- 'shoulds' and 'buts' and the influence of language on the way we tackle problems
- staying in the 'here and now'
- holes in the personality and blocks in thinking and feeling
- projections
- Topdog (who nags) and Underdog (who whines)
- Force Field Analysis
- time-limited work
- how these ideas are used in Gestalt groups.

This is only a start, and I have merely touched on some of the helpful ideas in Gestalt psychology. For further reading, try Harris' *Gestalt, An Idiosyncratic Introduction* and the other books recommended in Appendix B.

If you are interested in this approach, you can try some of the ideas out on yourself, listening to your own internal dialogues and the times you use 'you' instead of 'I', and 'should', 'ought' and 'but'. Some of the exercises can be used by anyone who has counselling and groupwork skills, particularly Force Field Analysis. Before practising other Gestalt techniques on others you *must* do more than just read about it. Take some further training. It is a technique that allows a worker to deal with some very deep and distressing personal situations in a constructive way, and is well worth undertaking seriously. Some organisations which offer training are listed in the final chapter on 'Developing Your Skills'.

OTHER APPROACHES

Practitioners are constantly developing new approaches and applying new theories. TA and Gestalt have stood the test of time. They have survived the demise of their charismatic leaders. They are both undergoing development and gaining from being tried out in new situations.

There are some modern approaches to counselling and therapy which integrate many of the ideas outlined here. Neuro-Linguistic Programming (NLP) is one example. NLP is largely the work of the Americans Bandler and Grinder whose ideas are expressed in entertaining and persuasive ways. (For an easy introduction to NLP, see Sinclair's *ABC of NLP*.)

Psycho-Synthesis is another example, based on the works of an Italian therapist, Assagioli, and is described well in Jean Hardy's book *Psychology with a Soul*. Both approaches integrate a variety of psychological ideas into a system of counselling and therapy. Such theories build on the insights from Behaviourism, TA and Gestalt. They add various other ideas from communication theory and cognitive psychology. If there is an accredited centre in your locality where you can learn something of these techniques, explore what they offer. See if they are what you need for professional and personal development.

A CAUTIONARY NOTE

Sometimes eager workers grasp a few concepts from a theory and rush into using these. This probably does not cause much harm to group members, who can protect each other against a new worker's over-enthusiasm. The worst effect is to undermine the hopeful leader's confidence, since the new 'magic' tool does not seem to have the same result for you as the book says it should: 'I tried it once and it did not work'. So the worker does not get the hoped-for boost to their skills, but instead arrives eventually at the position where 'None of these ideas actually works,' and the risk of burn-out looms. In giving a few of the basic ideas from a body of theory for your consideration, I am conscious that this is a risk. Each section has clear markers about further training and reading; hopefully you will get beyond the first stages where 'a little learning is dangerous', and continue to develop your skills.

Not all techniques and approaches are suitable for groups of agency users. TA and Gestalt are effective approaches for use in group counselling, with appropriate training. However, the next chapter describes T Groups which are a method of training in awareness of what is going on in a group, and of alerting participants to their own behaviour as group members. This is not a technique to use with vulnerable clients or patients, since it does involve ambiguity and stress for participants, but is valuable for those who are going to be using and working with groups.

WHICH THEORY SHALL I USE FOR MY GROUP?

It would be so convenient if it was possible to draw up a table that clearly showed which type of group was most suitable for which type of situation or client group. Unfortunately it is not that simple. Yalom tells a story about running a group for long-term hospitalised schizophrenics in opposition to the general idea that groups were not suitable for this type of patient. He used all his best therapeutic techniques, only to find that the members sat silently together. This confirmed the gloomy predictions made by colleagues. After a few weeks, he proposed that the group should disband, as it was getting nowhere. The members rounded on him in dismay. They maintained that they gained a lot from the group and found the sessions valuable!

Much depends on how comfortable you are with different types of groups. Your groups will reflect your levels of anxiety, and your confidence in using some methods will be communicated.

Feedback on how your groups have worked is vital if you are to assess the impact of the method you have used. It is essential to gain as much knowledge as possible from group members and those in close touch with them. The final sessions of any group should include some time for evaluating the experience, and members should be encouraged to report any changes that family and friends have noticed. Co-leaders are a valuable source of accurate feedback. I am slightly less confident about the accuracy of feedback from fellow-professionals, since I have known instances of inter-professional rivalry lead to failure to recognise or value any changes to clients or patients that might have occurred.

It is important to select a type of group and method of working which you feel suits your style. If you are sensitive to dynamics such as the stages of group development, and to individual needs within the group, then the basic ingredients of a successful group are present. An example of development could be the need to learn more confrontational skills if you are working with a group of alcohol or drug users, who have learned how to fend off ordinary counselling or therapy techniques. Experiment!

CONCLUSION

In this and the preceding chapters I have surveyed briefly Social Skills Training, Assertion Training, Transactional Analysis and Gestalt.

Social Skills and Assertion Training are useful tools to have at your command and if practised with sensitivity, can help group members and workers to make their personal interactions effective.

Transactional Analysis is set out in simple words and concepts that most people can understand and use. This includes children and adults with learning difficulties. Groupworkers can use TA both for their own understanding and to pass on to others. Gestalt is a particularly effective way of approaching counselling and therapy groups.

These ideas and techniques are valuable for groups with agency users. They also have a contribution to make to professional skill development and support groups. Ideas from TA and Gestalt are useful in understanding groups at work.

To make use of these approaches, be prepared to find and attend groups where they are practised. It is essential that group leaders get experience of being a group member, not just in training, but at regular intervals while working. Attending groups run by other leaders not only keeps you alert to your own ways of working, but is an excellent way of improving your skills.

A list of useful organisations is given at the end of this book (in Appendix A.) They organise training both for beginners and for the more experienced. Some have lists of accredited trainers.

Nine

Training in groupwork

There are many opportunities for training in groupwork, in varieties of styles, theories and techniques. Some are rooted in the psychoanalytic tradition, some in humanistic psychology, and some in behaviourism. A number concentrate on the skills needed to work with a group, and others on the importance for groupworkers of learning about their own behaviour, both as group members and group leaders.

It is vital that the intending student has an idea of what to expect when undergoing training. To some extent, all training groups utilise your presence, as a group member, to help you to see what is happening in the group. Understanding your own problems and particular ways of coping with these, helps you come to terms with what is holding your skills back. It also supplies material on which to practise counselling techniques. The caring professional's chief working tool is him- or her- self, so it is important to reveal and overcome personal difficulties in handling groups before practising on others. If you are going to counsel, it is important to explore the aspects of your own personality which could interfere with clear perception of others' problems. Skill in understanding yourself is the basis for understanding and helping others.

Courses differ in the emphasis they place on the trainee's personal material. They also vary in the help they give to trainees. Some take a stern, distant stance to the individual, and others lay great stress on a warm and caring environment. You should know the approach of a course before you commit yourself.

Sort out your goals in learning. Do you want to:

- find out about group dynamics to help you understand groups?
- learn specifics about running a group in a public service agency?
- study individual or group counselling skills?

These three aims are not independent of each other. Skill in running a group depends to a considerable degree on a grasp of group dynamics. Individual counselling skills are usually taught in a group, and an understanding of the group helps in finding ways in which the learning environment can be best utilised. Group counselling skills combine all the elements of the other aims. But there may be one aim appropriate to your own stage of learning and which you are particularly interested in pursuing.

In this chapter, I have outlined some of the approaches to training that are most frequently offered to intending groupworkers. My evaluations are based partly on personal experience and partly on feedback from students. Styles of learning differ, and what suits you may not benefit another. Obtain enough information to decide what is appropriate for you.

Do not attempt to learn everything about what is to happen in a group before you go. If you have information about general aims and methods of work, it is not necessary to know in detail each of the planned activities. Before you start the group, you are in the pre-group stage of development, in which there is much anxiety about how much you will be expected to contribute, and how safe the group will be for you. Once the group has developed to stage four, you may find yourself doing something that you would have considered highly anxiety-provoking before you started the group. To take an example, if you had been told that in one exercise, everyone is expected to write a poem, you may have thought that would be quite impossible for you to do. After you have gained confidence in the group and with the stimulus of events happening around you, it could happen without much stress, and you would feel a sense of achievement.

T GROUPS

These groups are frequently offered as a basic learning experience. The 'T' stands for training, or 'sensitivity training'. The T Group is not a counselling or therapy group. The aim of such groups is to help you learn about group dynamics and how you operate as a group member. The focus is on learning from what happens in the T Group. There are two principal types of T Groups, each with its own history.

THE TAVISTOCK TRADITION

In the 1940s in England, Bion, a psychiatrist, was working with members of the armed services who had suffered mental breakdown while on service. He found that they responded well to therapy groups and he became fascinated by the forces he saw developing in these groups. (The section on group development in Chapter Two refers to some of his findings.) He evolved a method of creating maximum ambiguity about the task and structure of a group, so that the strong feelings, or basic assumptions, around dependency, pairing, and fight/flight could be seen to develop.

The original aim of the groups was entirely therapeutic, with members looking at the ways in which they used essentially irrational ways of dealing with relationships. Bion worked, after the war, at the Tavistock Clinic in London, where his ideas are still used in analytic group psychotherapy, and by Tavistock-trained psychiatrists or psychologists practising outside the clinic. The usefulness of this approach for training therapists and groupworkers was soon evident, and T Groups were set up specifically for this purpose. The focus of the T Group is on group and interpersonal dynamics, not on personal issues. At first very widely used, there is now more caution about this technique as basic training.

The method involves setting a structure in which people meet as a group, with rigid time limits for the length and frequency of meetings. One of the significant notions is the importance of boundaries which mark the separation of the individual from the group and the group from the world outside. To emphasise this, the chairs are arranged in a circle, and the leader takes his or her place at the appointed time. There is no task, except the one laid down in the introduction to the T Group. That is, to study group process and oneself as a group member. The leader remains silent while the members struggle to find out about each other, what role the leader is playing, and what is expected of them. They project on to the leader all their own distress and aggression, attributing wide powers to the person occupying the position. Occasionally the leader may interpret what he or she thinks is going on in a group, for example that the members are seeking to regain power by pairing off, or organising fight reactions. Much of the time the focus is on the uses of power both within and between groups. At the exact time the group is due to end, the leader gets up and leaves, even if someone is talking.

This method can be highly stressful. Ambiguity gives rise to anxiety and the freedom of action is useless because every member is alone and, apparently, unable to agree with any other member. It is the classic 'Laissez-Faire' situation. Out of boredom or anxiety, members can be savage towards one another, or get upset about their inability to cope with this stressful situation. The situation is not novel, or unusual, only stripped of the normal structures and goals which conceal what goes on under the surface. It is a microcosm of the struggles of politics, work, and even the family, for which we develop rules and norms as a shelter from destructive behaviour. Beneath familiar ways of regulating the situation people are busy blaming all their ills on the leader, or other group members, and feeling dependent and powerless. Often much time and energy is devoted to fighting or fleeing from the leader's perceived powerfulness or refusal to exercise that power.

In 'real life' we develop defences that serve us well, and conceal our uncomfortable feelings, but these do not seem to work in the T Group. We cannot shelter behind status, or structure, or our preferred role. So there is much to be learned about ourselves and about the way the group affects its members. One problem is the difficulty of sorting out individual reactions from group phenomena such as scapegoating or power struggles. The maintenance of boundaries between the self and the group can seem an impossible task without assistance. Sometimes members lose confidence in themselves outside the group as well as within it. They can feel depressed by their inability to cope with the destructive behaviour they have experienced or of which they have shown themselves to be capable.

These groups have been widely used to train groupworkers, managers, and other professionals. A study done in America by Canavan found that participants rated the Tavistock groups more valuable for understanding issues from their work situations than other groups which concentrated on personal issues. There is much to be learned from such groups about the nature of power and leadership in the group, and the essentially irrational behaviour which everyone displays sometimes in groups. My own feeling about Tavistock groups is that understanding can be achieved without this deliberate creation of anxiety. Learning about group dynamics involves intellectual understanding as well as experiencing the full blast of the storm outside the harbour without any defences! Most groups create enough anxiety to provide good opportunities for learning without creating additional stress.

This type of group can be useful for further training for experienced workers, since it crystalises difficulties with groups and gives a sophisticated lesson in dealing with these under stress. In my opinion, such groups are not suitable for beginners.

THE NATIONAL TRAINING LABORATORY TRADITION

In the 1950s in America, Lewin and his co-workers set up some groups to see if these could be used to tackle prejudice and racism in the workplace. The plan was for the groups to be observed and researched. Observers met every evening to report progress. Participants in the groups were curious about these meetings and asked to be allowed to observe the researchers' discussions. Once they were there as observers, they wanted to join in. Finally the evening meetings became the focus of the day, with participants trying to discover the ways in which the groups were operating and the reasons for their very limited progress. This started the idea of meetings in which the focus was on what was happening in the group in the 'here-and-now' situation. Such a group could tackle issues of power and competition, and blocks to understanding and communication. Members could gain valuable feedback about their own behaviour.

These new groups were termed 'Laboratories' because they created a safe climate for experimenting with new behaviour and new understanding. A basic idea was that group members, instead of expecting the leader to be the 'expert' and do all the group's thinking and planning, should take responsibility for their own learning. The emphasis was on the effectiveness of learning at an emotional, as well as an intellectual level. The term 'facilitator' was coined to describe the leader's role.

Members were encouraged to look at their typical modes of behaviour; for example, how they communicate, whether the messages arrive as intended, what they hear, how they distort incoming messages, how others see them. Another aim was to increase the understanding of group dynamics to the point where the individual could recognise the forces at work and their own reaction to these forces. Learning was focused on the group and interpersonal situations, as in the Tavistock type of T Group, but the emphasis was on the wide range of dynamics in groups and a willingness to look at the personal issues that arise in this process.

The Tavistock type of T Group is usually led by one person, whereas the NTL groups tend to use two co-facilitators, giving balance and feedback to each other.

One of the important ideas which developed was the value of feedback from others in the group on one's own behaviour. Feedback is not the same as criticism. It gives data for learning by including evidence of behaviour, by avoiding judgements and projections and by including positives as well as negatives.

The Gestalt idea of projection is also valuable in the Laboratory context. In a group, if another member annoys you, or you feel negative about them, it could be that you are projecting on to them feelings which you reject in yourself. That means you are projecting some part of your own difficulties on to the other person. Another explanation might be that this person affects others in a similar way, so you need to check with others if they are having the same reaction. Members learn to make an 'I statement', such as 'I feel hostile when you don't talk to me', which avoids being judgemental and gives a specific example of behaviour.

This type of group was strongly influenced by Gestalt ideas. It recognised the strong forces of the field in which the individual operates, the influence of unfinished business on present behaviour and the need to make sense out of experience. It was also very influential for Rogers, whose own brand of 'person-centred' T Group is used for training counsellors and group therapists.

It is probably obvious from what I have said that I prefer the NTL groups, based on Lewin's work, and find them a good place to facilitate learning both for relatively inexperienced and more advanced workers. There is more emphasis on understanding what is going on, not only on experiencing it. Interpretations of the dynamics of the group are within the framework of the theories about groups which are outlined in the preceding chapters.

The Johari window

One of the notions that arose from T groups was the so-called 'Johari Window', named after it's inventors, Joe Luft and Harry Ingram. A window is a useful image for participation in a group, since only certain parts of our personalities are revealed in a public situation.

	Behaviour known to self	Unknown to self
Behaviour known to others	PUBLIC SELF	BLIND SPOT
Unknown to others	FACADE OR HIDDEN SELF	UNCONSCIOUS

This window diagram is a picture of the different visibility of our behaviour depending on whether it is being observed from within ourselves, or from the vantage point of other group members. It also illustrates how we hide what we know about ourselves from others. PUBLIC behaviour is known to myself and others. HIDDEN behaviour is known only to me. BLIND SPOTS are not known to me, but can be seen by others. UNCONSCIOUS behaviour is hidden both from myself and others.

Blind spots can be reduced through feedback from other group members on what they notice about my behaviour. For example, if I am told I am looking anxious about something that is happening in the group, I become aware of my anxiety. Increased ease about self-disclosure and less defensiveness results in a reduction in the hidden self. The area of the unconscious, known neither to myself or others, is the source of much apparently irrational or childish behaviour that surfaces in groups. As the known areas expand, this area decreases and becomes less menacing.

Can you rate yourselves on these dimensions? How much of yourself do you hide? How open are you to feedback that will reduce your blind spots?

T Group exercises

Laboratory situations often include set exercises which are designed to highlight the forces at work in the group and between groups. These exercises are based on theories about group dynamics. They deal with, for example, communication, competition and co-operation, trust building and drawing a group to a conclusion. Participants can practice skills such as role-play, or receiving and giving feedback.

One technique used is that of the 'Fishbowl'. For this, one half of the group sit in the centre, working on some aspect of group dynamics, while the other half sit around the edge, observing and later, giving feedback. Napier and Gershenfeld's book gives a rich variety of such activities which you may want to try for yourself.

ENCOUNTER GROUPS

These developed out of the original T Groups in America. The name is sometimes used confusingly as a synonym for T Groups, but the term implies more physical activity and less talking than in the T Group. The aim of the group is to produce 'personal growth' for participants. The focus is on oneself as a group member and less emphasis is placed on learning about group dynamics. Such groups are often a good way to accelerate learning by reaching to the feelings without intervening words. Sometimes people who are wrapped up in language and logic find that this type of group can shift a block that has been reinforced by too many words.

One of the tensions in the T Group movement has been the need for individuals to work on themselves and their own reactions as against the need to understand the use of group forces. Encounter Groups usually concentrate on personal issues, but they inevitably develop their own group process which influences participants.

CAN SUCH GROUPS HARM YOU?

When I first organised a T Group for students, I was met by the flat assertion from colleagues that such groups were dangerous! So I looked into the question of how dangerous?

I tested levels of anxiety in students who were about to participate in the T Group, and then measured this again when the T Group was over. For this I used a simple written test which asks for reactions to a list of words. A year later I gave the same group of students the same test before and after their finals examinations. Anxiety did rise before the T Group, but it had dropped again two weeks after the event. Levels rose far higher before finals and did not drop, even after results were known. The students confirmed that this had been their subjective impression. They had felt that finals were far more stressful. So it was clear that colleagues were willing to inflict anxiety-provoking situations on students for traditional and organisational reasons. Why was there such concern about the 'dangerousness' of the T Group?

The assertion that T Groups were dangerous was so prevalent in the 1970s and 80s that much research was devoted to proving the case for or against. The negative effects of the T Group became a thoroughly researched phenomenon. In this it differs from individual therapy, on which there is very little research about possible damage. (See for example, Dinnage's *One to One*.) When Cooper reviewed the investigations, he found that there were some personal stories about people who had been in T Groups and had subsequently had breakdowns, but that these cases were very few and usually concerned business people who had been sent on a group compulsorily.

Lieberman, Yalom and Miles did an extensive study on the effects of different kinds of sensitivity-training groups on undergraduates. They did find that some students suffered emotional upset though the majority said they had been helped by the groups. Two groups that caused noticeable harm were the impersonal Tavistock-type and an intrusive, high-energy 'therapy' group.

Most groups in the study had no casualties and were found to be helpful and stimulating by students. Leaders of these successful groups demonstrated a caring attitude, helped members to understand what was happening and kept an unobtrusive hold on what went on in their groups. The leaders whose groups produced the most casualties used either very high levels of stimulation, or were completely laissez-faire in their approach. They were low in caring and gave little guidance on what was happening in the group. Lieberman, Yalom and Miles concluded that the style of the group leader was more important than the technique he used, and those who were 'hard' and 'cold' did the most damage.

The researchers were looking at a wide variety of techniques, some of which were not particularly appropriate for use with students. An example was the 'therapy' group, which used techniques originally designed for drug and alcohol abusers. It was therefore directed at people accustomed to high levels of visual and auditory stimulation. The researchers did find some leaders who were on an 'ego trip' and whose behaviour was unlikely to help group members. This is a worrying phenomena in all counselling and therapy. Dinnage, in researching individual therapists also noted 'ego trippers'. The presence of some unsuitable leaders and therapists does not seem sufficient justification for condemnation of the whole process. (Other professions also suffer from occasional incompetent practitioners, but this is not a popular subject and receives little study!)

The research of Lieberman, Yalom and Miles confirmed my preference for less stressful learning groups, in which the leader uses some structure. It also confirmed Lewin's finding that the 'Laissez-Faire' groups were highly stressful. However, I felt that general hostility to T Groups was based more on people's past bad experiences in groups of all kinds, though some did have unpleasant memories of specific Tavistock groups. When an individual's facade slips in a group, it is so much more public than when working with just one other person!

In the general assertion that T Groups are harmful, there is no distinction drawn between different types of sensitivity training groups and differing levels of leadership skills. The research shows that the type of group, and skills of the leader, are important in determining the levels of stress. This makes it all the more important that you should experience a T Group as a member and get some of your own 'ego trips' and 'hang-ups' sorted out before you lead others!

However, these groups are intended as training groups, not therapy or practical skills courses. The unstructured and ambiguous atmosphere they create and the 'laissez-faire' nature of the leadership (particularly in the Tavistock T Groups) means they are quite definitely not for use with agency users with personal difficulties, or as a basic introduction to groupwork skills. They are, however, essential as further training for those responsible for leading groups of any kind, including managers. They can also help workers review their own behaviour as group members.

COPING WITH T GROUPS

T Groups and Encounter Groups are a valuable way of learning about group forces and the way in which you react in groups. Participation in these, or groups with a similar aim, is essential if you are to become a group leader in any setting. They are part of most training courses in groupwork and in management, where awareness about groups is vital.

Here are some strategies which are useful for coping with T Groups:

Saying 'NO' in a group

There may come a time when what is happening in a group is something you do not approve of, or want to do. I have personally walked out of two different groups because they were working against what I wanted and needed. Others seemed to be getting what they wanted, so I did not feel justified in making a protest. On other occasions I have protested about what was happening in a group and stayed. This is never easy, but always instructive! (In the next chapter the phenomenon of group conformity will be examined in greater depth.) Here I will just point out that being the 'odd one out' in a group is very disagreeable. Sometimes even the possibility of expressing a different opinion or objecting to an action is inconceivable. That is the moment when non-conformity is most needed! Take responsibility for yourself in any group, including a training group. Such groups provide good opportunities for practising assertive behaviour.

Saying 'YES'

Do not let the previous paragraph give you the perfect excuse for staying just as you are in a group, retaining all your defences in place and judging others to be foolish if they experiment. You might miss good opportunities for developing your skills and effectiveness.

Exercises which involve role-play, for example, are often embarrassing and feel 'unnatural' to begin with. But gradually you will find that they help you to understand what it is like to be 'in the other person's shoes'. Such exercises give a great opportunity to develop skills, even if it feels threatening when you are first asked to play a part. Interviewing or counselling in front of others can be anxiety-provoking, but is a valuable way of improving practice.

Let the idea of taking responsibility for yourself in a group include permission to experiment with some new behaviour.

After the group

At the beginning, a T Group may have members who are anxious and afraid of each other and the leader, but a good deal of feeling is generated, and participants get to know one another well by the end of the group. They also have the shared camaraderie of the intense learning experience. When a group of people get very close to one another, share their hopes and fears, open up about their real problems and difficulties, they experience the support that others can give. It is sometimes hard to return to the rigours of real life where one has to be on one's guard and perhaps manage unsatisfactory relationships either at home or at work. This is especially so when the group has been residential, taking you out of your normal surroundings. Here are some things you can do to ease the transition between the group and home after you have been in an intensive group experience:

1. Before you set out for the group, prepare those nearest and dearest to you for the fact that you will be tired when you return. They will have been missing you, and will be looking forward to telling you all their news, or may even have planned a celebration of your return. Persuade them to postpone such events until the next day, emphasising that you will then appreciate them more fully.

2. Keep in touch with other group members and discuss how you feel with them. But also recognise that the group has ended and that other members may not wish to be reminded about some of the events. Respect the confidentiality of the group and do not tell anyone, even someone close to you, names or any identifying details about other members. When you talk about the events of the group, you may not find others are as interested in detailed events as much as you are. Recollect that you would not like to be discussed in personal detail with a stranger.

3. Write down the essentials of what you have learned from the experience and what you want to continue work on. Follow it up by further reading so that you reinforce the benefits of what has happened.

4. If you do continue to feel tired, or even depressed, seek someone who can talk with you about the experience. It is quite usual to feel 'let down' after an intensive experience. If there is important 'unfinished business' from the group, seek ways to continue working on it. You may feel, for example, that you did not deal well with a particular situation. Is there a nagging internal voice telling you that you 'should' have been able to cope? Share these feelings, preferably with someone who has experience of groups.

These points apply to groups convened for counselling courses as well as to T Groups.

ARE T GROUPS FOR ME?

Does all this sound alarming? Essentially, T Groups intensify feelings about groups of which one is a compulsory member, such as the family or work. The point of undertaking group training is to help you deal with ordinary experiences in groups in a more positive way, and increase your effectiveness as a group leader and member.

If you have been under severe stress, or have been experiencing feelings of depression or de-personalisation, do not go to a T Group. Instead of attempting to deal with new stimulation and knowledge, seek a therapy group where you can come to terms with the difficulties you are experiencing. Later, you will be able to use your experiences constructively in the training group situation.

TRAINING FOR COUNSELLING USING GROUPS

Courses that offer training in individual counselling often use a group as a training method. Participants work on their own problems and life experiences. This enables each individual to learn more about themselves and their way of dealing with problems. Members of the group counsel each other, using the group as commentators on the way in which they do this. Thus training takes place in public, and people can try out new approaches and learn from each other.

Many of these groups used for training are intense and rewarding experiences for participants. However, they are not a training in groupwork, since the dynamics of the group are often neglected. Such groups do not deliberately use the positive and anxiety-provoking aspects of groups, nor do they focus on any understanding of the ways these can be used. They are simply using groups as a convenient method of learning counselling skills.

Such groups can therefore be valuable and important in dealing with one's own experiences and learning new counselling techniques, but they are not sufficient for a groupworker. The T Group is more valuable in this respect. (There is more information on counselling training in Chapter Twelve).

OTHER TRAINING OPPORTUNITIES.

The National Institute for Social Work runs short courses which focus on the particular problems and learning needs for workers engaged in the practice of groupwork. Other University and Polytechnic departments mount occasional courses, notably Bristol University, which is strong in groupwork specialists. The journal *Groupwork* originated from the Bristol Department of Social Work. A training video titled 'Developing your Groupwork Skills' can be obtained from that department. (There are further suggestions in Appendix A.)

To summarise, this chapter has dealt with:

- a definition of T Groups
- the British Tavistock tradition
- the American National Training Laboratory tradition
- Encounter Groups
- possible dangers of the T Group
- suggestions for coping with the T Group experience
- using groups for training in counselling
- other training opportunities (plus Chapter 12 and Appendix A).

CONCLUSION

T Groups are an exciting way of learning about oneself and groups. For example, to experience the enormous difficulty of standing out against group pressure makes a greater impression than lectures or books on the subject. T Groups can be difficult emotionally, especially the Tavistock variety, but can also give a boost to personal growth and learning. They provide the opportunity to experiment with new ways of understanding, and to put this new knowledge into practice. It is important to follow up the experience with reading and increasing theoretical knowledge. Also keep practising your new skills, otherwise knowledge evaporates.

One point of joining a T Group as part of your training is to give you a sharp experience of what it is like being on the receiving end of the group forces that you will be working with. Another is to help you deal with those parts of your own experience and learning which may block the development of your work.

You also need training which focuses on the practicalities of running groups. Such training provides valuable opportunities for sharing your experiences with others and learning from their experience. (Some methods of achieving this are outlined in Chapter Twelve.)

Can you afford to do without these opportunities?

Ten

Relationships between groups: prejudice, conformity and obedience to authority

This chapter examines the ways in which groups relate to each other and frequently conflict. This conflict is fostered and encouraged by prejudice against other groups and pressure to conform to group norms and decisions. Chapter One described how individuals differ in their ability to resist group pressure. This chapter will demonstrate that group pressure is insidious and difficult to withstand. This is particularly so when orders or strong suggestions given by powerful members of a group influence individuals to act towards other groups with aggression and oppression. The same individuals would seldom act in these ways when alone. Powerful influences on individual reactions also include obedience to an authoritarian figure and loyalty to the group.

RELATIONSHIPS BETWEEN GROUPS

So far the focus has been mostly on what happens in groups. Now the subject turns to what can happen between groups. The early chapters provided an over-view of the factors which shape and sustain groups. Further understanding is necessary if the factors which influence inter-group dynamics are to be explained. Events within a group can sometimes be understood only by reference to those that happen between groups.

The small group is a collection of people who belong to other groups and membership of a group outside (an out-group) can be used to discriminate against and oppress an individual. When a new group forms, members will need to weld a new bond which includes and contains this diversity with its potential for conflict. This is one of the factors that highlights the necessity for time in each group to build up trust between members.

Membership of the other group may be non-voluntary, amorphous, and only acknowledged when membership represents security. Membership of much larger groups such as nations and cultures can be a source of pride and guidance in social relationships. Cohesion is threatened by rivalries and disagreements based on membership of these larger groups. As a new group develops, other groups may appear threatening and hostile. One way to deal with diversity within the group is to emphasise the differences between this group and other groups. This can seem a depressing area of human behaviour, since conflict between groups and subgroups often appears to be the prevalent mode.

In Chapter Three, the way in which inter-group rivalry can be used to make a group more cohesive was described. The readiness with which groups start to compete with one another was noted. The section on co-operation and competition considered some of the forces that develop as part of the process of any group. Ideas about scapegoating and group conformity from Chapters Two and Three are also relevant.

When the relationship between groups is one of friendly rivalry, it can lead to increased pride in the group and enhanced self-esteem, particularly if one's own group is successful; village cricket matches are a good example. Huge numbers of people in towns and cities identify with their football teams. Mostly this is beneficial, but sometimes the rivalry spills into violence, usually against supporters of other teams. A partial explanation of the strong feelings engendered in team supporters can be found in some of the social-psychological theories about inter-group rivalry, prejudice and group conformity

I believe that each individual has a responsibility to be aware of the shadowy underside of human relationships. On the principle that forewarned is forearmed, knowledge of the impact of barely conscious forces which arise from group membership is an important safeguard against the conviction that one is always acting rationally and is free of prejudice. It also helps in understanding why it can seem that individual members, or whole groups, are easily able to dislike and distrust others and are reluctant to co-operate.

Is conflict inevitable?

In *Civilisation and its Discontents* Freud said: 'It is always possible to bind together a considerable number of people in love, so long as there are other people left over to receive the manifestations of their aggressiveness'. This implies that love of fellow group members is only possible if there is an out-group to hate. The experiments of Sherif seem to support this point of view, as he found it easy to get a group to be hostile to outsiders even without any interaction having taken place. Tajfel also showed that once a group is formed, there was a tendency to react to the out-group in hostile ways, emphasising their differences, while being blind to differences between people in one's own group.

But why does a group feel hostility to some out-groups and not others? For example, blue-eyed people do not normally band together against brown-eyed ones, although in the remarkable documentary film 'Eye of the Storm' children are persuaded to do this by allocating one eye colour to a powerful, favoured group and the other to a powerless group without status. Explanations of prejudice are therefore sought in social phenomena, for example in class conflict and power struggles. Sherif showed that it was easy to produce inter-group conflict when there was a struggle over scarce resources. However, even without this, the boys' groups disliked the other groups. In one of his experiments, the boys' camp was already divided into two groups before they arrived, each with equal provision. As soon as the groups became aware of each others' presence, hostility appeared. They behaved 'as if' they were in conflict.

Billig and Tajfel showed by their experiments that group members would even do themselves out of a reward in order to make sure that the out-group got less. So inter-group rivalry takes place even when the individual's own interest is not involved in favouring his or her own group. It also occurs where there is no apparent competition between the groups and no history of previous hostility between them. People seem to get involved very easily in projecting their hostility towards an out-group. Members of the out-group are seen as a threat, perhaps because of the numbers in the out-group, or the differences in their values and behaviour. The mechanism of scapegoating shows how

166

easily the conflicts and undesirable characteristics of a group can be denied and projected on an unsuspecting victim.

There are also examples of groups which have heroically defended other groups, or taken extraordinary measures to assist them. The resistance fighters in Europe during the second world war risked death to shelter persecuted Jews. However, one group in these extreme situations can identify with the other group, since both are being oppressed by a third group. The community of interest outweighs the differences.

All these factors mean that group members and leaders need to be realistic when seeking to build trust and co-operation between groups.

Prejudice

Where there are negative attitudes directed against other groups of people, these are termed prejudices. Prejudice need not be against a minority: in South Africa many minority whites are racially prejudiced against the majority blacks, and in sexist prejudice, there are approximately the same numbers of each gender.

Negative attitudes often apply to new groups who arrive amongst well-established ones, or old enemies who have a history of mutual aggression. Prejudice has to be against something or someone perceived as 'different'. It means that the evaluation and judgement of the 'other' is negative. There is an emphasis on the similarities of the out-group members (this is the practice of stereotyping), and exceptions are said to prove the rule. It is a comforting delusion to look at one's own group and reflect how well everything is managed in it, ignoring the wide divergences within the group and the manifest failures to cope. It is also an excellent way of justifying possession of more resources than are available to people from the other group.

Prejudice leads to oppression of those perceived as belonging to another group. Prejudiced attitudes and feelings are therefore a common source of injustice. Where this prejudice is backed up by possession of power, the dominant group with the most power can use their prejudice to justify oppression of the out-group. This is one of the mechanisms at work in sexism and racism, in which these ideas are harnessed into structural systems of oppression and where more powerful men oppress women and white people oppress black people.

If a group has oppressed another through a period of history, when the power relationships are reversed, the newly dominant group appears often to seek to dominate and discriminate against the old oppressors. Apparently inexplicable savage behaviour towards out-groups is often rooted in historical oppression.

Personality and prejudice

Adorno's study of the authoritarian personality was referred to in Chapter One. Among the Americans he investigated in the 1940s he found those who had an exaggerated respect for authority were also very prejudiced. He thought that they were basically insecure and directed intolerable negative feelings to an outside source. They often reported harsh, rigid and threatening home environments and severe or inconsistent discipline as children. They were pre-occupied with surface conformity. He thought that such people had an 'authoritarian personality'. Those with unthreatening home backgrounds were much less likely to be prejudiced. This study has been repeated several times in different cultures (for example by Ray in 1980) and its truth still holds.

Members of fascist groups perceive other groups as a threat to existing beliefs and privileges and use this as justification for their hate campaigns. They may have a majority of authoritarian personalities in their ranks, although many will themselves be underprivileged and victims of discrimination. Whereas the evidence described later in this chapter demonstrates that quite ordinary people can become oppressors when caught up in situations of strong group pressure, an already prejudiced person will be more easily influenced to commit violence towards an out-group.

STEREOTYPING AND OPPRESSION

One of the elements of prejudice is the way in which people tend to place reliance on simple messages about out-groups. They are willing to believe statements that are easily refutable, or can only be proved by trying them out. Before women became newsreaders on radio and TV, many believed that women would not be able to read the news without trivialising it. As soon as women did read the news, they were shown to be well able to do so. When the available evidence does not support the prejudiced point of view it tends to be excluded.

The person in the out-group is seen as belonging exclusively to that group, and having no other attributes. The discriminated-against group of people are allocated unpleasant characteristics, such as cowardice or ugliness. Many individuals in the out-group may be heroic and beautiful, but that is not taken into account in categorising them. Moreover, as in scapegoating, the attributes given to the other group members are supposed to be absent from the group to which the prejudiced person belongs. Those doing the discriminating do not see themselves as having any undesirable attributes.

It is therefore easy to persuade prejudiced people that the group against whom they are discriminating are barely human. Prejudice thus grows into racist oppression. The world has many appalling instances of one group trying to extinguish another as a nuisance, as the Australians and Americans did with people whom they called Aborigines and Indians. Those with the power to do so, exploited powerless groups unmercifully, as in slavery, convincing themselves that the out-group members did not have human feelings.

Other factors at work in such situations are demonstrated by Milgram's experiments, described below. People obeyed instructions to inflict pain on someone who was slow to learn, sometimes explaining this by saying that stupidity deserved punishment, justifying their own actions by blaming the victim. Milgram also demonstrated that obedience to authority, or to a group norm, is a vital factor in such behaviour.

Prejudiced behaviour within groups

Within a new group, or one formed without free choice of membership, there is therefore likely to be prejudice against other members. Some of this is due to the identification of a member with an out-group. Probably most of us have many more prejudices than we admit to. We are even unaware of some of our prejudiced feelings, which only surface under pressure.

This can produce painful relationships between some group members, or the scapegoating of someone who is different. It is particularly difficult to be the only person who is seen as an object of prejudice in a group. It helps to have two or more from a group which attracts discrimination, as they can offer each other some support against prejudiced remarks or behaviour. To have equal numbers can lead to difficulties of entrenched sub-grouping.

Prejudice is one of the most intractable and difficult issues to deal with in groups. In groups which are specifically set up to tackle racist issues there is at least an agreement to come together and consider these. In groups in which this is not the specific aim, prejudiced remarks and behaviour still erupt. Prejudice is aggressive and embarrassing when openly expressed, since it contravenes the acceptable norms of social relationships. Prejudiced behaviour therefore often operates at the edge of awareness and this makes it even more difficult to deal with. People are often unaware that they are expressing views which are hostile to another group, or they cover up the underlying idea by pretending that what they are saying is a 'joke'.

It is not surprising that people who share a common experience of discrimination and oppression often insist on setting up their own groups. Groups which give support to people who experience the effects of prejudice, such as those for disabled people, or offenders, give a collective sense of protection which is valuable.

There is also great need for mixed groups to work on prejudice, stereotyping and value judgements in members. These attitudes are sometimes the product of ignorance and mis-information, but such ideas are strongly inculcated by the structures of our society. They are likely to be experienced as deeply held, primitive feelings about an out-group who are perceived as threatening and different. The presence within a group of members of the out-group is seen as a threat to these strongly-held beliefs, since in the new group, there is an expectation that a new relationship will be built up.

So all-pervasive are these attitudes, that members of groups who are themselves discriminated against can hold similar feelings for another group of similarly oppressed people.

Taking some personal responsibility for overcoming prejudice

Brittan and Maynard, in their book *Sexism, Racism and Oppression*, recognise the huge weight of institutional oppression but also ask individuals to take some responsibility for their own attitudes and behaviour. Many of us can look at the organisations in which we work and see that there are very few black people, or women, who get promotion. Some groups may never be properly valued within the organisation. As long as that situation is accepted as an organisational hazard, there will be no progress. Who is responsible for this state of affairs within the organisation? What is each individual doing about it?

The issue of racial prejudice and oppression is difficult to tackle for a writer who is herself white and therefore a member of the wider group which discriminates and oppresses. With trepidation, I have attempted to set out some of the pitfalls which can beset a white worker, following the precept that each of us needs to assume responsibility for this difficult and painful situation and not leave responsibility entirely to others.

Groupworkers who are black are grappling with racism every day of their lives, but how can a white worker understand the effects of prejudice and discrimination? How can white workers make their groupwork more sensitive and appropriate to black members? Hopefully you will already be aware of books such as Devore and Schlesinger's *Ethnic Sensitive Practice* and d'Ardenne and Mahtani's *Transcultural Counselling in Action*. Devore and Schlesinger have a section in their Chapter Seven on 'Adapting Strategies and Procedures for Ethnic-Sensitive Practice' which considers social groupwork.

The journal *Groupwork* has published articles about the issues involved. (For example, the articles by Muston and Weinstein, and Mistry and Brown mentioned in Chapter Four). So the first step is to reflect on the information these contain.

There should also be an obligation to work on one's own language, that subtle betrayer of hidden attitudes. If all powerful people are called 'he' and all subservient ones 'she', and the word 'man' embraces 'woman', what message is conveyed? If bad things are 'black' and good ones are 'white', what does that say about black people? There is much evidence that the language we use helps to form our attitudes, so, although this may sound trivial, in practice a language change can be a positive step forward.

One route that may help is to seek ways of conveying to the groups of which you are a leader or member that it is important to value and work for other groups. If a group of people accustomed to discrimination can feel positive enough about themselves to reach towards another group, that is a great step forward. A group of people with experience of mental illness with whom I worked finally felt confident enough to offer to help a local group for people with learning difficulties. It was a small step that marked a large development.

Academics are themselves liable to divide into deeply entrenched groups when they theorise about oppression and discrimination. One type of explanation attributes the source of the problem to society and its structural inequalities. Another places reliance on individual and small group explanations. There are many sub-categories of explanations. Rival factions devote much energy to proving each other mistaken. Since human behaviour and society are so complex, it may seem to a practitioner who has to find ways of facilitating work between those from different groups in society that multiple explanations are needed. It is in the interactions of the individual, the group and the community that practical solutions can be found.

Improving relationships between groups

When Sherif had produced a powerful dislike between members of different groups in the course of his study on inter-group rivalry in a boys' camp, he was faced with the task of healing these rifts before returning them home. It is likely that he would have found that dislike and distrust would have persisted if they had returned straight after the first part of the exercise. In an exercise I use in group training, the groups have to divide into 'Reds', 'Blues', 'Greens' etc. and compete for hypothetical points (this is the Power Game, from Napier and Gershenfeld). Long after students have returned to other college work, references can be heard to those dreadful 'Blues', or someone may be accused of having belonged to the 'Green' group and therefore not to be trusted! This highlights the importance of debriefing after every exercise: that is, giving participants an opportunity to come out of role and discuss their feelings while in the exercise. Even when some time has been devoted to debriefing, some of the feelings of group rivalry still persist.

Sherif dealt with the problem by contriving a situation in which the Eagles and the Rattlers were made to work together if they were to get food and find their way back to camp. Gradually, as they came to rely on each other, and were forced to contend with a broken truck, lack of food and being a long way from home, their hostility evaporated. It seemed that the enforced interaction on an important task healed the rift. In the same way, students who had been in the Power Game forgot their rivalry when they were working together in seminar groups and on joint projects.

So it seems the situation is simple: get members of groups in opposition to work together, to interact with one another, and soon understanding and tolerance will prevail. Unfortunately this has proved to be only a small part of the solution. Of course there is some truth in it, but as social psychologists have studied the real-life situations of, for example, mixed housing estates where inter-group clashes can be prolonged and lethal, they have realised that proximity and interaction are not enough. After all, men and women live together and that does not cure sexism!

Amir studied inter-ethnic conflict and co-operation in depth. He suggested that contact between different groups can reduce prejudice *only* when the following conditions are also in operation:

- the groups are of equal status
- there is a social climate, backed by authority, in favour of reducing prejudice
- the contact is fairly intimate
- the contact is fairly pleasant
- the members cooperate for the attainment of a common goal
- the contact does not lower the status of either group
- neither group has practices which are morally offensive to the other

Note that they do not all have to operate simultaneously, or we should hardly ever be able to overcome our prejudices, but they are a salutary reminder that huge difficulties have to be surmounted if barriers are to be safely reduced.

It is not enough to like one or two members of the out-group which is being discriminated against. There is evidence that this simply categorises these friends as 'exceptions' and leaves the stereotyping intact. It is important for as many as possible of the whole group to abandon their prejudices and provide a support group for each other in these new attitudes. Unfortunately the dissolving of one boundary with the out-group, results in the creation of another; the people with changed attitudes are now a threat to those who retain their prejudices.

So it can be seen that the topic of discrimination is likely to be a source of deep and painful conflict in groups. If there are members present from groups which are discriminated against, they will detect many subtle ways in which prejudice manifests itself. If they speak out, they are assigned the role of 'the angry one'. If they stay quiet, nothing changes.

It is often assumed, quite wrongly, that black members of groups should be responsible for educating and changing white members, or that women should take responsibility for changing male attitudes. Members of groups which practise discrimination need to work on their own attitudes. Some of this process involves becoming aware of the ways in which social structures condition us into out-group hatred. We also need to be aware of how we justify this and manage to live with our own prejudices, while deploring these in others.

It is true that a member of a group which is discriminated against is an expert on the problem. It is also true that such a person will have a vast store of information on the differences between their culture, background and way of life. It does not follow that this person is to be at the disposal of every member of other groups whenever needed. If a white worker has a specific need for information, to ask for this is legitimate, but the problem is that people from dominant cultural groups may not know what they do not know. They should not put others in the position of having to point this out continuously. I have observed white workers neglecting a source of information because they were of higher status than the possible source of knowledge. I have also seen situations in which, when the information is proffered, it is dismissed.

I have come to think that white people should be hesitant to ask black people to be present when they are working on their own feelings and attitudes about prejudice, racism and inter-ethnic conflicts. Even when well-intentioned, white people say and do things that offend black people, who get very tired of trying to show others the offensive nature of what they are doing. The same applies to issues around sexism.

Those who are members of a society, organisation or group which discriminates against another group should take responsibility for raising their own levels of consciousness. A wide variety of material is available, from books, TV and films, which educates and illuminates. Read these, watch TV programmes on these issues and be aware of prejudice, discrimination and oppression. Try not to use a group of which you are a member to gain confirmation and agreement on your own prejudices. Expect this to be an uncomfortable process.

A powerful stimulus towards changing prejudiced attitudes arises when the group which is prejudiced begins to realise the damage their prejudices are doing to themselves. Scorn of emotion as a 'female' attribute can rob those men who profess such ideas of the ability to express their feelings. Increasingly, many men are realising that their lives are lacking in appreciation of the power of their emotions and this damages their ability to create close relationships. Becoming more open to emotion, however, exposes men to the charge of 'not being a real man', in other words, they are up against the stereotype of male behaviour which many peer groups impose on men. Gender stereotypes are a powerful demonstration of the huge impact of group conformity on each individual.

GROUP CONFORMITY OR INDIVIDUAL INDEPENDENCE?

The social psychologist Codol described the dimension of conformity and difference in social relationships. He noted a constant tension between the desire to be one of the group, to be a social being, whilst at the same time, to be a strong, individual, differentiated person, with a sense of unique identity. To be too close to others in a group leads to a sense of being stifled and robbed of individuality. To be alone is to be abandoned and lost.

Milgram, whose work is described below, pointed out that we are all brought up to conform to our important reference groups, especially the family. This is often a source of pride. This contrasts with feelings about conformity to peer-group norms: to acknowledge influence from other group members of equal status amounts to a confession of weakness. Nevertheless, group pressure is often strong and difficult to detect. It feels as if we are making up our own mind about our actions and beliefs, but in practice we pay a lot of attention to what others around us are doing or saying we should do. The people who took part in Asch's experiments (described in Chapter One) did not seem to realise how much they were influenced in judging the length of the line by the others in the group. This is a partial explanation of some crowd behaviour, where individuals can act in ways they would never do alone, either aggressively or heroically.

Seeking and achieving approval from others is an important part of social bonding. Outsiders can be seen as 'deviant', outlaws, of no importance. This is risky for the individual. So we seek others who are similar to us, who will approve of us because we are like them. Anyone wanting to join this group must become like us. Those who are similar are liked, and those who are most similar are most liked.

But we also yearn to be different. Being too similar reduces our sense of being unique. Having the courage to 'stand out' is also valued. This is especially so if it is not a stand against one's own group (for example, we value dissidents in communist countries, but disparage them in Britain).

So we swing between the two poles of conformity and individualisation. In a threatening environment, conformity is a good defence, but when the social climate is favourable, differentiation takes place. When neither is operating strongly, we vary between a wish to please others and the need to develop ourselves.

175

Some cultures place great emphasis on group identity with the family, clan or tribe. Individual needs and aspirations are seen as subordinate to those of the group. This is an excellent defence against a hostile world, where there are life-threatening scarcities and a real danger of deprivation if group resources are not shared. It is also imperative to band together when under threat of racial violence, as many black families do in Britain. Cultures with strong group ties point accusingly at the way in which those which emphasise individuality allow defenceless members of the group such as children and the elderly to suffer alone. Individualist cultures make a fuss about the suffering of less powerful people within strong group cultures, citing the problem of young women, whose individual aspirations may be neglected because the group needs to create new family ties. It seems there are advantages and disadvantages to both systems.

To summarise, so far this section has examined ideas about inter-group relationships from the perspective of:

- whether conflict is inevitable
- prejudiced behaviour and its causes
- how authoritarianism and prejudice are often linked
- the need to take some personal responsibility for overcoming prejudice
- ways of improving relationships between groups

The tension between group conformity and individual independence has been outlined. This leads from consideration of the conflict between groups to the influence of feelings of loyalty and obedience to the group which often lie behind inter-group prejudice and oppression.

OBEDIENCE TO AUTHORITY

This topic has already been referred to, particularly in Chapter One, when considering the characteristics of individual group members, and the influence this has on the group. In the section on leadership in Chapter Two the effect of authoritarian styles of leadership was examined. Obedience to authority is included in this discussion about inter-group dynamics because it plays such an important part in the treatment of the out-group. The preceding section looked at the way in which people with an exaggerated respect for authority are often prejudiced. The suggestion has been made that people are much more influenced by group pressure than they would like to think. An important component of that pressure is the respect for authority. Both designated leaders and those who are 'experts' seem to attract obedience.

Milgram's experiment

Milgram was a Professor of Social Psychology at Yale University in America. He set up the following experiment: an advertisement was circulated for people to come and take part in an experiment on learning. When volunteers arrived, they were immediately paid a small fee for the time they would spend. They then took part in a selection of who was to be the 'subject' of the learning experiment, and who was to be the 'experimenter'. They invariably found they were the 'experimenter'. The 'subject' was taken into another room and strapped to a chair. Electrodes were put on his arm, and the 'experimenter' was placed before a panel which contained a scale for administering electric shock. The scale was not only in numbers, but indicated in words how slight, serious, dangerous, etc. the shock would be. The 'experiment' began, and quite soon the 'subject' started to forget the words he was asked to learn. The laboratory technician asked the 'experimenter' to give a shock to the 'subject', to help him remember better. The forgetting got worse, and the 'experimenter' was asked to increase the dose of shock, until soon they were at the 'dangerous' end of the scale. At first, the 'subject' screamed and pleaded to be let off, then he fell silent.

Unknown to the volunteer 'experimenter' he or she was actually the person being studied, and the 'experiment' was to see how long he or she would continue to press the button. The selection process was rigged, and the 'subject' was a 'stooge'. The button they were pressing was not connected to any shock machine, and the 'subject's' cries were good acting. Not one of the people who participated in the experiment realised this. They all thought they had been selected by chance, and could have been the 'subject' receiving the shocks, and they were all convinced they were actually administering shocks.

The results of the experiment

When Milgram asked people outside the laboratory if they would give shocks to someone to the point of danger, they all said, as you are saying to yourself, 'Never'. But this reaction only follows after you are aware of the nature of the experiment. In the early stages, when Milgram was still looking for the set-up that would lead to maximum information, every volunteer pressed the button marked shock for as long as they were asked to do so; there was a 100% response. Milgram was forced to include indications like the crying of the 'subject' to see whether this would prevent everyone pressing the button.

When they could hear the cries, 60% still carried on to the point of 'severe shock'. Many of them did so with a great deal of anxiety, but when the laboratory technician in charge of the experiment said they would spoil the experiment if they did not go on, they continued. Milgram introduced variations: when the 'experimenter' was sitting in the same room as the 'subject' and could see the effect of his shocks, 30% still pressed the button, and when asked to press the 'subject's' arm down on the electrified plate, 10% still complied.

The people who participated were ordinary citizens of the town where Milgram worked. They came from all sections of society, and included men and women, young and old, black and white people. Milgram wanted to see whether the prestige of the university was an important part of the influence, so he moved the set-up to a nearby small town and made it much less 'official'. This reduced the numbers of those who continued to press the button, but not by a significant amount.

Only 10% of 'experimenters' continued to give shocks when they were placed with two others who were acting the part of rebels against the instructions. Afterwards, they said they did not feel they could continue when the others had stopped, even though they themselves would have like to go on helping out with the experiment. It seems this placed them in a position where two sources of authority were giving conflicting instructions, but the group of which they felt they were a member became more important than the group for whom they thought they were working.

When the person conducting the experiment left the room, very few people went on giving shock, although they often pretended that they had, when he returned. More people were ready to defy authority when they could do so without confronting the authority figure. They became quite kind when they thought nobody was watching.

Milgram's experiment showed that people were willing to hurt others badly at the request of a rather low-status 'scientist', in a laboratory coat. Some would not carry out the task, but the majority did. Why did they bow to his instructions?

The people who took part in the experiment

All participants were carefully interviewed both immediately afterwards and between six to twelve months later. One woman who had refused absolutely to continue with the shocks after they passed 'mild', said that she was a refugee from Germany, and recognised the situation as one that she had had to learn to resist under the Nazis. Milgram admired her, she was just as he had hoped the vast majority would be. Another participant who had refused to continue, appealed to a higher authority. He was a minister of religion, and he said that the Lord would not allow him to participate in such a cruel experiment.

Were those who did go on, cruel, mentally disturbed people? Milgram found one or two who appeared to enjoy the experience, or expressed no emotion at all. But most were anxious about what they had done, and extremely relieved to hear that the 'subject' had received no shock. Here are two of the 'profiles' that Milgram made of people who participated.

> **The Social Worker**, 39 years old, male: appears intelligent and concerned. As the experiment proceeds, laughter intrudes into his performance. The laughter seems triggered off by the learner's screams. Afterwards he says he feels the experiment may have been designed to 'test the effects on the teacher of being in an essentially sadistic role, as well as the reactions of a student to a learning situation that was authoritative, rigid and punitive'. His conversation after the experiment is relaxed and sedate, though he describes his inner tensions during the experiment. 'There was I, I'm a nice person, I think, hurting somebody, and caught up in what seemed a mad situation ... and in the interests of science, one goes through with it. At one point I had an impulse to just refuse to continue with this kind of teaching situation ... my impulse was to plead with him, talk to him, encourage him, try to ally myself with his feelings, work on this so we could get this through together and I wouldn't have to hurt him ... my laughter was a sheer reaction to a totally impossible situation.' A year later he says 'I hope I can deal more effectively with any future conflicts of values I encounter'.

Does this bring the situation nearer home? It is easy to think 'That was America', or 'People like me do not do these things'. But this is reminiscent of what happened in Germany, where there were many who justified their behaviour by claiming they had only obeyed orders, or the 'authorities'. It was also found that people became very intrigued with the mechanisms of the experiment, latched on to the technicalities, and conveniently forgot the person on the receiving end. This is a risk for all who work in settings which require technical knowledge.

The other profile was slightly different:

> **The Voluntary Social Worker** This woman was very nervous during the experiment but continued to full shock. Afterwards described her work with 'dropouts' as 'teaching them manners ... respect for people ... respect for society'. She claims she does this 'Through love, not punishment'. But she complied, she says, 'I had to do it, I'm here for a reason. You said so. So I didn't want to ... I'm softhearted, a softy ... I was tempted so much to stop and say 'Look, I'm not going to do it any more. Sorry. I'm just not going to do it' ... but I know you wouldn't let anything happen to him. So I went on with it, much against my will. I was going through hell. ... I don't think others would be as nervous as I ... I don't think they would care too much'. A few months later, she asserts that her 'mature and well-educated brain had not believed the learner was getting shocks.'

Here the very urge to help the people she worked with become 'social beings' worked against her humanity. She was caught in the conformity/individuality dimension. And she later rationalised her behaviour out of existence.

Explaining the results

This experiment has been described in detail because it shows so clearly what monsters quite ordinary people can become once they have ceased to identify with the weak and the different. Another experiment by Zimbardo confirmed this and showed how power and the opportunity to discriminate can change behaviour for the worse. He used students, one group of whom he designated as 'jailers' and another as 'prisoners'. The 'jailers' quickly became sadistic guards of the unfortunate 'prisoners' when they were given unlimited power and instructed to 'keep order'.

Milgram thought that there were major difficulties in overcoming one's tendency to be obedient. The problem is that obedience receives so much approbation in society, starting with the family, going through school, in the armed forces and in many jobs. Duty is a virtue. Devotion to one's country, family, clan and religion is much admired. Even loyalty to a gang or group of friends is an important source of social approval from peers.

Religions especially demand obedience to a higher will. Unfortunately this does not always ensure better behaviour. The minister in Milgram's experiment, who claimed a higher authority, did use his religious conviction for the benefit of the victim, but many thousands have suffered from belonging to the 'wrong' religion or the 'wrong' sect. Obedience to a higher will is no guarantee that others will be well treated.

Obedience differs slightly from conformity. The person who conforms can be thought of as weak and lacking in moral fibre. People do not like to admit that they are conforming to group norms. But they will boast about being loyal to the group and obedient to a leader.

Milgram concluded that we easily bypass common humanity when we do not feel responsible for the set-up. This happens when we follow a leader's authority, or attribute authority to the expert. The people who gave shocks simply assumed that the subject was 'dumb' and that someone else, the 'expert', was in charge. They also distanced themselves from any possible suffering that their actions were causing. Even if they did not like what they were doing, their anxiety did not prevent them from carrying out the order. They were particularly influenced by what other members of the group were doing, or advising them to do, and would only become kinder if they thought no-one else was watching.

To summarise, this section has described Milgram's experiment, outlining:

- how the experiment was set up
- the results, in which 60% of participants were prepared to give severe shock to another person
- details about the participants and their reasons for conformity or refusal to conform
- how the results can be explained by reference to the value placed on obedience and conformity by authoritarian elements in society

CONCLUSION

There are many situations in which we are insulated from someone who is the sufferer as a result of our actions, and where the responsibility for the order to act is not ours. Sometimes we feel we have to carry out the actions to preserve ourselves, our job, or our prestige.

How can we use knowledge about conformity and prejudice to avoid being drawn into these situations ourselves? Just having the knowledge is a good start. The German woman in the study quoted above, recognised the situation and refused to participate. Be alert to signs that undue pressure is being exerted on you to reduce the status of another, or treat someone as less than human. Easy to say, but we all get caught up in situations where there seems to be no alternative.

Recognise stereotypical thinking in yourself and others. One indication is that nice, comfortable feeling that we get when we know that our group is right and the others are wrong. Mistrust that feeling.

Even if you are a member of an oppressed or a newly-liberated group, and are clear about your own values, you can oppress others with your definitions of what is wrong and what is right. Your scorn of those who do not conform to your perceptions of acceptable behaviour or permitted status may lead to further alienation. Being a member of an oppressed group yourself does not give you automatic understanding of someone else's experience of oppression.

Work towards tolerance and understanding; do not assume that it will automatically happen. Achieving tolerance often requires much hard work. Refuse to be discouraged when intolerance arises, and understand that those who are insecure or deprived will often voice deeply disturbing opinions about out-groups. Do not expect that your overtures to other groups will be met with trust; there is too long a history of oppression for that to happen easily.

Look at your own comfortable opinions and be willing to change these. The alternative involves building barriers between your group and other groups and putting great trust in membership of a group of people whom you see as similar to yourself. To do that means to submerge your own individuality. The swings between emphasis upon the individual and upon the community are a source of stress and upheaval. It is to be hoped that these stresses can also lead to creative solutions.

Eleven

Groups at work

You may work in an organisation which provides day or residential care; it could be as formal as a school or hospital, or as informal as a youth club. The setting will influence the nature of the work group, but all employees have to work in some kind of group, whether this is closely integrated and clearly defined, or a loose aggregate of people who work alongside each other.

Everything said so far applies as much to groups of workers as it does to any kind of work with agency users. The dynamics of work groups will be different, but they will still centre on the same three elements of structure, members and process. Once you can perceive the impact of these elements, you will be able to see them operating in all groups, whether at work, in organisations, at home, or in leisure.

ORGANISATIONS

Organisations contain collections of different groups. These all owe their existence to the organisation. They are closely interconnected, so that the decisions of one group strongly influence other groups. Within the organisation, groups vary structurally. There are groups of managers, liaison groups, departmental staff groups and teams.

Since most organisations are hierarchical, groups differ profoundly in their power. Public service agencies are accountable to other groups and committees, which co-ordinate their work with other agencies, influence planning, and control resources. These are often perceived as out-groups, sometimes thought to be hostile and often held to be out of touch with those workers who have contact with agency users.

Within the organisation, workers tend to have only a shadowy sense of the large group which constitutes the organisation as a whole. The immediate work group is usually experienced as an important part of working life. Although all workers are members of the large group, they seldom meet as such and communications with other groups are usually by memoranda or telephone.

Organisations can be viewed as a large group in which, instead of individual members, the units of which they are composed consist of teams of workers. In this way it is possible to identify the patterns of communication of an organisation, the flow of communication and information, the sub-groupings, methods of dealing with conflict and anxiety, and roles played by individual units.

The size of any organisation is one of the major influences on the kind of experience it is to work within it. Just as in the small group, too many units mean that the group, or the organisation, fragments. Large organisations tend to split up into smaller, specialist units which provide a more satisfactory and comprehensible working situation. Nevertheless organisations and departments continue to grow, and the units of administration get bigger, so working in them is a fact of life.

In theory, organisations do not have to be hierarchical. It is possible to envisage an organisation which does not have bosses, directors or team leaders. This would be the circle pattern of communication, in which every member has an equal voice; this type of organisation can be seen in co-operatives. It is seldom used in organisations of any size, as communications tend towards chaos if too many people are involved. Interesting experiments have been tried with smaller units within large organisations operating co-operatively, even if the larger organisation is set up in a more conventional way.

Identifying the style and characteristics of an organisation

Each organisation has an individual style of administration and leadership. Sometimes this is a help in carrying out the task, and at other times, a hindrance. To analyse the style of the organisation in which you work, try answering some of these questions: How would you draw up the communication lines of your organisation? Is there agreement on aims, or would different parts of the organisation have different aims? What picture do outsiders have of your organisation, and how is this created? Do you play any part in this picture?

How often do crossed transactions occur between teams or departments? Do you feel that your needs as a worker and your views on the job are listened to? Do you feel a valued member? When units conflict, what decides the outcome? How do decisions get made? Do they actually get carried out? How does your organisation deal with changes that have to be made?

Is there evidence in your organisation of discrimination? For example, how many black people and women are there in senior positions; are the numbers in proportion to the numbers engaged in work lower down the hierarchy? Do resources go to sports fields, technology and administrative buildings, or to a nursery for workers' children, extra training for those who need it, and services for workers? Who gets the best buildings and the best offices? Answers to these questions give a good indication of who is most valued by the organisation. Lip-service to equal opportunities can be used to conceal underlying values.

Influencing organisations

It is rarely possible for one worker, or even one department, to make an impression on any organisation. What is needed is an analysis of the system and how it operates. This indicates where to look for alliances in order to make a concerted effort for change. Most organisations work on the principle of 'divide and rule'. This means that each unit is in competition with other units for scarce resources. Co-operation is difficult to obtain when units have to compete with each other regularly.

Napier and Gershenfeld's 'Power Game' is useful for learning about the ways in which power can be used and manipulated in groups and organisations. In it, teams work against each other for negligible rewards. Some groups choose to play co-operatively, but that is not an easy option, as co-operation has to be worked at in order to succeed. Others experience the problems involved in making alliances and negotiating contracts with others that are likely to endure. Many people are surprised at how competitive they become, even in a situation with little at stake. Once the rewards of 'fighting for one's corner' are substantial, most of us automatically go into battle mode.

Chapter Ten demonstrated how easily competitive feelings and dislike of other groups can be aroused.

Devoting time to attending committees, writing papers, and lobbying, seems time-wasting and onerous when the organisation is devoted to public service. But the units of the organisation have to assume some responsibility for ensuring that communications are not only one-way. When individuals are subject to role conflict they often respond to the demand that clamours loudest. Organisational groups can suffer from role conflict too. Does your work group have a voice that can be heard? Influencing organisations is very up-hill work, but it is the organisation that sets the structures of the work group.

To summarise, in this section, a brief indication has been given of how some theories about groups can be applied to organisations. This involves:

- looking at ways in which the dynamics of organisations determine the types of group in which we work
- the question of whether, and in what ways, groups of workers can influence organisations

The next section considers how the three factors of structure, membership and process apply to work groups within the agency.

STRUCTURES

The structure of the group you work in is determined by its size, its rules and aims and who decides these, the nature of the contract with the individual workers and the group, the physical space it occupies and the patterns of communication that are laid down.

Patterns of communication in larger organisations are mostly those of the star or Y. (See Chapter One.) It is usually only the smaller organisations, or sub-groups of larger ones, which see any advantages in using the circle pattern. In your work group, who controls the flow of information? Is communication one-way only, or can you communicate with people who issue the orders?

What type of leadership is imposed on the group? Do you see yourself only as a member of a group composed of your immediate colleagues? Or do you feel like a member of a larger organisation? Could you make a clear statement of the aims of your part of the organisation, and would others agree with you? Are there 'official' and 'unofficial' aims for your work?

The membership of work groups is seldom decided by those who make up the group, since employees are chosen by those higher in the hierarchy. Exceptionally, a work group is allowed to choose a new member. Occasionally there is some consultation but the staff group decision is given little weight in the final selection. The method of selection of new workers is a good indication of the real power structure within the organisation, and shows clearly whether communication is one or two way. A team engaged in running a group for agency users is more likely to be able to choose fellow workers in the light of the needs of the group. How much can you influence the composition of your work group?

The ways in which these questions can be answered have a tremendous influence on the efficiency of a group and the satisfaction to be gained from working in it. Often what seems like a problem over membership, or process, is rooted in the structures, and effort needs to be spent on creating a structure which fits the task.

INDIVIDUAL MEMBERSHIP

Roles

Chapter One looked at individual differences in the roles people feel comfortable in playing. This is one of the main contributions that individuals make to the group. A group struggles if members are not able or willing to play appropriate or complementary roles.

Think about your fellow workers. What roles do they like to play? Could you rank each one on a line going from 'never responds to group pressure' to 'always responds to group pressure'? Or rank them on 'attitudes to authority' and 'attitudes to intimacy'. And how about you? Where do you rank on these factors? How would others rank you, do you think? If you did this together, how much agreement would there be? Would you change your ranking if other team members were working on them with you?

Does your group agree about who has the status in the group? And is this the same person as the official leader? Is there a problem of too many people of the same status, or a lack of anyone with enough status to run the group or have influence in the organisation? Are there some who will play the roles the group needs to function well? Do you have too many jokers, or silent ones, or individualists?

You may note the lack of evaluative words in all these questions. It is usually not productive to ask 'Who do you like best?'. You may feel very friendly towards someone and enjoy their company outside work, but not want to work with them. Or you may dislike a leader but find that they have a beneficial effect on the group. If you find it difficult to work with a colleague, can you list the positives they have, as well as the negatives? If you feel very negative about another worker, does this tell you anything about yourself?

Role conflict

Chapter Two described how the group imposes roles on members. Sometimes this is done in a way that overrules their individuality and provides a false solution for the management of group conflict. In work situations, roles are formally imposed and workers are considered to accept the prescriptions for the roles by virtue of having accepted the job.

However, workers are not only occupying work roles. They are also in partnerships, families and friendships. In addition, they occupy religious, political and leisure-time group roles. When these roles conflict, much anxiety is generated. An example would be the conflict that can arise between your role as a groupworker and as a member of a team which is mainly dealing with individuals. You need to prepare for the group, but an individual needs attention. Which role wins?

When roles conflict in this way, one solution is to do half of both roles, leaving you feeling dissatisfied with your performance in both. If you continue to do a bit for one and a bit for the other, you are likely to be responding to the one who is clamouring loudest for your attention.

For some, the work group is of little importance because they belong to a reference group which has greater significance and to which they give priority. This can mean that there is no interest left over for relationships in a work group with people who do not belong to the same reference group. Strong messages can come from political or religious groups, or a family one. This is not just a clash of roles, but also a clash of values. Can you think of an example of a value clash which has affected your relationships with others in your work group?

If the person occupying a role has strong convictions that arise from membership of another group, such as a religious or political organisation, they can find that their role at work conflicts with their values. A worker dedicated to both anti-racism and user self-determination can experience such conflict when an agency user expresses racist views, for example.

Another source of role conflict occurs when there are different expectations of the way a role is to be carried out. One of the sources of burn-out at work arises from a situation in which the worker is doing their best to fill a professional role according to their values, training and job description, only to find that the expectations of the role from seniors or other professionals is quite different. A groupworker can find that agency expectations about his or her role can conflict with a sense of professional competence.

If you are leading a group, there may be different expectations from members about the way in which you should lead. Someone used to an authoritarian leader expects you to give orders and be firm about deviants. You may prefer to play the role in a more democratic style. Disagreements of this kind can be useful in helping a group to move from early developmental stages. How do you resolve such conflicting expectations?

Cliques and reference groups

Is subgrouping a problem in your work group? Do you belong to a clique? Do you feel loyalty to those you are close to in the group and none towards the whole group? If any of these factors operate, you can be sure that the group is not satisfying the needs of its members.

It is inevitable that friendships will form in work groups and that some members will find another person particularly easy to work with. In some work groups, such alliances can become sources of tension. The reasons for destructive subgroup formation may lie with the way the group members relate to each other. Is there any prejudice operating? Are members being discriminated against? Are some members thought of as more valuable than others? Are some members being held in rigid roles? If any of these are operating, then the member will naturally turn to an alliance within the group for support, and if this is not available, to a reference group outside the work situation.

It is important to tackle the problem of subgroups and cliques in any work group since these can mean that the group as a whole is missing out on the energy and skills of members. Naturally people who share an interest, or a common background, feel easy about working together, but if the work group is to function efficiently, members should be prepared to work with others who do not share these interests.

One exercise that can be done in sessions where teams take time out to look at their own functioning is a 'group sculpture'. This seeks to clarify the relationships and sub-grouping within the group. For this, one member of the group arranges others by moving them around, until they are placed in positions which indicate the relationships within the group as the person in charge of the sculpture perceives them. This person then joins the group to indicate their own place. Thus a group with many subgroups would look fragmented. A member who felt isolated would place themselves outside the group. A leader may be put on a pedestal (or a chair if there is no pedestal handy), or just be seen as one of the crowd.

Each sculpt needs to be discussed thoroughly. Group members can be surprised or hurt to learn how they are perceived, and each person needs to be allowed time to explain their sculpt, and possibly re-arrange it in the light of members' comments. If others do not agree with the first sculptor, then they should re-sculpt the group according to their own view. This exercise gives a dramatic picture of the way members of a group are seen as close or distant from one another and usually gives rise to much discussion. It can be done with pencil and paper as well as with real group members. How would your work group look if you sculpted it on paper?

PROCESSES

The processes that develop in work groups are crucial to their efficiency in getting the task done and their ability to sustain individual workers. The most difficult and dangerous work can be a positive experience in a good work group, whereas even routine tasks become onerous in a group which is experiencing difficulties. So it is worth spending some time on analysis of the processes in your work group.

A newly formed work group has to develop ways of operating. It goes through all the stages of development listed in Chapter Two. Has your group arrived at stage four, where you can agree on aims and ways of working? Do you feel you use all the resources that are available from all the group members? Are you stuck at an earlier stage, where there are still disputes going on for power and control? Is your group so intent on imposing group standards that progress is stifled? If a new member comes to join you, what sort of experience will they have? Will the group feel warm and welcoming, or cold and pre-occupied?

Are members content with the roles they are playing, or are some forced to operate roles they are unhappy with? Is there a good balance between those who concentrate on the task and those who can see the process of the group? Is the group giving the leader room and authority to lead? Is leadership spread around when the task allows this? Has anyone been forced into being a scapegoat? If so, what problem are they solving for the group by occupying this role?

The group will have worked out rules for the management of their anxieties, and for conflict situations. Could you say what these are in your work group; humour for example, or real concern for each others' feelings? Are you content with these rules? If not, how could they change? Is yours a competitive or a co-operative group? How do decisions get made?

The factor that will provide you with the best test of how well your group fulfils the needs of its members, is the degree to which it has developed cohesion; (Chapter Three has a section on this). That is, there is a definite pay-off for being a member. This could be evident in the support that workers get in their job, the ways in which their individual needs are met, or the prestige of belonging to a successful group. The emotional feel of the group is important in developing a sense of belonging. It needs to match the style of the member. Remember the differences in the way people feel about intimacy? If a member feels better with distance between self and others, then a cool emotional atmosphere in which members are not very involved with one another, will suit them well. What are your needs and how well are these being met in your group?

If you want to assess how effective a group is, look at how well it fulfils its aims and whether the decisions that are made actually get carried out and further the aims. Remember that being efficient and being effective are not the same. A task may be carried out efficiently but group members may feel badly about the way it has been done. This can build up resistance to other tasks. It can also effect agency users. Task and process both need to be dealt with for real effectiveness.

How do you rate your work group in this respect? If you are not entirely content with what is happening, what do you think is preventing the group from fulfilling members' needs and from being effective? How would you want to see it change? How would you go about changing it? Would you have any support in doing this?

To summarise, this section has looked at the ways of increasing understanding of the groups in which you work by using the ideas about structure, membership and process which were described in the early chapters. It has considered:

- ways in which structures influence work groups, including size, rules, aims and contracts, and patterns of communication
- ways in which membership of the work group can affect job satisfaction and efficiency, such as the impact of non-voluntary membership, role preferences, role conflict, and the influence of membership of out-groups
- processes that influence the work group; for example, the stage of development of the group, the roles imposed on workers, rules and norms, and the development of cohesion

Knowledge about the influence of structure, membership and the processes that develop, can help to analyse why a group is satisfying or frustrating to work in and successful or not in carrying out its task. The three factors are not always easy to separate out; the aim is not so much doctrinal purity as using an aid to understanding and intervening. For example, if one member seems to be causing the group to fall apart, decide whether this is because:

- the group has a structural flaw in composition; for example, this member is the only person from an out-group which is viewed with suspicion by the majority
- this person is unsuitable for this type of group: for example, they may be the kind of person who likes clear, autocratic structures, but this group prefers a democratic approach
- an example of the scapegoating process: is the member being blamed for something the group cannot face up to?

TEAMS

Structural factors and team processes

Teams come in many varieties. The word 'teamwork' implies co-operation, continuity, a common goal and agreed methods of achieving the goal. In the helping professions it is common to find work groups organised into officially-designated teams with workers allocated to these. Whether they feel they belong is another matter. Often it is only the physical structure of the team that is provided: a place to work, means of communication (such as telephones and forms to fill in), a designated leader and team members. A typical team organisation is one which contains qualified workers of all grades plus ancillary workers. This can lead to status problems and rivalry.

In large cities, area offices are often split into several teams; an example would be Social Service Department 'patch' sub-teams. In modern hospitals, teams are often quite self-sufficient, and may feel a psychological separation as real as if they were separated by being in different buildings. Some teams are fragmented, because they may belong together as a profession, but be allocated out to other work groups. This means that they are simultaneously members of more than one team and may have divided loyalties.

The term 'team work' also implies that people are welded together in a group which will offer them support for their work and opportunities for skill development. But this is not always the situation. Anyone working with organisations, and able to listen attentively, hears questions such as: 'How can I get my team to be more effective?' or 'How can I get more support from my team?'

It is useful to consider your own definition of a team. To what extent does the team in which you work coincide with your definition?

Parsloe, who studied teams in Social Service Departments, quotes an observation that these often resemble tennis teams more than football teams. That is, they are collections of individuals and not dependent on each other's ways of working. Such loose teamwork may suit some situations and people, but there are advantages in the type of team in which people work together, relying on each others' skills and drawing strength from the group.

One advantage of a good team is that it provides a wide range of skills and information to draw on. Individual members may know part of the situation the team is dealing with, but when they pool their information, a picture of the whole problem emerges. If a team includes members with different skills, then a variety of approaches are accessible to those who come to use the agency; users will get a service suited to their particular needs. For example, if a team of social workers or health visitors consists only of workers who are skilled in individual methods, then someone who might profit from groupwork will not be offered that alternative. So by definition, a good team contains members with differing experience, qualifications and methods of working. This means that they will not always agree on aims and methods, so some work has to be done on these issues.

If the team includes people from different professions and with different training, it is vital that they learn to respect each others' values and language. Sometimes people seem to feel they belong much more to their professional group than they do to the team they are working with, and this leads to difficulties over status. Inter-professional co-operation is notoriously difficult.

Individualistic teams and collective teams

Parsloe describes a continuum of different types of group, going from the 'individualistic' at one extreme to the 'collective' at the other.

The individualistic team is defined as a collection of people whose work is allocated to them by a team leader. They are responsible individually for their cases and any supervision is in sessions alone with the leader. Such teams will not need to meet frequently, or may never meet as a group. Their communication pattern is that of the Star.

The collective team has some influence over the composition of the group, controls the allocation of work as a team and tends to work together on cases. Members of such teams often develop special interests and skills, and are encouraged in this by other members. The skills are recognised, acknowledged and used by the team. The meetings of such a team will tend to be regular and include group supervision and group discussion about issues such as training and management. Their communication pattern is the Circle.

Not all teams will be at these two extremes, many will have only a tendency to be like one or the other. Both types of team have advantages and disadvantages.

The individualistic team may be poor at communicating with each other about work issues and problems. Thus the wider implications of their work is not considered. This renders them vulnerable to anxiety about what is happening in other sections of the organisation. Members of these teams tend to feel helpless and powerless in the path of changes made by the hierarchy and to attribute unshakeable power to management and other groups. Conflicts are projected on to events and people outside their team and the leader is not overtly criticised. Such a team can be wasteful of the potential of individuals in it, and it keeps members at a level of dependency which prevents them from campaigning to change anything outside their own group. When individualistic teams work well, they can nurture high quality individual work. Little time is used in team building and more time can be spent with agency users.

The collective team's great strength is that it can ensure a diversity of skills and care plans. It can also address problems engendered outside the immediate working situation, for example in management or in the community. The team can plan and execute strategies for dealing with pressures of this kind. Members can support each other in this, for example, by freeing time for one worker to attend committee meetings or by spending part of team meetings preparing a good case for the changes they want to see. The disadvantages are that all this takes time away from working with agency users. The team can devote so much of its resources to team building that the task of the team gets lost.

Collective teams can also provide support and feedback for each other. In individualistic teams the only source of such support is the team leader, and much depends on the skill of that one individual.

The individual in the team

Individuals can have preferences for the type of team in which they wish to work, but not always be able to control where they are placed. Some people like to share their skills, but this can threaten others. Which type of team member are you? Does your team give you the support you need for your style of work? Does your team feel supported by the environment of the organisation in which it operates?

It is possible to work in an individualist team and yet have the opportunity of setting up a collectivist team for a special project, for example, in running a group. That gives a good opportunity to discover which kind of team you prefer to work in.

After Masson worked with the NSPCC, she realised how vital collective teamwork is for survival in stressful work. She found she was a member of a team which worked hard at team building, devoting one morning a week to this. Personal situations and feelings were explored and respected. Tensions between members were openly discussed, with the aim of resolving these as far as possible. She had previously worked mostly in individualistic teams; at the NSPCC she discovered how much, in other jobs, she had missed this provision of a secure base from which difficult and innovative work can be undertaken with increased confidence.

It is important to analyse the ways in which a team can provide workers with a situation conductive to doing good work, or cramp their efforts. Consider the ideas about work groups already mentioned and ask yourself how these apply to your team.

Typical issues that arise are around roles, power, cliques and rules. Teams can be difficult to work in if they pressure a member to play a special role, such as to become the representative to a committee. Or they can neglect the potential for development of a low status member. Power issues and rivalry can make the work place a misery. Teams can split into competitive cliques. Members may be discriminated against because they are black, or women, or disabled or over fifty. Teams can pretend that the rules by which they operate are written in tablets of stone and can never be changed, even if they wrote the rules themselves only a few months ago.

Remember that teams are not an entity separate from the people who compose them, though these people are strongly influenced by their membership of a team.

Team building

Some teams take an 'away-day' regularly to have a look at the way the team is working. Both Woodcock and Dyer have devised methods for team building and analysing team dynamics. This may be stressful at first; a start needs to made with caution, and some easy and pleasant team activity can break the ice. If examining the way the team functions is seen to promote better team feeling and help with the task, they can become popular events. If more negative feelings are generated than can be easily tolerated, an outside consultant is useful.

Another format for team building is to take several days together and employ an outside facilitator. If the facilitator is skilled in this work, they can help a team overcome some quite difficult situations. But not always. There are some teams that are so preoccupied with rivalry, status and poor management that nothing will change until some or most of the team members change, or the organisation changes. I hope you are not a member of such a team, they provide distressing environments for work.

A consultant from outside the organisation brings a new perspective, has no personal issues around the work or the team, and is an unknown entity, so that no preconceptions have built up around them. Such people are usually found by personal recommendation, but directories of such facilitators are being compiled: an example is the one recently issued by the British Association of Social Workers (see Appendix B).

The main gain from such team building is that the myths about each other that grow up in working environments can be explored and often, dissipated. I may believe that you would be offended if I say that I have difficulties over some way in which you are treating me. But you may be relieved to hear exactly what the problem is. You may have sensed some irritation but not known what it was about. You may have thought the situation was much worse than it turns out to be. Knowing the reality of the situation is usually not as bad as living with the fantasy. People may know that there are criticisms of them around, but be surprised to learn that there are also many ways in which their work is appreciated. A criticism may be based on a complete misconception, which can be remedied.

Part of team building is to bring to the surface all the strengths and skills of the group, and see where these fit the task and where some changes are needed. A team may find that it has someone with skill and experience, but that person is not being asked to contribute nearly enough. This is just one of the many factors that can be explored, given time and some trust between team members.

Exercises in careful listening can also be useful. If two people are in dispute, what often happens is that they have stopped listening to each other. Asking them to give an account of what the other person is saying before they give their counter-arguments is usually an eye-opener. Giving controlled feedback (not judgemental criticism) is another technique to explore.

Some independent consultants find that Transactional Analysis is helpful in understanding the ways in which crossed transactions can arise in work situations and develop into Games. To spend some time socialising together, for example, means that team members can get out of the responsible Adult and Parent positions which they normally occupy with respect to each other, and show they have a fun-loving Child in their repertoire. People in the helping professions need to understand the Drama Triangle notion, of Helper, Rescuer and Persecutor, described in Chapter Three, and how these can spill into each other as team members try to 'help' each other. The Game of 'Ain't It Awful' (where worries are rehearsed with no intention of doing anything about them) is played frequently. How many other games can you observe within your team?

There is also a tradition of Gestalt team and management training, in which the aim is to uncover the real feelings experienced in the work situation, as distinct from those which Topdog thinks we ought to have.

The idea is that authentic transactions, based on real experiences, lead to more nurturing and therefore more efficient working relationships.

It can be useful if team members have some T Group training, even if they are not intending to do groupwork. The learning that takes place in a T Group can usually be seen to be relevant to work situations. The aims of the NTL model of sensitivity training are to enable participants to learn how to assess situations accurately, increase their interpersonal skills and improve communication. This should have a beneficial impact on the way in which someone who has been in a T Group relates to his or her team on return to work. However, if only one of the team goes to a T Group, it is difficult to maintain more open and trusting behaviour if others cannot also change their interactions.

Some commercial workplaces offer opportunities for teams to undergo a T Group experience together, though this is rare in the caring services. I have some question about the wisdom of this, since it is difficult to practise new behaviour with the people you have to work with after the group. But for several people in a team to go to T Groups independently often helps the team open up new ways of working.

To summarise, so far in this chapter the application of theories about work groups to teams has been considered. The points covered have been:

- types and characteristics of teams
- individualistic/collective continuum
- advantages of different styles of teamwork
- team building exercises
- fears around the use of team building
- using consultants from outside the organisation
- application of theories from Transactional Analysis, Gestalt and T Groups to team work

THE LARGE GROUP

A form of meeting sometimes encountered in work situations is the large group. Groups of twenty or more are too big for effective group problem-solving. A large group has some uses, and can advance a project and disseminate information quickly. However, such a group needs careful preparation if it is to achieve sufficient unity to accomplish a common goal. Occasionally a large group achieves a sense of trust and coherence.

This can happen when members share a common sense of simultaneously belonging to smaller groups with similar ideas and values, or where everyone is following a leader whom they all admire.

Even if you feel at home in small group situations, the large group can be baffling and frustrating. It demands different skills, since members cannot know one another well and every contribution is in the nature of a public pronouncement. Most of us are not used to speaking in front of large numbers of strangers. It is much more difficult to give individuals the consideration and assistance in getting their point across that can be easily managed in the small group.

The large group particularly highlights the tension between the individual and the collective (referred to in Chapter Ten). It is very difficult to reach a point where the individual's perspective, personal and professional needs and ability to contribute are in balance with the needs and task of the group. There is a longing for structure, but at the same time, the need for autonomy and dislike of rules is also operating.

Issues of power, its misuse, and the need to empower group members are at the heart of the large group situation. When the group is going well, members get a sense of cohesion with others. This means they are sensitive to group pressure, and with so many participants, decisions start to be made which do not serve the interests of the minority. Group pressures operate strongly and withstanding these can seem quite impossible, even dangerous.

Individuals can dominate, especially if they are powerful people outside the meeting. It is difficult for a chairperson to ask a high status speaker to restrict what they are saying and give others an opportunity to speak.

Many large groups have no agreed structure and rules of procedure, and it is a lengthy business to get agreement to any rule where so many interests are represented. Where a group does operate by the rules of formal meetings, speaking through the chair and having a formal agenda with points of information and procedure, these can be the merest shell and the underlying rules may be quite different. Large groups can use the rule book to give a cold, hard feel to the meeting and to stifle individual contributions.

There is always the potential for disorder in large groups. Agreement over aims and values is notoriously difficult to achieve. All behaviour in such groups is designed to influence the whole group and there is a powerful need to make an impact and have others follow. The alternative is to be ignored, overruled, rendered powerless. Interactions have a dramatic quality which is not called forth by smaller groups.

When studies of groups began, it was the large group, the mob, the crowd, that fascinated the early theorists. Trotter's book, *Instincts of the Herd in Peace and War* was an example of this early work. Why should normally peaceable citizens bay for blood when under the sway of mass psychology? Freud was particularly interested in examples of mass altruism and heroism, looking at the ways in which the leader became the ego-ideal for a mass of disparate people.

The large groups of ordinary citizens normally encountered at meetings of fellow-professionals seem far from the notion of a herd or a mob. If people are assembled to work on issues such as the future of professional education, or in plenary sessions of conferences, surely they will behave politely to one another? But beneath the surface there are profound conflicts of interest, and some of the exchanges can be identified as knife-thrusts. Power struggles can be intense, but unacknowledged. Face must be saved in so public a forum, and acknowledging that one may have been wrong is out of the question. Recognising the existence of a process as well as the task becomes difficult in a climate where feelings are ignored. The expression of discomfort or sorrow at what is happening is risky and may give the appearance of being weak and ineffectual.

Most members of large groups do not have the opportunity to speak, and it is easy to claim a majority when this is not measured. To say nothing is to give consent, but it may be impossible to catch the eye of the chairperson. Frustration at not being noticed or heard can lead to shouting and walk-outs even among the normally unemotional.

All this means that large groups are usually convened with caution. Organisations tend to avoid bringing everyone together, as the outcome is uncertain. It is difficult to make contact with others who may share your interests and concerns, and this helps to inculcate a feeling of powerlessness in making any changes from the 'shop floor'.

Influencing a large group

Structural factors are important in large groups. For example, seating arrangements are usually in rows, often with the Chair and other important officers on a raised platform. Those facing the officers have to look up to them. This makes difficulties in communication, especially if the chairs are fixed to the floor, as in some educational establishments.

All lines of sight go forward, and contortions are required to get communication going with those at the side, or behind.

Another seating pattern is that of the very large circle, which means that from one side, participants can hardly see the other side of the ring. People seem to freeze in these situations. If possible, get members to change these pre-arranged settings. For example, those agreeing with a particular point of view, or a common interest, could group together. Once inertia and embarrassment are overcome, this can lead to some creative work in large groups.

In public meetings on issues that concern us as workers, such as the provision of hostels in a neighbourhood, it may seem as if only a vociferous minority are involved. No-one appears to be able to argue against them. It takes courage to stand up against prejudice when it is backed up by numbers. Identify the prejudice and get a significant number of people who oppose the view to attend, so that the meeting is more representative.

Who sets the boundaries of the large group, the times it meets, the membership, the extent of its influence? In groups where this is all organised in advance and the large group is expected to keep to the arrangements, it may be possible to do some preliminary work on these boundaries, for example by setting the task and planning some follow-up.

It is instructive to be in a large group which has no ground rules and see what develops. The need for structure is immediately apparent, but difficult to achieve. While some are trying to establish rules, rules develop by themselves. Some members seem to have higher status; rules appear out of the blue, such as 'don't interrupt'; communication structures evolve, so that some members are in receipt of many communications and others are ignored. The first step in being able to work in large groups is to understand the dynamics that develop.

Learning about large groups

Most people have to be involved in large groups from time to time. To help participants cope with these, T Groups usually have some sessions which are 'plenary'. Plenary groups gather together the whole body of participants. The aim of such groups within the T Group 'Laboratory' is for participants to experience the dynamics of the large group. These sessions can be frustrating and participants may skip these or leave early rather than attempt to get further learning out of a situation that is either frightening or seems to have no purpose. But if feelings of helplessness and anxiety are to be overcome, it is useful to be involved with large groups and get practice at analysing their dynamics.

One way of practising more effective behaviour in large groups is to attend a T Group which focuses on the large group. There is less at stake, compared to the pressures of the work situation. Experimentation is easier. If the group seems slow to start, what can an individual do to get interactions going? If a few are dominating it, how do you get allies and challenge this? Can you see one member playing a 'Game' to get others upset? Any 'Sabotage' around? Or 'Let's You And Him Fight'? Study the dynamics of what is happening.

Another form of large group experience is described by Thorne in *Group Therapy in Britain,* a book edited by Aveline and Dryden. Inspired by Rogers, the Facilitator Development Institute (FDI) convenes large groups of between twenty and one hundred people and experiments with a person-centred approach to finding a way of managing the self and the group under these conditions. There are no set procedures, and everything has to be worked out as the group develops. Thorne says that although the experience is stressful, most of these workshops make progress towards a new and fresh approach to managing oneself and the group which 'confirms and illuminates the uniqueness of individuals, while at the same time establishing beyond any shadow of doubt their inter-connectedness.'

Such workshops could be useful learning experiences for those who work with large groups, such as a therapeutic community. Organisations profit when the notion that people respond well when they are listened to and respected as individuals is put into practice. The ability to use the large group as a forum for new ideas and a possible means of support is a rare skill.

You need to select for yourself the strategy that enables you to work most effectively within the large group. The rhetoric and panache required to sway a group successfully need a great deal of practice, and may never be your style. If there are issues needing intervention and action, it may be possible to do some planning beforehand and gather a few like-minded people around, strategically placed, who can follow a pre-arranged plan. Those who have chosen to work in one of the helping professions may feel reticent about engaging in such 'underhand' behaviour. If you do not exercise influence, others will, and sway the large group in ways that you feel are mistaken. Study the skills used by others to influence large groups and use these for more positive ends. The charismatic leader uses his or her own personal magnetism, a record of past successes, and carefully rehearsed rhetoric to exercise influence. Less spectacular influence can be practised from among the ranks.

To summarise, large groups can be frightening and are difficult to handle. Some of the reasons for this have been outlined:

- the necessity for unfamiliar skills in public speaking
- tension between identification with the group and maintaining the self as an individual
- power and influence in a large group
- lack of agreed norms and methods of working
- over-reliance on rules
- dramatic possibilities of winning or losing
- the similarity between some crowd behaviour and the large working group
- the presence of strong emotions

Some suggestions for dealing with large groups have been made:

- influencing arrangements such as seating and membership
- pre-planning of strategies
- the need to apply knowledge of group dynamics to the large group

Finding safe learning environments to facilitate skills in dealing with large groups can include:

- using plenary sessions of T Groups
- attending large group training events

CONCLUSION

This chapter has looked at some applications of group theory to organisations and groups of workers. It has also briefly described teams and teamwork and some of the difficulties inherent in operating in a large group.

The aim has been to arm the ordinary worker with tools that help to understand and influence groups at work. A basic knowledge of the dynamics of the work place is as essential for the worker as for those in management.

Twelve

Developing your skills

This chapter considers some of the practical points about training. It needs to be read in conjunction with Chapter Nine on 'Training in groups' and with Appendix A, which gives names and addresses of training resources.

FINDING OPPORTUNITIES FOR TRAINING

First stages

Bearing in mind the type of learner you perceive yourself to be, as outlined in the introduction to this book, how do you acquire a training in groupwork?

The first place to try is your own organisation. Could a course be set up within the establishment? It would mean finding people within the organisation who have experience, and know something about communicating their skills. Not everyone who does a task well can analyse and train others in their skills, so it may be that an experienced practitioner would be able to team up with an experienced trainer. If that is not practicable, your organisation can find such a person from outside the agency. There are many able trainers located either in local Technical

Colleges or Universities, and others who are freelance. The BASW Directory is another source of information about trainers. (See Appendix A.) An advantage of training on an inservice course is that it gives you a ready-made group of people with similar interests with whom you can continue to meet.

This may not be considered as practicable by an agency, perhaps because there are not enough people who can be freed to take a course simultaneously. In that case, ask your agency to send you on a course run by one of the organisations listed in Appendix A. If the agency will not make resources available for this, there is still the possibility of resourcing yourself. There are many groupworkers who have taken annual leave and paid for their own courses. This is a sign of the low priority given to training and to groupwork by some agencies. The satisfaction of feeling your skills grow and your competence develop will compensate for the inconvenience of self-funding.

With the new arrangements for training and qualification which are planned in social work and nursing, it may be possible to find a unit of training which is being provided as part of a basic qualifying course but which is available to workers not taking the whole course. The aim of the reorganisation of training is to enable agencies to provide tailor-made units of both pre- and post-qualifying training. Press your agency to take advantage of this.

The new training arrangements will make it easier to provide short courses for both social work and health care personnel. However, organisations outside mainstream educational institutions such as the Group Relations Training Association (see Appendix A), have recognised the community of interests that enable people from industry, government, mental health care, teachers and social workers, to learn groupwork skills from each other. An advantage of taking a course which invites applicants from different professions is that participants become aware of the wide number of settings in which groupwork can be practised, and can look for allies from other areas of work.

A course which lasts only a few days can be valuable, but is by no means enough. Following it up with other short courses consolidates and develops learning. This has the advantage of enabling you to find short patches of time when you can be away from home and work. It also means you can choose courses to make up the pattern of training that suits you. Some courses, usually in group counselling, go on for a year or more on a part-time basis, but these are not commonly provided for basic groupwork. Since your skills need time to develop, it is a pity that more basic courses do not extend over a period of time.

You may already have some knowledge of group dynamics gained through a qualifying professional course. Some courses are excellent in providing this training, but there is so much ground to cover in professional qualifications that the space given to groupwork is under continual pressure. Perhaps you have some memory of having done groupwork while training professionally. Re-read any handouts or notes you may have made and refresh your memory.

Find some books that are written in ways to which you can relate. Busy workers do not have time or much inclination to read, but if you are reading this, you are already demonstrating your commitment. If possible, get your training department to set up a resource centre for groupwork which stocks a good variety of up-to-date books.

See if it is possible to join others who are interested in groupwork. Mutual training is exceptionally valuable. Early in your planning, locate a suitable consultant. Seek out supervision from within the agency if you can find someone already running a group. If you have some experience, offer to share this with newer workers.

Fitting the course to your level of experience

Make an honest assessment of your stage of learning and take appropriate steps to find opportunities for skill development. It is important to find a course that fits your developmental needs. Those with experience need different courses from beginners. It is difficult for a short course to cover both early and further stages of learning. Dividing the group into beginners and experienced workers at a training event presents difficulties. If the trainer attempts to provide more advanced work, meeting the needs of one subgroup, there is a feeling among the others that they are being deprived of the knowledge contributed by the more experienced workers. If there is no separation, the experienced workers feel they are being asked to start on basics again. If the work is too advanced, beginners feel out of their depth. A mixture of experienced and inexperienced workers therefore often leaves people feeling they have not gained much from the training.

Read very carefully any brochures that give information about courses. If a course says it is for experienced workers and you are a beginner, do not join it; you are likely to be confused and baffled. A course may specify that it is designed for basic groupwork, but be joined by experienced workers seeking support. This adds to the range of needs to be met. Neglect of this basic attention to information has made some courses in which I have participated into more difficult learning environments than necessary.

It is well worth spending time and effort on finding out more about a course before you join it. Usually courses will spell out their aims and methods for prospective members. The chapter on 'Training in Groups' in this book will help you to recognise which type of group is being offered.

On any course, if you have taken note of what the aim was and think it fits with your requirements, you will still find that there are ways in which the course does not meet your needs. It may be that the setting in which you work makes special demands, or your style of learning is not being taken into consideration. Express these needs and take responsibility for making others aware that your particular requirements are not being fulfilled. If you have given your time and energy to a course, it is important to get the most out of it. Sometimes you can take steps to get what you want: calling together a small group of like-minded people, for example, and doing some mutual training and exploration of issues.

Both during and after a course write down what you are learning and reflect on it. This is one of the most important ways in which you can further your own learning. It means that when you are back in practice, you can review the learning and determine how it can be applied to your present situation.

Remember the point made in Chapter Nine about sorting out your goals of learning, and defining what you want to find out. Do you require further information about group dynamics, or contact with others running specific groups, or do you want to study group counselling? Although these are not mutually exclusive, it is important that you bear in mind these broad distinctions when planning your training.

TRAINING FOR LEADERSHIP OF GROUPS WHERE COUNSELLING IS THE MAIN FOCUS

If you are to be involved in a group where the aim is counselling and personal problem solving, it is particularly important that you get the training, co-leadership and supervisory back-up that is essential in this kind of group.

Assessing the training you have had so far

Have you any training in counselling? Some basic qualifying courses in social work seem to omit any formal learning of these skills, entrusting the practice teacher to provide what is required. But in the agency there is much to be learned and counselling may take a back seat, or there may not be the opportunity to find and participate in good counselling practice. Indeed, some social work agencies now say there is no room for counselling in their work, and refer those who need it to other agencies. Conversely, those who realise counselling skills are a vital part of the work, bemoan the lack of people who are qualified to undertake counselling. Experienced practice teachers can often demonstrate many of the necessary skills, but it is unfair and impracticable to expect them to teach basic counselling to individual students.

On nursing and teaching courses, there may be very short introductions to counselling, which are not an adequate preparation. There are so many other skills to be learned that these are not given priority.

Many courses for social workers and health care professionals include the basics of interviewing. Interviewing can have a variety of aims such as collecting information, or trying to discover if there are difficulties in relationships which may lead to dangerous situations. Developing skills involved in such work is an avenue not necessarily related to counselling.

There are opportunities for teachers, nurses and others in caring professions to take courses which give an introduction to individual counselling. These are often provided on an inservice basis. There are also courses in counselling where non-professionals can gain basic knowledge. These can be offered by further and higher education colleges; some of these are carefully set up and supervised by the RSA. Agencies such as Relate or the Samaritans provide a good training in the type of work they undertake, much of which takes place in groups.

You will need to find out which theoretical orientation the course follows. Ideas based on Freud, Bion and Rogers are those most commonly used. My own preference is for courses based on TA and Gestalt ideas. It is worth seeking out courses that teach these approaches (see Appendix A).

Undertaking one of these courses will provide a useful groundwork of knowledge and skill, but probably will not cover counselling in groups. However, if you have training in counselling which involves listening, helping the person you are working with to reflect on what they have said, or left unsaid, avoiding collusion and direct advice, this is an excellent start. Such skills are needed in groups which use counselling approaches. Further skill development can build on this.

With training and experience in groupwork and counselling, you are well on the way to familiarity and competence in group counselling situations. Most counselling courses use groups as a medium of training, but it is quite rare for them to take into account the dynamics of the group during the learning. It is difficult to keep the individual and the group in mind simultaneously. If you are in a learning group try to keep your knowledge about groups to the forefront of your mind, so that you can recognise what is happening as the group develops. If a group is concentrating on individual situations and problems, it is doing so through the medium of group processes.

Finding a course on counselling in groups

Courses in group counselling, as distinct from those which use groups to train counsellors, are quite rare. This is strange, given the number of ways in which counselling in groups is currently developing. Courses in group psychotherapy tend to use the theories of Freud and Bion, or of Rogers. The scarcity of courses which specifically teach TA and Gestalt group counselling reflects the fact that, in spite of their value, they have not yet been widely adopted by educational and health service establishments. (This may be the result of the anti-expert stance adopted by these newer approaches!) The Manchester Gestalt Centre is developing groupwork courses and it is worth finding out about developments in your own area from the Gestalt Psychotherapy Training Institute.

Philippson and Harris's short book on *Gestalt: Working with Groups* and Houston's current work on ways of increasing the uses of group dynamics in counselling groups within the Gestalt framework, show how the two branches of knowledge can be integrated. Hopefully, future training courses in counselling will develop awareness of group dynamics, and there will be a wider choice of courses for groupwork counsellors.

TRAINING FOR MANAGEMENT

In general, training and experience in any of the helping professions are an insufficient preparation for a manager's job. It is important that managers share the specialist knowledge of the workers they are going to manage, but it is equally important that they have further training in management. Training as a groupworker is a good start in acquiring managerial skills, but again, it is not enough by itself.

Some authorities understand this, but many still expect managers to learn enough simply from experience. This probably accounts for the popular strategy of employing managers who have already had some experience in another authority. Presumably the hope is that they will have made all their worst mistakes in the other job. This reflects the state of affairs prevalent in business and industry until the last decade. Now the knowledge that amateur managers can do a great deal of damage has become widespread, and training is highly valued in the field of commerce.

If you are about to be promoted, insist that you get some further training with the new job. Remember that bosses are in a position of power and can damage workers, even if they are seen as efficient by higher management. There is a world of difference between being efficient and being effective.

Training can be on an in-service basis, but if you are sent to an outside source you are more likely to learn about ways of working that are not yet being used in your own area. Available courses range from a few weeks to a year or two, part-time or full time, from giving no recognised qualification to a Master's Degree. Once you start, you will find there is much relevant knowledge which you can use, so go on adding training to experience as you get promoted. Try to find a course that is not all book learning, and teaches practical skills.

My recommendation is that you get some training in the NTL type of T Group, even if this is not part of the managerial course which you are offered. This will open your eyes to the way in which you are seen by others in group situations.

SELF-ASSESSMENT

Assess your own strengths and where you lack training, or would like to develop your work.

Ask yourself some searching questions. Do you know enough theory? Reading is a start, but can you use theoretical knowledge to understand what is happening in the groups of which you are a member? Hopefully, if you have read this book, the answers to these questions will be at least a tentative 'yes'. So what is needed next?

Maybe you have done some basic work and are gaining confidence in your skills. Make a list of what you do well, and where you would like to feel more confident. Are you now at the stage where a support group would be the best step, or the opportunity to take some further training? What needs would you meet by such training? If you have a supervisor or a colleague who knows your work well, ask their opinion about further training. If you list the results of your evaluation, you have the basis for an appeal to your agency to resource your training.

As an experienced professional interested in advancing your skills, you will be to some extent self-training. This happens when you think about what you are doing and use these reflections to extend your competence. If you set goals for your work, you can see when these are being met and if not, why not. You will know how to re-negotiate goals so they are more realistic, or look around for other methods of achieving the goals you have set. You will be asking yourself 'Why did that work?', or 'What happened there?'. This way, experience becomes not just time spent on the job, but a means of increasing competence.

USING SUPERVISION AND CONSULTATION

Group supervision is particularly valuable for groupworkers. If each worker brings their current concerns before other workers for comment, these can be given in ways that fit the ground rules for groupwork. This avoids criticism and unhelpful comments such as 'Have you tried ... ?', which is nearly always followed by 'Yes, but ...'. It permits the discussion of personal issues which may be holding a worker back. The group is available to roleplay a knotty situation and experiment with alternative solutions. In group supervision, it is important that all members take a part in sharing the work they are doing, so that no-one sits back in the observer role. Once trust has developed, such groups are a creative method of skill development.

If you are using a consultant, prepare carefully for the sessions you have. Do not think of your group entirely in terms of the problems it raises. Take time to think through the structural, individual and process factors in your group. Then you will already have accomplished half the work towards solving any problems. If possible, give the consultant relevant material before the session.

A record of group sessions gives valuable information about ways of improving practice. It is time-consuming, but a quick record of the main events of each meeting is better than nothing. Over the weeks it will give you a picture of the way the group is developing. If you can make fuller records, concentrate on finding out what triggered key events and what followed them. This will give you further insights into the interactions in the group. Video recording is also useful, but has the disadvantage of taking as much time to play as the group took to run. Once recorded, do not let the work you have done gather dust. Read it again before the next session and discuss it fully with co-workers, or a consultant if available.

CONCLUSION

I have concluded this book with a section on skill development, knowing that if you have had the persistence to read to the end, you will be one of those valuable workers who is not content with what you know now. You will have managed to keep your enthusiasm and idealism; are seeking ways of being more effective and of reaching out to the people you encounter. I trust that this book will help with your work.

Working in groups is exciting, stimulating, absorbing and instructive. You never stop learning. It is the very stuff of living and working together. As your understanding of groups develops, you will find they become increasingly effective, productive and creative experiences.

Good luck with your groupwork.

Appendix A
Useful organisations

This appendix lists some contacts which you may want to pursue in the interests of further learning. The list is by no means definitive. I have included organisations of which I have had some experience, but there are many others. The 'Publications' section of this Appendix, and several of the books listed in Appendix B, will give you some leads to further opportunities.

Addresses alter as organisations evolve and their officers move or change. The addresses given are those known to be up-to-date at the time of publication.

ASSOCIATIONS
Group Relations Training Association
GRTA is an association of people who are interested in groups. Members are from public services, counselling, business and industry. It provides experiences in groups at reasonable cost both for newcomers and more experienced workers. It organises two events each year in different locations around the country. These are the annual Training Laboratory in January and the Conference in September. These last for four or five days.

The Training Laboratory is set up along the lines of the NTL to enable participants to learn about group dynamics and themselves as group members. It provides a setting for experimenting with new ways of relating to the group, using T Groups and inter-group exercises.

At the Annual Conference workshops provide examples of the ways in which group theory and groupwork is being developed. Participants can undertake several different workshops. There are also large group events. Members also use the Conference to present their ideas to peers and try out new applications.

Address for information: Jill Brooks, Secretary, GRTA, Gala House, 3 Raglan Road, Edgbaston, Birmingham B5 7RA

British Association for Counselling

BAC's aims are to promote counselling generally, but they have some events which are useful for groupworkers.

Address: BAC, 37a Sheep Street, Rugby, Warwickshire CV21 3BX. Telephone: 0788-578328

BEHAVIOURAL WORK AND SKILLS TRAINING

British Association for Behavioural Psychotherapy

BABP provides workshops on a variety of topics for those interested in using behavioural methods, including skills training.

Address: 59, Revelstoke Road, Wimbledon Park, London SW18 5NJ

Centre for Fun and Families

The centre provides specialist training for practitioners to enable them to run groupwork programmes in parenting skills. It also provides a consultancy service providing advice and support on different aspects of behavioural work with families.

Address: 25 Shanklin Drive, Knighton, Leicester LE2 3RH
Telephone: 0533-707198

Lifeskills Associates

Lifeskills runs courses in skills training and publishes workbooks for use in individual and groupwork.

Address: Clarenden Chambers, 51 Clarenden Road, Leeds LS2 9PJ

GESTALT

Gestalt Psychotherapy Training Institute

The Institute will have information about training courses available in centres throughout Britain.

Address: Sandy Elstrob-Johnson, Administrator, GPTI, 273 Wick Road, Brislington, Bristol BS4 4HR.
Telephone: 0272 710 527

The Gestalt Centre, London

The Centre provides courses in Gestalt work and is developing the theory and practice of Gestalt to group dynamics.

Address: 64 Warwick Road, St. Albans, Herts, AL1 4DL
Telephone: 0727-64806

The Manchester Gestalt Centre

The Centre provides qualifying courses in Gestalt counselling. It also hosts short courses in groupwork, stress management and organisational skills.
Address: 7 Norman Road, Rusholme, Manchester, M14 5LF.
Telephone: 061-257-2202

TRANSACTIONAL ANALYSIS

Institute of Transactional Analysis

The British ITA publishes three newsletters annually, with details about training workshops and other TA groups.
Contact address: ITA, Box 4104, London WC1 N3XX

ORGANISATIONS OFFERING TRAINING IN GROUPWORK

Eigenwelt

Eigenwelt runs courses in Hampstead, Worcester, Derbyshire, Newcastle, Edinburgh and Glasgow on groupwork, counselling and psychodrama.
Address: 40 Grosvenor Place, Jesmond, Newcastle-upon-Tyne NE2 2RE.
Telephone: 091-2816243

Facilitator Development Institute

Provides workshops on the Large Group and FDI Counsellor and Psychotherapy courses.
Address: The Administrator, Norwich Centre for Personal and Professional Development, 7 Earlham Road, Norwich NR2 3RA

Institute for the Development of Human Potential

The IDHP runs courses on humanistic psychology, including groupwork, in three locations:

- *Department of Education Studies, University of Surrey, Guildford, Surrey GU2 5XH*
- *CAER, Rosemerryn, Lamorna, Penzance, Cornwall*
- *Leeds, care of C. Bostock, 5 Hawthorne House, Regent Street, Leeds L87 4PE*

Institute of Group Analysis

The Institute, which is based on group-analytic psychology, runs both introductory and qualifying courses, in London, Cambridge, Glasgow, Manchester, Northampton and Oxford.
Address: 1 Daleham Gardens, London, NW3 5BY

The Minster Centre

Provides workshops and training courses in psychotherapy and counselling, including group therapy.
Address: 57 Minster Road, London NW2 3SH

Oasis

Provides a three-month part-time course in groupwork skills. Also has courses in counselling.
Address: Beechwood Conference Centre, Elmete Lane, Leeds LS8 2LQ. Telephone: 0532-736765

The Richmond Fellowship

The Richmond Fellowship is responsible for many facilities for people with mental health problems, run on therapeutic community lines. They undertake groupwork and leadership training in London and Manchester.
Addresses: 8 Addison Road, Kensington, London W14 8DL
Telephone: 071-603-6373
Richmond Fellowship College, North: Brian Jackson Centre, New North Parade, Huddersfield, HD1 5JP.
Telephone: 0484- 434866

TRAINING FOR MANAGEMENT

Many Universities and Technical Colleges offer part-time training in management. These can lead to a Certificate or a Diploma in Management Studies. Some Universities offer Master of Business Administration or Management courses. Some professional bodies are starting to offer NVQ training and assessment in managerial skills.

The Institute of Personnel Management

The Institute of Personnel Management has its own professional qualifications.
Address: IPM House, 35 Camp Road, Wimbledon, London SW19 4UW.
Telephone: 081-946-9100

Institute of Management Services

Institute of Management Services are another source of information:
Address: 1 Cecil Court, London Road, Enfield, Middx, EW2 6DD. Telephone: 081-946-9100

PUBLICATIONS

British Association of Social Workers

BASW published a Directory of Consultancy and Training, entitled *Search* in 1991.

Obtainable from: BASW, 16 Kent Street, Birmingham, B5 6RD.

Cahoots

A quarterly magazine which lists groups and training events in the North-East, centring on Manchester.

Subscriptions from: PO Box 12, Levenshulme PDO, Manchester M19 2EW

Groupwork

A British journal for those working with groups, set up in 1988. The editors are Allan Brown, from the University of Bristol, and Nano McCaughan, consultant with The Children's Society. It can be obtained through Whiting and Birch, 90 Dartmouth Road, London SE23 3HZ.

Human Potential

A quarterly magazine which lists many groups and training events, largely in London and the South-East.

Subscriptions from: HPM Subs, 3 Netherby Road, London SE23 3AL

Changes Bookshop

This bookshop specialises in books on humanistic psychology, counselling and groups. They publish a comprehensive catalogue and will post books to purchasers.

Address: 242 Belsize Road, London NW6 4BT. Telephone: 071-328-5161

Appendix B

Recommended books

GROUPWORK

Brown, A. *Groupwork*. Third Edition. Ashgate, 1992.

Brown, A. and Clough, R. (eds.) *Groups and Groupings: Life and Work in Day and Residential Settings*. Tavistock/Routledge, 1989.

Heap, K. *The Practice of Social Work with Groups*. Allen and Unwin, 1985.

Hodge, J. *Planning for Co-Leadership*. Groupvine, 1985 (43 Fern Avenue, Newcastle-upon-Tyne NE1 7RU).

Lennox, D. *Residential Group Therapy for Children*. Tavistock, 1982.

Whitaker, D.S. *Using Groups to Help People*. Routledge and Kegan Paul, 1985.

ACTIVITIES AND EXERCISES TO USE IN GROUPS

Brandes, D. and Phillips H. *Gamesters Handbook*. Hutchinson, 1977.

Brandes, D. *Gamesters Handbook Two*. Hutchinson, 1982.

Dearling, A. and Armstrong, H. *The Youth Games Book*. IT Resource Centre, 1980 (21 Atholl Cresent, Edinburgh)

Dynes, R. *Creative Games in Groupwork*. Winslow Press, 1990.

Jennings, S. *Creative Drama in Groupwork*. Winslow Press, 1986.

Napier, R.W. and Geshenfeld, M.K. *Groups: Theory and Experience*. Houghton Mifflin, 1973.

Scannell, E.E. and Newstrom, J.W. *Games Trainers Play: Experiential Learning Exercises* .McGraw Hill, 1980.

Scannell, E.E. and Newstrom, J.W. *More Games Trainers Play*. McGraw Hill, 1983.

GROUP COUNSELLING

Aveline, M. and Dryden, W. (eds.) *Group Therapy in Britain*. Open University, 1988.

Corey, G. *Theory and Practice of Group Counselling*. Brooks Cole, 1990.

Yalom, I. *Theory and Practice of Group Psychotherapy*. Second Edition. Basic Books, 1985.

Appendix B: Recommended books

ETHNIC-SENSITIVE PRACTICE
d'Ardenne, P. and Mahtani, A. *Transcultural Counselling in Action*. Sage, 1989.
Devore, W. and Schlesinger, E.G. *Ethnic-Sensitive Social Work Practice*. Merrill, 1987. (Chapter Seven on 'Adapting Strategies for Procedures for Ethnic-Sensitive Practice: Direct Practice' contains a section on 'social groupwork').
Mistry, T. and Brown, A. 'Black/White Co-working in Groups', Groupwork, 4:2, 1991.
Muston, R. and Weinstein, J. 'Race and Groupwork: Some Experiences in Practice and Training', *Groupwork*, 1:1, 1988.

SKILLS TRAINING
Beech, R. *Staying Together*.Wiley, 1985.
Gordon, T. *Parent Effectiveness Training*. New American Library, 1970.
Goldstein, A.P. and Glick, B. *Aggression Replacement Training*. Research Press, 1987.
Hopson, B. and Scally, M. *Build Your Own Rainbow: A Workbook for Career and Life Management*. Lifeskills Associates, 1984 (Clarendon Chambers, 51 Clarendon Road, Leeds LS2 9PJ).
McGuire, J and Priestley, P. *Offending Behaviour: Skills and Strategies for Going Straight*. Batsford, 1985.
Nelson-Jones, R. *Human Relationship Skills, Training and Self-Help*. Cassell, 1986.
Phillips, K. and Fraser, T. *The Management of Interpersonal Skills Training*. Gower, 1982.
Priestley, P. and McGuire, J. *Learning to Help*. Tavistock, 1983.
Priestley, P. and McGuire, J. *Life after School: A Social Skills Curriculum*. Pergamon, 1981.
Priestley, P. et al. *Social Skills and Personal Problem Solving: A Handbook of Methods*. Tavistock, 1984.
Priestley. P. et al. *Social Skills in the Prison and Community: Problem Solving for Offenders*. Routledge and Kegan Paul, 1978.
Smith, M. *The Best is Yet to Come: A Workbook for the Middle Years*. Lifeskills Associates, 1989 (from Branching Out, 34 South Lane, Holmfirth, West Yorkshire, HD7 1HJ).

ASSERTION TRAINING
Cotler, S.B. and Guarra, J.J. *Assertion Training*. Research Press, 1976.
Dickson, A. *A Woman in Her Own Right*. Quartet Books, 1982.
Fensterheim, H. and Baer, J. *Don't Say Yes When You Want To Say No*. Future Publications, 1976.

219

Smith, M.J. *When I Say No I Feel Guilty.* Bantam, 1975.
Sundel, S. and Sundel, M. *Be Assertive: A Practical Guide for Human Service Workers.* Sage, 1981.

TRANSACTIONAL ANALYSIS

Berne, E. *What Do You Say After You Say Hello?* André Deutch, 1974.
Harris, T. *I'm OK, You're OK.* Pan, 1973.
Freed, A.M. *TA for Tots and TA for Teens.* Jalmar Press, 1977.
James, M. and Jongeward, D. *Born to Win: Transactional Analysis with Gestalt Experiments.* Addison-Wesley, 1976.
Jongeward, D. and James, M. *Winning With People.* Addison-Wesley, 1977.
Pitman, E. *Transactional Analysis for Social Workers and Counsellors.* Routledge and Kegan Paul, 1984.
Pitman, E. *This Won't Change Your Life (But it Might Help!).* Channel View Books, 1991.
Steiner, C.M. *Scripts People Live.* Bantam, 1974.

GESTALT

Harris, J.B. *Gestalt: An Idiosyncratic Introduction* Manchester Gestalt Centre 1992 (7 Norman Road, Manchester, M14 5LF)
Houston, G. *The Relative-Sized Red Book of Gestalt.* Rochester Foundation, 1990 (8/9 Rochester Terrace, London NW1 9NJ).
Houston, G. *The Red Book of Groups: And How To Lead Them Better.* Rochester Foundation, 1990 (for address see above).
Houston, G. *Being and Belonging: Group, Intergroup and Gestalt.* Wiley, 1993.
Perls, F. *Gestalt Therapy Verbatim.* Bantam Books, 1969.
Perls, F., Hefferline, R. and Goodman, P. *Gestalt Therapy: Excitement and Growth in the Human Personality.* Penguin, 1973.
Philippson, P. and Harris, J.B. *Gestalt: Working with Groups.* Manchester Gestalt Centre, 1992 (for address see above).

SELF-HELP GROUPS

Wilson, J. *Self-help Groups: Getting Started - Keeping Going.* Longman, 1986.

TEAMWORK

Adair, J. *Effective Teambuilding.* Gower, 1986.
Dyer, W.G. *Teambuilding.* Addison-Wesley, 1977.
Fisher, R. and Ury, W. *Getting to Yes.* Hutchinson, 1982.
Tropman, J.E. *Effective Meetings.* Sage, 1980.
Woodcock, M. *Team Development Manual.* Gower, 1979.
Woodcock, M. and Francis, D. *Organisational Development Through Team Development.* Gower, 1981.

Glossary

Assertion (or assertiveness) training A method of learning to value the personal rights of the self and others, act positively without aggression, and negotiate where these rights are in dispute. The training is designed to overcome inhibitions about expressing feelings and needs and reduce anxiety about being assertive.

Authoritarian leadership A style of leadership which is based on unquestioned right or power to enforce obedience.

Authoritarian personality Someone who solves personal problems about power by seeking security within authoritarian structures.

Basic assumption group Used by Bion to describe the three ways (dependency, fight/flight and pairing) in which members unconsciously take refuge to avoid facing the problems posed by the group.

Behaviourism A branch of psychology which takes behaviour as the unit of study. Initiated by Watson in America in the early Twentieth Century, its chief exponent in recent years, Skinner, maintained that emotions and feelings were irrelevant.

Behaviour modification A therapy based on the idea that all behaviour is learned and therefore can be unlearned.

Burnout A destructive process caused by stress, overwork, undervaluation, etc. in which the worker's enthusiasm, competence, health and psychological responses are affected adversely.

Cognitive therapy A method devised by Beck in America for use in counselling and psychotherapy. It is based on the idea that negative thoughts produce negative behaviour. This leads to negative relationships with others. It aims to alter the perceptions and thoughts of people who have a negative opinion of themselves and others, replacing these notions by restructuring their images and ideas.

Cohesion A term for the forces which induce the individual to remain a member of the group. Generally, cohesion is equated with the 'attractiveness' of a group, which is a combination of many factors.

Contingency theory of leadership Devised by Fiedler as a view of leadership which relates leaders' styles and success to the characteristics of the group.

Counselling A form of psychotherapy by non-medical practitioners. It is designed to help anyone in crisis or with a personal problem. Practitioners can be voluntary workers or professionals. They have usually undertaken training, some at a basic level, while others will be intensively trained. The theoretical basis of the work is varied, but all counsellors learn to listen carefully, treat communications as confidential, and refrain from judgement. They can then sum up and feed back what has been said and lay out the advantages and disadvantages of any possible decisions or actions, while refraining from giving direct advice.

Cybernetics The comparative study of systems of communication and control in living organisms and machines developed in America by Weiner.

Deviants Those whose behaviour disturbs prevailing norms within a group.

Drama triangle An idea developed by Karpman within the framework of TA in which the relationship of those who habitually play Rescuer, Victim and Persecutor is examined.

Encounter group A form of sensitivity training designed to enhance interpersonal communication and the quality of relationships. More attention is given to personal growth and development than in a T Group. To avoid over-emphasis on words, there are usually activities and exercises designed to involve participants in physical action.

Exercises Pre-arranged activities to enable group members to learn about group dynamics or their reactions to the group.

Experiential Subjective data obtained as a result of undergoing an experience. A method of learning through action and experience rather than from books or formal instruction.

Feedback A term borrowed from cybernetics referring to the relationship of the input of a system to its output. In relationships between people, it infers that intelligent use of experience can be used to affect future behaviour. In groups it applies to information given to a member about the impact of his or her behaviour upon another member. It is not the same as criticism, as the reaction is couched in terms of the impact of the behaviour on the individual, not as a judgement.

Gatekeeping A process by which people are selected for or kept out of groups, particularly those groups with prestige. Also used to describe ways of managing the boundaries between a group and the world outside the group.

Gestalt From the German word meaning a 'configuration, whole or pattern'. This approach emphasises interactions between individuals and their environment and the importance of processes, rather than component parts. The essential unity of the person means that a full response to the environment should involve ideas, feelings and actions. If this does not happen, there will be troublesome 'unfinished business' creating difficulties in relationships.

Group development The stages that a group goes through in its progress from being a novel experience for participants in which members are unsure of what will happen, to becoming a fully-functioning group which deals with internal processes and accomplishes the set task.

Group dynamics The study of the way people behave and the interactions which develop in groups, particularly small or face-to-face groups. Associated with the pioneering work of Lewin.

Hidden agenda Motivations or intentions not obvious from the exhibited actions or behaviour. The hidden element may be intended to operate in a different direction to the overt contribution.

Humanistic psychology A branch of psychology set up to counteract the impersonal and dehumanising effect of the modern technological and fragmented society. The impetus for the individual's behaviour and development is seen as the need for personal growth, or 'self-actualisation'. The main inspiration derives from Maslow and Rogers in America, but the term is now used to describe approaches to psychology which seek to develop each individual as a whole person.

Johari window The name derives from its originators, Joe Luft and Harry Ingram. It is a four-compartment box diagram, illustrating the extent to which behaviour is hidden or revealed to ourselves and others.

Laissez-faire leadership A form of leadership in which the leader takes no action or responsibility but trusts the members to provide these. Laissez-faire can be loosely translated as 'let (people) do (as they think best)'.

NLP or Neuro-Linguistic Programming A modern synthesis of therapeutic approaches, psycho-linguistics and semantic theory. It was devised by Bandler and Grinder in America. It emphasises the difficulty of communication between people who operate in different sensory modes (visual, auditory or tactile). It also demonstrates the ways in which a change in the habitual use of words can alter thinking.

Norms Unwritten rules of the group which are devised and enforced without conscious thought or negotiation.

Patterns of communication A description by Bavelas of the channels of communication that are formed when members of a group communicate. Bavelas found that different patterns produced different effects on speed, efficiency and effort involved in communicating. He also noted that some patterns made group membership more interesting or boring and coerced members into roles.

Prejudice An attitude, opinion, belief or assumption with a heavy emotional overlay making it generally inaccessible to reason or evidence to the contrary.

Prisoner's dilemma A contrived situation derived from Games Theory used to study bargaining behaviour.

Psychoanalysis A form of psychotherapy devised and developed by Freud. Its emphasis is on uncovering and understanding unconscious motivation. Practitioners have a long training at a recognised institute which involves a full personal training analysis.

Psychosynthesis A recent development in psychotherapy, pioneered by Assagioli in Europe, which blends several strands of psychological thinking and practice. The aim is to help the individual develop a harmonious and balanced personality. Particular attention is given to spiritual development.

Psychodrama Developed by Moreno in America as a method of group psychotherapy, in which people act out scenes in their own lives to enable them to deal more constructively with personal and social conflicts. Under Moreno's direction the acting took place on a small stage, which enabled people to distance themselves from their life histories and feel free to express their emotions. It is now practised in less formal settings.

Psychotherapy The talking therapy. A method of treating psychological disturbance by helping the individual to understand and deal with problems and difficulties. Psychotherapy can take place over a longer period than counselling although techniques for short term therapy have been developed. Psychotherapists are likely to have had more training than counsellors, but this is not an invariable rule. A wide variety of approaches come under this term, including those from psychoanalysis, from cognitive theory, from TA and Gestalt.

Reference group A group which is influential in determining the values, attitudes and beliefs held by the individual.

Rogerian counselling A method of non-directive and client-centred therapy pioneered by Rogers in America.

Roles A term used with a special meaning in psychology which refers to the behaviour expected of a person occupying a position in the family or wider society. Roles can be filled with varying degrees of skill and seriousness of approach.

Scapegoating An individual within a group singled out to be the focus for frustration or anger not of their making. The object of displaced aggression or blame. In inter-group relations, it can be another group which is scapegoated.

Social-emotional leaders Individuals who emerge in small groups as the members who keep up morale and who facilitate the personal interactions within a group.

Social skills training A method of developing skills in everyday interactions or specialist situations. It is derived from the behaviourist idea that behaviour can be separated into component parts and relearned.

Sociometry A method designed to measure how people in a group rate each other. It was originated by the American psychotherapist Moreno and involves asking group members to rank themselves and others for various attributes and preferences.

Stereotyping An over-simplified perception of another person which is one factor in prejudice.

Stress Physical and psychological strain, threatening the capacity of a person to go on coping with the prevailing circumstances.

Styles of leadership A description of various approaches to leadership which appear to proceed from individual personality factors rather than the demands of a particular group.

TA (Transactional Analysis) A therapeutic approach in which the interactions of people are analysed and attributed to ego-states called 'Parent', 'Adult' and 'Child'. These three states are further sub-divided into positive and negative aspects. The transactions between these ego states are seen as the basic units of communication. Devised by the American psychotherapist Berne.

T Groups A method of sensitising people to group dynamics by participating in groups in which the focus is on what happens in the group. These groups are designed to improve interpersonal communication and ability to deal constructively with group situations. The group leader, known as a facilitator, aims to encourage open and honest discussion of feelings within the group and render the transactions of the group visible to all participants. Tavistock T Groups were developed in England; the NTL approach originated in America.

Task leader An individual in a small group who maintains group attention on the task or job to be done.

Therapeutic community A residential or day care facility which assumes that the total environment contributes to psychological disturbance or well-being. A therapeutic situation is generated which is designed to enhance interpersonal communication and relationships.

Abbreviations

BAC	British Association of Counselling
BASW	British Association of Social Workers
BBC	British Broadcasting Corporation
CCTV	Closed Circuit Television
FDI	Facilitator Development Institute
GRTA	Group Relations Training Association
NSPCC	National Society for the Prevention of Cruelty to Children
NTL	National Training Laboratories
NVQ	National Vocational Qualification
RSA	Royal Society of Arts
TA	Transactional Analysis
TV	Television

References

Adorno, T.W. et al. *The Authoritarian Personality*. Harper, 1950.

Amir, Y. 'Contact Hypothesis in Ethnic Relations', *Psychological Bulletin*, 1969, 71, pp.319-342.

d'Ardenne, P. and Mahtani, A. *Transcultural Counselling in Action*. Sage, 1989.

Argyris, C. *Management and Organizational Development*. McGraw Hill, 1971.

Asch, S.E. 'Studies of Independence and Conformity: A Minority of One Against a Unanimous Majority', *Psychological Monographs*, 1956, 70:9.

Assagioli, R. *Psycho-Synthesis*. Thorson Publishing Group, 1965.

Bales, R.F. and Slater, P.E. 'Role Differentiation in Small Decision-Making Groups' in Parsons, T. et al. (eds.) *Family, Socialisation and the Interaction Process*. Free Press, 1955.

Bales, R.F. and Strodtbeck, F.L. 'Phases in Group Problem Solving', *Journal of Abnormal and Social Psychology*, 1951, 46, pp.485-495.

Bandler, R. and Grinder, J. *Frogs into Princes*. Real People Press, 1979.

Bavelas, A. 'Communication Patterns in Task-Oriented Groups' in Cartwright D. and Zander, A. (eds.) *Group Dynamics*. Tavistock, 1960.

Beech, R. *Staying Together*. Wiley, 1985.

Bennis, W.G. and Shepard, H.A. 'A Theory of Group Development', *Human Relations*, 1956, 9, pp.415-437.

Berne, E. *What Do You Say After You Say Hello?* André Deutch, 1974.

Berne, E. *The Structure and Dynamics of Organisations and Groups*. Ballantine, undated.

Bernstein, S. (ed.) *Explorations in Group Work*. Bookstall Publications, 1972.

Bernstein, S. (ed.) *Further Explorations in Group Work*. Bookstall Publications, 1972.

Billig, M.G. and Tajfel, H. 'Social Categorisation and Similarity in Intergroup Behaviour', *European Journal of Psychology*, 1973, pp.27-52.

Bion, W. *Experiences in Groups*. Tavistock, 1961.

Blaug, D.R. 'Staff Anxiety and its Management in a Day Nursery', *Journal of Social Work Practice*, 1989, 3:4, pp.1-10.

Bristol University Department of Social Work Video *Developing Your Groupwork Skills,* 1984.

Brittan, A. and Maynard, M. *Sexism, Racism and Oppression.* Blackwell, 1984.

Brandes, D. and Phillips H. *Gamester's Handbook.* Hutchinson, 1984.

Brown, A. *Groupwork.* Third Edition. Ashgate, 1992.

Brown, A. and Clough, R. (eds.) *Groups and Groupings.* Tavistock/ Routledge, 1989.

Burgess, R., Jewitt, R., Sandham J. and Hudson, B. L. 'Working With Sex Offenders', *British Journal of Social Work,* 1980, 10:2, pp.133-142.

Canavan, (unpublished, quoted in) Cooper, C.L. and Aldenfer, C. *Advances in Experiential Social Process.* Wiley, 1978.

Cartwright, D. and Zander, A. *Group Dynamics: Research and Theory.* Tavistock, 1960.

Codol, A. 'Social Differentiation and Non-Differentiation' in Tajfel, H. (ed.) *The Social Dimension* Vol. 2. Cambridge University Press, 1982.

Cooper, C.L. *T Groups, A Survey of Research.* Wiley, 1971.

Cooper, C.L. and Aldenfer, C. (eds.) *Advances in Experiential Social Process.* Wiley, 1978.

Cotler, S.B. and Guarra, J.J. *Assertion Training.* Research Press, 1976.

Devore, W. and Schlesinger, E.G. *Ethnic-Sensitive Social Work Practice.* Merrill, 1987.

Dickson, A.*A Woman in Your Own Right.* Quartet Books, 1982.

Dinnage, R. *One to One.* Penguin, 1989.

Duck, S. *Human Relationships.* Sage, 1986.

Dyer, W.G. *Teambuilding.* Addison-Wesley, 1977.

Fiedler, F.E. 'The Contingency Model: A Theory of Leadership Effectiveness' in Proshansky, H. and Seidenberg, B. (eds.) *Basic Studies in Social Psychology.* 1965.

Fisher, R. and Ury, W. *Getting to Yes.* Hutchinson, 1982.

Freud, S. *Group Psychology and the Analysis of the Ego.* Complete Works Volume XVIII. Hogarth, 1922.

Freud, S. *Civilization and its Discontents.* Vol. XXI of Complete Works Hogarth. 1961 (passage quoted is from p.114).

Garland, J.A., Jones, H.E. and Kolodny, R.L. 'A Model for Stages of Development in Social Work Groups' in Bernstein, S. (ed.) *Explorations in Group Work.* Bookstall Publications, 1972.

Golembiewski, R.T *The Small Group.* University of Chicago Press, 1962.

Golembiewski, R.T. and Blumberg, A. (eds.) *Sensitivity Training and the Laboratory Approach.* Peacock, 1973.

Gordon, T. *Parent Effectiveness Training*. New American Library, 1975.

Groupwork, a journal edited by Brown, A. and McCaughan, N, published by Whiting and Birch (PO Box 872, 90 Dartmouth Rd, London SE23 3HZ), 7 volumes of 3 issues, 1988-1994.

Heap, K. *The Practice of Social Work with Groups*. Allen and Unwin, 1984.

Hardy, J. *Psychology with a Soul*. Routledge and Kegan Paul, 1987.

Harris, J.B. *Gestalt, An Idiosyncratic Introduction*. Manchester Gestalt Centre (7 Norman Rd, Manchester M14 5LF), 1992.

Hartford, M.E. *Groups in Social Work*. Columbia University Press, 1971.

Henry, M. 'Revisiting Open Groups', *Groupwork*, 1:3, 1988.

Hewstone, M. and Brown, R. *Contact and Conflict in Intergroup Encounters*. Basil Blackwell, 1986.

Hodge, J. *Planning for Co-Leadership*. Groupvine, 1985.

Houston, G. *The Red Book Of Groups*. Rochester Foundation, (8 Rochester Terrace London NW1 9JN), 1990.

Houston, G. Workshops in 1989 and 1990 given with the Gestalt Centre, London.

Houston, G. *Being and Belonging: Group, Intergroup and Gestalt*. Wiley, 1993.

Hudson, B.L. and Macdonald, G.M. *Behavioural Social Work*. Macmillan, 1986.

Jongeward, D. and James, M. *Winning With People*. Addison-Wesley, 1977.

Karpman, S. 'Fairy Tales and Script Drama Analysis', *Transactional Analysis Bulletin*, 1968, 7, pp.6-16.

Kennard, D. 'The Therapeutic Community' in Aveline, M. and Dryden, W. (eds.) *Group Therapy in Britain*. Open University, 1988.

Lennox, D. *Residential Group Therapy for Children*. Tavistock, 1982.

Lewin, K. *Field Theory in Social Science*. Harper, 1951.

Lewin, K. Lippitt, R. and White, R.K. 'Patterns of Aggressive Behaviour in Experimentally Created Social Climates', *Journal of Social Psychology*, 1939, 10, pp.271-299.

Lieberman, M., Yalom, I. and Miles, M. *Encounter Groups: First Facts*. Basic Books, 1973.

Luft, J. *Group Processes*. 2nd Edition, Chapter 3, 'The Johari Window - A Graphic Model of Awareness in Inter-Personal Relations'. Paola Alto National Press, 1970.

Masson, H. 'Training for Competence in Child Protection Work', *Social Work Education*, 1990, 9:1, pp.35-43.

Menzies Lyth, I. 'The Functioning of Social Systems as a Defence Against Anxiety' in *Containing Anxiety in Institutions*. Free Association Books, 1988.

References

Milgram, S. *Obedience to Authority*. Harper and Row, 1974.

Mistry, T. and Brown, A. 'Black/White Co-working in Groups', *Groupwork*, 4:2, 1991.

Moreno, J.L. 'Psychodrama' in Arieti, S. (ed.) *American Handbook of Psychiatry*. Basic Books, 1959.

Muston, R. and Weinstein, J. 'Race and Groupwork: Some Experiences in Practice and Training', *Groupwork*, 1:1, 1988.

Napier, R.W. and Gershenfeld, M.K. *Groups: Theory and Experience*. Houghton Mifflin, 1973.

Nelson-Jones, R. *Human Relationship Skills: Training and Self-Help*. Cassell, 1986.

Novaco, R.W. 'Anger and Its Therapeutic Regulation' in Chesney, M. and Rosenman R.H. (eds.) *Anger and Hostility in Cardiovascular and Behavioural Disorders*. Hemisphere Publishing Corporation, 1985.

Novaco, R.W. 'Anger as a Clinical and Social Problem' in Blanchard, R. and Blanchard, S. (eds.) *Advances in the Study of Aggression*. Volume 2. Academic Press, 1986.

O'Byrne, P. 'Personal Communication'.

Parsloe, P. *Social Service Area Teams*. Allen and Unwin, 1981.

Perls, F.S. *Gestalt Therapy Verbatim*. Bantam, 1971.

Perls, F.S., Hefferline, R. and Goodman, P. *Gestalt Therapy: Excitement and Growth in the Human Personality*. Penguin, 1973.

Philippson, P. and Harris, J.B. *Gestalt: Working with Groups*. Manchester Gestalt Centre, 1992.

Pitman, E. *Transactional Analysis for Social Workers and Counsellors*. Routledge and Kegan Paul, 1984.

Pound, A. 'Development of Attachment in Adult Life: The Newpin Experiment', *British Journal of Psychotherapy*, 1990.

Pound, A. and Mills, M. 'A Pilot Evaluation of Newpin: A Home-Visiting and Befriending Scheme in South London', *Association of Child Psychology and Psychiatry Newsletter*, 1985, 7:4, pp.13-15.

Priestley, P. and McGuire, J. *Learning to Help*. Tavistock, 1983.

Priestley, P. et al. *Social Skills in Prison and the Community*. Tavistock, 1978.

Randall, R. and Southgate, J. *Co-operative and Community Group Dynamics*. Barefoot Books, 1980.

Ray, J.J. 'Authoritarianism in California 30 Years Later: With Some Cross-Cultural Comparisons', *Journal of Social Psychology*, 111:9, 1980.

Redl, F. 'Group Emotion and Leadership' in *When We Deal With Children*. Free Press, 1966.

Rogers, C. *On Encounter Groups*. Penguin, 1970.

Rogers, C. *Client-Centered Therapy*. Constable, 1951.

Ross, E. 'Personal Communication'.

Sherif, M. *Group Conflict and Cooperation*. Routledge and Kegan Paul, 1967.

Sinclair, J. *An ABC of NLP* . Aspen, 1992.

Smith, M. *The Best is Yet to Come: A Workbook for the Middle Years*. Lifeskills Associates, 1989.

Smith, M.J. *When I Say No I Feel Guilty*. Bantam Books, 1975.

Stammers, R. and Patrick, J. *The Psychology of Training*. Methuen, 1975.

Steiner, C.M. *Scripts People Live*. Bantam, 1974.

Stewart, J. 'The Development of an Intermediate Treatment Scheme for Girls' in Marshall, M. et al. (eds.) *Social Work in Action*. BASW, 1979.

Tajfel, H. and Fraser, C. *Introducing Social Psychology*. Penguin, 1978.

Tajfel, H. (ed.) *Differentiation Between Social Groups*. Academic Press, 1978.

Thorne, B. 'The Person-Centred Approach to Large Groups' in Aveline, M. and Dryden, W. (eds.) *Group Therapy in Britain*. Open University, 1988.

Tropman, J.E. *Effective Meetings*. Sage, 1980.

Trotter, W. *Instincts of the Herd in Peace and War*. Benn, 1916.

Tuckman, B.W. 'Developmental Sequence in Small Groups', *Psychological Bulletin*, 1965, 63, pp.384-399.

Vinter, R.D. *Readings in Group Work Practice*. Campus Publishers, 1967.

Welford, A.T. *Fundamentals of Skill*. Methuen, 1968.

Wertheimer, M. 'Gestalt Theory', *Social Research,* 1944, 11.

Whitaker, D.S. *Using Groups to Help People* .Routledge and Kegan Paul, 1985.

Woodcock, M. *Team Development Manual*. Gower, 1979.

Yalom, I. *The Theory and Practice of Group Psychotherapy*. Third Edition. Basic Books, 1985.

Zimbardo, P.G. Ebbeson, E.B. and Maslach, C. *Influencing Attitudes and Changing Behaviour*. Addison Wesley, 1977.

Lightning Source UK Ltd.
Milton Keynes UK
UKOW02f2152300916

284225UK00001B/61/P